Living Beyond Brain Injury

Living Beyond Brain Injury: A Compassionate Resilient Guide for Survivors is a practical guidebook for people living with brain injury.

Rooted in neuropsychological theory and drawing on cognitive behavioural models, including third-wave approaches, this book introduces a values-based mindset called the Compassionate Resilient Mind (CRM). This balances compassion and resilience to support Brain Injury Survivor's (BIS's) recovery, adaptation and growth.

This book explores common post-injury challenges, such as memory difficulties, fatigue, emotional regulation and changes in identity, using the CRM framework and metaphors to help readers understand what is happening and how to respond. Through the use of practical metaphors, complex neuropsychological processes are made more understandable and easier to work with, supporting insight without overwhelm.

These ideas are translated into action through easy-to-use worksheets, clear comparisons and step-by-step strategies that encourage more flexible and compassionate ways of thinking and responding. The CRM framework and metaphors act as shared reference points, helping readers notice unhelpful patterns, practise alternative responses and apply strategies in everyday situations.

This book is for BISs and the professionals who support them, such as clinical psychologists, neuropsychologists, case managers, occupational therapists and rehabilitation support workers, to work together towards lasting recovery and adjustment. Whilst the guidebook can be used independently in some situations, it is most effective when used alongside therapists as a shared, structured resource to support self-understanding, navigate setbacks and rebuild a meaningful life.

Vicki Hall is a consultant clinical neuropsychologist and a chartered clinical psychologist. She is the owner and director of Neuromindworks Limited.

Co-authors

Cathy Grant is a consultant clinical psychologist and neuropsychologist. She is also an independent consultant at Neuromindworks Limited.

Selina Holmes is a neuropsychologist, clinical psychologist and independent consultant providing specialist neuropsychological rehabilitation for people with traumatic brain injury as well as individual assessments of cognition and mental capacity.

Stephanie Keay is a clinical psychologist with a specialist interest in neuropsychology and promoting well-being at work. She is an independent consultant at Neuromindworks Limited and the co-founder of The Core Collective.

Emma Nicholas is a chartered clinical psychologist specialising in neuropsychology, registered with the Health and Care Professions Council. She currently works as an independent consultant for Neuromindworks Limited.

Katie Venables is a registered clinical psychologist working at Neuromindworks Limited providing assessment, therapy and rehabilitation services for patients with acquired brain injury and neurological disorders.

Living Beyond Brain Injury

A Compassionate Resilient Guide for Survivors

Vicki Hall with Cathy Grant, Selina Holmes, Stephanie Keay, Emma Nicholas, and Katie Venables

Routledge
Taylor & Francis Group
LONDON AND NEW YORK

Designed cover image: Getty Images via Twenty47studio

This edition published 2027
by Routledge
4 Park Square, Milton Park, Abingdon, Oxon OX14 4RN

and by Routledge
605 Third Avenue, New York, NY 10158

Routledge is an imprint of the Taylor & Francis Group, an informa business

For Product Safety Concerns and Information please contact our EU representative GPSR@taylorandfrancis.com. Taylor & Francis Verlag GmbH, Kaufingerstraße 24, 80331 München, Germany.

First published 2014 by Routledge

British Library Cataloguing-in-Publication Data
A catalogue record for this book is available from the British Library

ISBN: 9781032735320 (hbk)
ISBN: 9781032735313 (pbk)
ISBN: 9781003464655 (ebk)

DOI: 10.4324/9781003464655

Typeset in Galliard
by codeMantra

Access the Support Material: www.routledge/9781032735313

Contents

About the Author and Co-authors

Dr Vicki Hall is the owner and director of Neuromindworks Limited. She is a consultant clinical neuropsychologist and a chartered clinical psychologist. She has a doctorate in Clinical Psychology, a postdoctoral diploma in Clinical Neuropsychology, and the British Psychological Society Qualification in Clinical Neuropsychology (obtained with distinction). She is on the British Psychological Society Specialist Register of Clinical Neuropsychology; an associate fellow of the British Psychological Society; registered as a clinical psychologist with the Health Professions Council and a member of the Expert Witness Institute. She has worked in neuropsychology and clinical psychology settings since 2001. She has worked in a range of private and National Health Service (NHS) settings in a variety of neurological services spanning the whole care pathway and across the lifespan. She currently provides neuropsychology rehabilitation and medicolegal services for Neuromindworks Limited.

Dr Cathy Grant is a consultant clinical psychologist and neuropsychologist. Prior to her clinical training, she completed her PhD at the University of Sheffield in 1999, examining moral understanding in children with autism. She held a lectureship in Developmental Psychology at the University of Hull from 1999 to 2001, before holding a research position at the University of Nottingham from 2021 to 2022 on a project examining the DAT1 genotype in relation to inattentive behaviour. She has worked in paediatric neuropsychology services since completing her clinical training at the University of Birmingham in 2005. She has worked within the NHS with children and their families affected by a range of neurological conditions, including acquired brain injury. She currently works part time at Alder Hey Children's Hospital on the epilepsy surgery programme and also works part time as an independent consultant for Neuromindworks Ltd.

Dr Selina Holmes completed her PhD in Cognition at the University of York and worked as a research psychologist before training as a clinical psychologist at the University of Manchester, qualifying in 2007. She went on to complete a Master's in Clinical Neuropsychology at the University of Nottingham, later gaining the British Psychological Society's (BPS) Qualification in Clinical Neuropsychology (QICN). She is included on the BPS Specialist Register of Clinical Neuropsychologists. She has held a range of NHS posts in inpatient and community services, working extensively with people living with dementia, stroke, neurological illnesses and traumatic brain injury. Alongside her clinical practice, she has experience in higher education and held a part-time lectureship in Clinical Psychology, where she led the development of the university's clinical neuropsychology training pathway. She also completed a Postgraduate Certificate in

Continuing and Higher Education with Staffordshire University. Now working in independent practice, she provides specialist neuropsychological rehabilitation for people with traumatic brain injury, as well as individual assessments of cognition and mental capacity. Her therapeutic approach is influenced by Schema Therapy, Compassion-Focused Therapy and Acceptance and Commitment Therapy.

Dr Stephanie Keay is a clinical psychologist with a specialist interest in neuropsychology and promoting well-being at work. She is an independent consultant to Neuromindworks Limited and the co-founder of The Core Collective who provide well-being services to a range of organisations. She is a registered clinical psychologist with the Health and Care Professions Council (HCPC). She has worked in clinical psychology and neuropsychology settings for over 12 years and has experience working in a variety of settings, both in the NHS and private sector. She has worked with people in inpatient and community settings, as well as in the corporate domain. In her clinical work, she uses a range of psychological models with a particular interest in utilising Acceptance and Commitment Therapy (ACT) principles.

Dr Emma Nicholas is a chartered clinical psychologist specialising in neuropsychology and is registered with the Health and Care Professionals Council (HCPC). She has doctorate in clinical psychology (2012) and a post graduate diploma in clinical neuropsychology with distinction (2019). Since commencing her psychology career in 2006, she has worked in a number of psychological and neuropsychological settings in both NHS and the private sector, including inpatient brain injury rehabilitation, acute neurosurgical ward, dementia assessment service and community brain injury rehabilitation. She currently works as an independent consultant for Neuromindworks Limited. Therapeutically, she draws on compassion and values-focussed models, including acceptance and commitment therapy, cognitive behavioural therapy, solution-focussed therapy and mindfulness strategies.

Dr Katie Venables is a registered clinical psychologist working at Neuromindworks providing assessment, therapy and rehabilitation services for patients with acquired brain injury and neurological disorders. She has worked in a range of clinical psychology services since 2007 and has experience of working with a wide range of neurological conditions, including stroke, traumatic brain injury and progressive conditions, such as dementias.

Acknowledgement

For my son, Charlie, whose presence in my life has shown me that we are constantly evolving on our journey, learning and reshaping ourselves with each step. You have been both my greatest teacher and my quiet inspiration.

Living Beyond Brain Injury

A Compassionate Resilient Guide for Survivors

Vicki Hall

Introduction

A brain injury refers to damage to the brain. This damage can result from a range of causes, including:

- Trauma, such as a blow to the head or complications following surgery (e.g., tumour removal)
- Stroke, caused by restricted blood supply (e.g., ischaemia) or bleeding on the brain (e.g., haemorrhage)
- Lack of oxygen to the brain (hypoxia), such as after cardiac arrest, surgery, or substance misuse
- Toxic or metabolic insult, for example, from a hypoglycaemic episode associated with diabetes
- Infection, such as meningitis or encephalitis

Brain injuries vary in severity and outcome, and some (e.g., mild traumatic brain injuries) tend to resolve within days to months. This manual is not intended for brain injuries that do not have persistent symptoms, and you should consult your doctor about your brain injury severity and prognosis.

Purpose of This Manual

This manual is designed to support individuals who are living with the lasting effects of brain injury. It aims to build understanding of how injury can impact areas, such as thinking skills (e.g., memory, attention), emotional responses, sleep, fatigue and daily functioning, and how these challenges affect life at home, in relationships and in work or community settings.

Rooted in neuropsychological theory and informed by therapeutic approaches (particularly those within the cognitive behavioural therapy tradition, including third-wave approaches), this manual offers a structured yet adaptable guide to recovery. More than just a collection of strategies, it introduces the Compassionate Resilient Mind (CRM) as a recovery and adaptation philosophy. CRM is a values-based way of approaching life after brain injury. This philosophy provides a guiding compass through which to meet the challenges of recovery and adaptation. It emphasises compassion and resilience as complementary values that shape how you respond to setbacks, adapt to symptoms, and rebuild a meaningful life. Instead of focusing on symptom control, CRM encourages a shift in mindset: from fighting or denying difficulties to working with them in ways that foster growth, adaptation, and self-kindness.

Through this framework, this manual invites you into a practical, compassionate and adaptive recovery process that addresses not only what you do to navigate difficulties, but also how you relate to yourself and your recovery journey as a whole.

A Compassionate Resilient Mind (CRM)

The two complementary values of the CRM are compassion and resilience. These values work in dynamic balance:

- **Compassion** provides warmth, self-reflection and acceptance. It listens to your needs, allows space for rest and softens the struggle by responding to harsh self-criticism with understanding and kindness.
- **Resilience** brings flexibility, determination and drive. It supports you to adapt, persevere and keep moving forward, even when life feels uncertain or overwhelming.

When compassion and resilience work together, they create an inner balance that sustains recovery. Compassion fuels resilience by protecting against burnout, whilst resilience channels compassion into purposeful action.

Developing this mindset means shifting from rigid resistance (e.g. characterised by denial or self criticism) towards a more open, adaptive way of responding. It allows you to make space for challenges, learn from them and keep taking steps, however small, towards a meaningful and valued life.

Why This Mindset Is Crucial after a Brain Injury

Brain injury can bring sudden and disruptive changes to a person's sense of self, daily functioning and future plans. Familiar abilities, such as memory, speech, mobility or emotional regulation, may feel unreliable or lost altogether. These changes can awaken what we call the "Gatekeeper" mindset. This is the mind's protective response to threat ("survival mode"). The "Gatekeeper" is a harsh, rigid inner voice that tries to keep you safe in the face of uncertainty, discomfort or loss, but often does so in unhelpful ways. Sometimes it compares you to "how you used to be," guarding the doorway back to your old life with impossible standards: "You should be able to do this by now," "You're failing," "Don't bother if you can't do it perfectly." In other cases, the "Gatekeeper" pretends nothing has changed, fights against symptoms, or urges you to avoid challenges. Instead of making space for difficulty, it pushes against it or tries to get rid of it.

When setbacks are common and progress is uneven, the "Gatekeeper" can become especially loud, leaving Brain Injury Survivors (BISs) stuck in cycles of self-criticism, avoidance, denial, or relentless over-pushing that leads to exhaustion and feelings of hopelessness. This, in turn, blocks meaningful adaptation.

In contrast, the CRM (represented through the character "Eve Olve") takes a softer and more flexible, adaptive, stance. Instead of fighting symptoms or pretending they do not exist, it helps you to make space for them, respond with balance, shift how you respond, and gradually adapt. Compassion and resilience enable this by working together to create an inner equilibrium.

For BISs, adaptation can begin with compassionately accepting what cannot currently be changed. This is not passive resignation. Rooted in compassion and resilience, acceptance becomes a form of psychological strength, creating space to adapt, evolve, shift direction and grow in new ways. Together, compassion and resilience form the psychological scaffolding that enables BISs to persist, adapt and rebuild a meaningful life in the face of change. This may involve regaining abilities, adapting to ongoing challenges, and learning to accept aspects of life as they are now.

Putting the Mindset into Practice

In the face of disruption to familiar routines, habits or abilities, this mindset does not simply "accept and endure." Instead, it encourages BISs to use strategies and worksheets to enable them to make change, self-reflect and purposefully adapt; to develop, trial and refine strategies that help them function and reclaim a sense of identity and control. Many chapters in this manual focus specifically on strategy use, such as tools for memory, pacing techniques for fatigue and communication scaffolds. These are not "workarounds" for weakness; they are adaptive tools that form part of a new, empowered way of living.

What This Manual Offers

This manual is designed to equip you with knowledge, guidance and practical strategies that support recovery and long-term adjustment and to help you:

1. Understand common difficulties experienced after brain injury
2. Develop a CRM to navigate those difficulties
3. Use strategies to adapt to and manage symptoms in everyday life
4. Rebuild a meaningful, values-aligned life across relationships, routines and roles

It includes metaphors, exercises, real-life stories and worksheets to help you personalise your learning, and apply it directly to your circumstances.

The Use of Metaphors in This Manual

Throughout this manual, metaphors are used as a central tool for learning and reflection. Brain injury can make it harder to grasp abstract concepts, hold onto complex ideas, or apply strategies across different situations. Metaphors bridge this gap by turning difficult ideas into concrete, memorable images that are easier to recall and put into practice.

For example, you will meet the "Gatekeeper" (representing the mind's rigid, self-critical "survival mode") and "Eve Olve" (representing the flexible, adaptive qualities of the CRM). You will also encounter the metaphor of water softening rock**,** which illustrates how patience and compassion can gradually wear down resistance, and create new pathways for recovery and evolution.

The function of these metaphors is as follows:

1. **Clarity**: They simplify complex neuropsychological processes into everyday language.
2. **Memory Support**: They provide visual and emotional anchors, making ideas easier to remember and apply when challenges arise.
3. **Perspective-taking**: They encourage you to step outside your immediate struggles, viewing your reactions and choices through a gentler, more flexible lens.
4. **Containment**: Some metaphors in this book act as containers, offering a safe mental space in which intense thoughts, feelings, bodily sensations, or urges can be held.

Rather than trying to suppress or push these experiences away, the metaphors invite them to exist within a steadier, more supportive framework. This makes it possible to acknowledge and observe what is uncomfortable without becoming overwhelmed by it. Containment provides reassurance and perspective, helping you recognise that inner experiences, even when powerful or distressing, can be noticed, held, and carried alongside you, without taking over or pulling you under.

Metaphors in this manual are therefore not just illustrations; they are practical tools for reframing your experience, softening rigid patterns of thought, and opening up space for compassion and resilience to guide adaptation. By working with these images, you can more easily spot when the "Gatekeeper" is active and call upon the qualities of "Eve Olve." This is why the CRM is introduced, not only as a concept, but as a living metaphor - one that brings its qualities to life in ways you can carry with you, recall in moments of difficulty and practise in your everyday journey towards acceptance, adaptation and evolution (personal growth).

How to Use This Manual

This manual is not a substitute for medical or psychological care. Ideally, it should be used alongside the support of a clinical psychologist, neuropsychologist or rehabilitation therapist, who can guide you in applying the strategies in your life.

Some BISs may be able to use this manual independently, particularly if they have relatively intact executive skills (e.g., problem-solving, planning, self-monitoring, goal setting and flexibility of thinking). However, this manual is likely to have most benefit when worked through with a therapist. The various worksheets may require differing levels of cognitive abilities, and they can be selected as appropriate. Some BISs may also not be able to independently understand all of the chapters, and they may require a brain injury professional to support their understanding. The metaphors can be used by therapists in the context of therapy to support BIS's understanding and adapted to individual needs, preferences and circumstances accordingly.

Support Required

After a brain injury, you may experience executive functioning difficulties, such as problems with initiating tasks, shifting mental focus, or recognising and monitoring your thoughts, emotions and behaviours. These challenges can make it harder to apply key components of the CRM, particularly:

- **Compassionate Persistence**: Sustaining effort during difficulty, whilst showing compassion and taking breaks when needed
- **Self-awareness**: Noticing inner experience without judgement
- **Flexibility**: Adapting thinking and behaviour
- **Purposeful Action**: Acting in line with values

When these executive functions are impaired, it may become difficult or not possible to implement CRM strategies without external support, especially in everyday environments or under stress. This manual offers structured tools, strategies, and worksheets designed to help you gradually build these CRM capacities in a manageable and meaningful way. However, some individuals may require more structured and sustained support to benefit from these strategies. For example:

- You may not be able to independently implement strategies on your own.
- You may have difficulty recognising your limitations or when you make mistakes.
- You may not be able to generate alternative perspectives on your own.
- You may struggle to formulate CRM statements.
- You may find it difficult to shift out of rigid or self-critical thinking, or unhelpful behavioural patterns due to reduced self-awareness, abstract reasoning or cognitive flexibility.

In such cases, a Rehabilitation Support Worker (RSW) or another trusted support person can play a vital role. They can help apply strategies in real-life contexts, scaffolding your independence by modelling skills, offering adaptive interpretations and CRM statements, and gently guiding compassionate thinking. Over time, if skills improve, the level of support may be gradually reduced. However, in cases with severe impairment, these strategies may not be applicable. The suitability of the strategies can be assessed by a qualified neuropsychologist.

The level of support needed may vary based on your level of thinking skills, emotional resilience, and ability to tolerate and work through difficult experiences. Support may range from light prompts and reminders, to full scaffolding and guided implementation of strategies.

The process of acceptance, adaptation and evolution may not be a solo journey. Drawing on the insight, encouragement and structure provided by others can be a vital part of rebuilding your own resilience and self-direction.

Expanding Support in Volume 2

Volume 2 of this manual provides detailed guidance for RSWs, therapists and family members on how to implement strategies in everyday settings, including the home, social situations and the broader community. It also offers additional resources and adaptations for BISs with more significant cognitive limitations, ensuring that recovery tools are accessible and appropriately tailored to different levels of need.

1 Lighting the Way

Navigating Depression and Low Mood in Early Recovery

Vicki Hall and Emma Nicholas

The Control Tower in a Storm

Imagine your recovery as the work of a control tower at a busy airport. Each plane in the sky represents a meaningful, purposeful action (i.e., things you need or want to do in everyday life). When the skies are clear, planes take off and land with ease; you connect with loved ones, keep up with routines, enjoy activities and steadily move towards your goals.

After a brain injury, the airport infrastructure itself may have been affected. The control tower may become overloaded more easily and have fewer cognitive resources available to coordinate incoming demands. Tasks that were once automatic may now require far more effort and energy, especially when the skies are already stormy. Fog, crosswinds and turbulence (in other words, difficult thoughts, feelings and sensations, such as pain and fatigue) can obscure your radar and leave the control tower feeling overwhelmed. Some planes circle endlessly waiting for clearance, some fail to land and others are knocked off course. This is what depression can feel like: a storm that slows traffic and clouds your sense of direction. Here is where the Compassionate Resilient Mind (CRM) comes in. The CRM is like your co-controller in the control tower, offering a calm, steady presence. Its qualities can be remembered with the acronym ACCEPTS, and each one has its role in keeping the airport running:

The ACCEPTS Control Tower Metaphor

ACCEPTS	*Metaphorical role in the control tower*
A—Awareness and acceptance	With your radar, you notice changing weather conditions, such as mood, fatigue or pain, and recognise programming glitches (e.g., memory problems) with awareness and acceptance, rather than resistance or harsh judgement.
C—Cognitive flexibility	The ability to change your line of thinking adjusts flight paths when storms block the usual routes, helping you replan and adapt goals, whilst still moving towards your values and what matters most.
C—Compassion	The co-controller's steady voice, encouraging, rather than criticising when landings are rough, especially during slips or setbacks.
E—Effort with balance (compassionate persistence)	Keeps the airport moving with steady energy, fuelling flights without burning out, pacing effort with rest.
P—Purposeful action	The flight schedule, giving each plane its destination and ensuring energy is spent on meaningful journeys connecting you to what is meaningful to you, such as connecting with loved ones, caring for your health, contributing to your community, pursuing hobbies or working towards personal goals.

DOI: 10.4324/9781003464655-1

ACCEPTS	*Metaphorical role in the control tower*
T—Tools and strategies	The runway lights and safety procedures that guide planes down in poor visibility: memory aids, routines, mindfulness or therapy skills.
S—Self-reflection	Your observations from the control tower allow you to conduct post-flight reviews, helping you learn from experience, refine your strategies and grow stronger over time. From this vantage point, you can hold space for experiences and purposefully respond to them, without being swept away by them.

Just like any airport, the control tower is never left to function without support. Ground crew (i.e., family, friends and therapists) provide encouragement and practical help when traffic feels overwhelming. Beacons and safety checks (practices like mindfulness and gratitude) shine through the fog, reminding you of connection, calm and hope even in difficult conditions.

As the airport image has many moving parts, here is a simple airport map that shows how each part of the metaphor links to recovery after brain injury:

Airport Overview

Airport metaphor	*What it means in recovery*	*Examples after brain injury*
Storms, fog, turbulence	Difficult thoughts, feelings or symptoms	Feeling anxious about the future, sadness after losing independence, fatigue clouding concentration
Control tower	Your mind trying to guide daily life	Trying to plan meals, keep appointments or manage emotions, whilst feeling overwhelmed and experiencing cognitive difficulties.
Radar	Awareness and acceptance of your current state	Noticing "I feel exhausted today" without harsh judgment
Runway lights	The basics: sleep, food, routine	Getting into a regular bedtime routine, eating balanced meals, creating a daily structure
Flight schedule	Purposeful action and activity pacing	Setting small daily goals, like going for a short walk or calling a friend
Planes	Meaningful actions or goals	Spending time with loved ones, doing hobbies, looking after health, working towards independence
Co-controller (CRM)	CRM qualities (ACCEPTS)	Awareness and Self-kindness when you forget something; choosing compassionate, resilient behaviours that help you cope, compensate, and continue moving towards your goals
Ground crew	Family, friends, therapists, support workers	A partner reminding you to take breaks, a therapist teaching memory strategies
Beacons and safety checks	Mindfulness, gratitude, calming practices	Taking a mindful pause during difficult experiences, noticing small positives, like a laugh or a sunny day
Post-flight review	Self-reflection and learning	Looking back on what worked (e.g., pacing activity) and adjusting for next time

With this map as a quick reference, you can easily check which system might need attention: are your runway lights (sleep, food, routine) dim? Are there too many planes (daily demands) circling? Does the radar (your awareness) show only storms? Using ACCEPTS as your compass, the CRM steadies your hand, cuts through the fog and helps you guide planes safely towards destinations of connection, growth, recovery and adaptation. Even in poor weather, you can keep landing one plane at a time, moving steadily towards what truly matters.

Adapting to a Brain Injury in the Early Stages Post-Injury

When the control tower is shaken by stormy weather, recovery and adaptation is not simply about waiting for the skies to clear. It also requires strengthening the systems that keep planes moving, i.e., switching on runway lights, refining flight schedules and training ground crew to handle new conditions. In the same way, recovery and adaptation after brain injury are not just about what has changed, but also about what can be discovered, rebuilt and transformed.

Over time, some abilities may return, whilst new ways of adapting emerge. Along this journey, you may uncover inner strengths and strategies that support resilience, personal growth and emotional well-being. The most rapid brain healing usually occurs within the first six months to a year following your injury, and physical recovery may plateau after around two years. Yet, this is far from the end of the story; progress continues through adaptation, rehabilitation and the mindset you bring to your recovery.

By developing a CRM, you can navigate with greater clarity and steadiness. Compassion and resilience become the compass that helps you steer through uncertainty, guiding you towards flexibility, self-kindness and purposeful action.

Emotional Responses to Injury

When the skies above the airport darken, the control tower feels the strain. A sudden storm may bring heavy turbulence, crosswinds may force planes off course or thick fog may obscure the radar. In the same way, the circumstances of your injury can cause difficult feelings and sensations (e.g., fatigue and pain) and push normal everyday routines or plans off course.

If someone else caused your injury, such as in a car accident or an assault, you may experience powerful feelings of injustice, anger or grief, both towards that person and towards the changes in your own life. You may also feel anxious about the future or unsettled by changes in your abilities. These emotional storms are human and understandable responses, but they can leave the control tower feeling overwhelmed, struggling to manage traffic safely.

The good news is that even in poor weather, flights can still land at a destination that matters. With compassionate strategies, it is possible to steady the radar, adjust the flight paths and guide planes safely through turbulence. In practice, this means loosening the weight of anger, injustice or anxiety and gently redirecting your planes towards the runways that matter most, i.e., the people, values and activities that bring meaning and purpose to your life. See Chapter 5: *Living Beyond Anxiety: A Compassionate Resilient Approach* and Chapter 6: *The Weight of Injustice: Finding Freedom through Compassion*, for practical support on these issues.

The Role of Family and Support

A control tower never works in isolation. Behind every safe landing are ground crews, engineers and support staff who keep the airport running. In the same way, adaptation after brain injury may not be a journey you have to take alone. Family members, friends and wider support networks also need time and guidance to adjust. Open, honest conversations about the effects of brain injury can help everyone involved understand what is happening and how best to respond. Supportive relationships become like the ground crews of your airport, a vital source of encouragement, hope and shared resilience when the control tower feels under strain.

If you have children, they too may face challenges in understanding and adapting to the changes. With sensitive guidance, children can learn the same skills of resilience and compassion that help the control tower weather difficult skies. See Chapter 15: *Supporting Relationships with Your Children*; Appendix 41: *Key Points for Your Family to Understand about Brain Injury* and Appendix 42: *Relationships with Children Worksheet (to Complete with Your Family*), for practical strategies to empower family communications and strengthen your relationships.

Loss, Growth and Adaptation

Even with the best support teams, storms can disrupt the airport. Brain injury can bring undeniable losses, such as changes in thinking skills (e.g., memory or processing speed), physical ability, independence or social roles like being a worker, parent or caregiver. These disruptions can affect confidence and self-identity, and feelings of grief, sadness, anger or frustration are natural responses when the skies no longer look as clear as they once did.

Yet, alongside these difficulties lies the possibility of growth and adaptation. Just as airports adapt by building new runways, updating technology or redesigning flight paths, people can also discover fresh ways of connecting with others, rediscover hidden strengths or create new purposes and values in life. Emotional adaptation often comes as some abilities are regained or improved, but it can also arise from learning to adapt in meaningful ways. Even when grief feels overwhelming, compassionate support and reflection can help you move from a place of loss towards one of empowerment and adaptation (see Chapter 2: *Flowing Forward: Compassionate Resilient adaptation to Brain Injury,* for further guidance on this).

Recognising Depression

Sometimes, the storm does not pass quickly. Instead of brief turbulence, low clouds may settle over the airport for days or weeks, making it harder for the control tower to keep traffic moving. This is what depression can feel like after brain injury, i.e., a prolonged storm in the skies that leaves the controller drained, uncertain and struggling to trust that planes will land safely.

Depression is not a sign of weakness. It is a common response to a major life change, and it is treatable. It is characterised by a persistent low mood most of the day, nearly every day, for at least two weeks. Other signs may include:

- Loss of interest in activities you once enjoyed
- Frequent feelings of worthlessness, hopelessness or guilt
- Low energy or lack of motivation
- Persistent sadness
- Changes in sleep patterns (sleeping much more or much less than usual)
- Episodes of crying

After a brain injury, these signs can be complicated by overlapping causes. For example:

- Crying may be related to emotionalism, a common post-injury condition, rather than a sign of depression (see Chapter 3: *Riding Emotional Waves: Navigating Emotionalism after Brain Injury*).

- Sleep changes may stem from brain injury–related factors (see Chapter 7: *Resting with Resilience: A Compassionate Guide to Sleep*).
- Fatigue can be part of brain injury (see Chapter 8: *Pacing with Purpose: A Compassionate Guide to Navigating Fatigue*).
- Reduced motivation may reflect damage to brain areas involved in initiating actions (see Chapter 12: *Executive Skills after Brain Injury: A Compassionate Guide to Planning, Problem-Solving and Self-Control*).
- Loss of interest may result from physical or cognitive limitations, rather than depression itself.

The key symptoms to watch for are persistent low mood and feelings of guilt, worthlessness, helplessness or hopelessness. These are like the fog and turbulence which may not clear on their own, leaving the airport struggling to function. Recognising them early matters because, just as airports switch on extra runway lights and call in support when storms drag on, depression can be managed with help and treatment.

Your doctor should be your first point of contact, and they may recommend therapy, medication or both. With the right support, many people find that the fog gradually lifts, motivation returns, the control tower regains its rhythm and the airport begins to run more smoothly again.

Navigating Depression and Low Mood

When storms linger over the airport, the control tower cannot rely on clear skies to manage flights. Instead, it turns to the building blocks and procedures that keep the airport safe and operational in difficult conditions. In the same way, when depression lowers your mood and clouds your thinking, structured strategies become the supports that steady your recovery.

Addressing Symptoms Related to Brain Injury

Sometimes the fog that is interfering with the smooth running of the control tower comes not only from the weather but also from changes in the radar or slowed communication systems. After a brain injury, challenges, such as fatigue, memory slips problems planning or slowed thinking can naturally influence how smoothly the control tower runs and can directly affect mood. These are not faults, but signs that some systems may require updated programmes or procedures to work efficiently again. Learning new strategies is like updating programmes or adjusting procedures in the control tower, ensuring that flights can continue to run safely and purposefully. Many of these strategies are introduced throughout this book (e.g., see Chapter 10: *Catching the Slips: A Compassionate Resilient Guide to Remembering*, for how to develop new procedures to improve your ability to remember things).

Getting the Basics Right

Runways cannot function without power, lighting and regular maintenance. Likewise, your mind and body cannot function well without attention to the basics: food, sleep and daily structure. A brain injury can disrupt your routine and lifestyle, which can negatively impact your mood. Being compassionate towards yourself and attending to these needs is like switching on the runway lights and ensuring the tarmac is clear for landings. Focusing on diet, sleep and daily activity (see Appendix 1: *Building the Basics for Recovery and adaptation*) creates the essential infrastructure for recovery and adaptation.

Managing Your Activity Levels

If too many flights are grounded, the airport quickly falls behind schedule, and it may be difficult to get it back to a working rhythm; the rhythm may need to adapt to the conditions (see Appendix 28: *Breaking Out of the "Boom-Bust" Cycle – Pacing Activities*, for how to pace activities in the context of pain and fatigue), but it is important that planes still take off. Depression often works the same way, leading to withdrawal, avoidance and fewer opportunities for connection or achievement. When you stop doing things, it can feel difficult to get going again, which deepens the low mood. Setting small goals to engage in activities that bring both enjoyment and a sense of mastery is like reopening the flight schedule and gradually getting planes back in the air. Even one safe take-off or landing can restore momentum and confidence.

Appendix 4: *Enjoyment and Achievement: Activities to Lift Mood and Motivation* and Chapter 2: *Flowing Forward: Compassionate Resilient adaptation to Brain Injury*, provides guidance on how to set goals that are aligned with your values and what you enjoy.

Navigating Difficult or Gloomy Thoughts

Sometimes the control tower's radar becomes distorted, showing storms that are bigger or closer than they really are. Depression can act like these faulty readings, filtering your perspective through "gloomy glasses" and biasing your thoughts towards unhelpful beliefs about yourself and the world. If you act on these distorted signals, you may steer away from your intended flight paths, aligned with your values and goals.

Here, the CRM functions like a skilled co-controller, i.e., it helps you pause, recheck the radar and realign your compass with compassion and resilience before selecting new routes. Updating your "radar software" (see Appendix 7: *Navigating Mind Influencers: Guidelines for Adaptive Thinking*, to update your thinking with adaptive thinking guidelines) strengthens your ability to think and respond more adaptively. Compassion brings kindness to your experience of slips and setbacks, whilst resilience fuels persistence and purposeful action. Mindfulness (see Appendix 14: *Switching off Automatic Pilot: The Art of Mindfulness*) helps you step out of "automatic pilot," notice the weather (e.g., pain, fatigue, memory slips) without judgment and guide your focus back to what matters. Gratitude practice (see Appendix 5: *Shifting Focus: Building Resilience through Gratitude*) means actively noticing and appreciating small moments of value, such as a kind word, a shared laugh or simply a moment of calm. This practice is helpful because it shifts attention away from the storm and gently reorients your focus towards what is still good and sustaining in life. Enjoyment and achievement activities (see Appendix 4: *Enjoyment and Achievement: Activities to Lift Mood and Motivation*) add a sense of mastery and pleasure, like beacons in the storm, reminding you of the safe landings and meaningful journeys still taking place, even in difficult conditions.

Bringing It All Together: Airport Storm Protocol

This map shows how the CRM and its core ACCEPTS qualities guide recovery when depression or low mood feels like a storm in the skies. Each part of the airport represents a principle or strategy to help you keep moving towards what matters.

- **Runway Lights = Basics (Awareness and Acceptance)**
  Notice how well your runway lights are working (e.g., exercise, nutrition and daily routines) and ensure that they are being maintained—this provides the steady light that grounds recovery.

- **Flight Schedules = Activity Planning (Purposeful Action and Effort with Balance)**
  Small, achievable goals keep you active and steady activity levels restore rhythm, and prevent withdrawal.
- **Radar Systems = Navigating Thoughts (Cognitive Flexibility and Self-Reflection)**
  Spot distorted signals, adjust flight paths and update your radar software to enable flexible, balanced thinking.
- **Ground Crews = Support (Compassion and Tools/Strategies)**
  Family, friends and therapists provide encouragement and share practical strategies.
- **Beacons and Safety Checks = Mindfulness and Gratitude (Awareness and Compassion)**
  Simple practices that shine through fog, reminding you of safe ground and meaningful moments.
- **The Co-Controller = The CRM (All of ACCEPTS)**
  A steady presence in the control tower, guiding with compassion, resilience and direction, whatever the weather.

Quick Reflection

- Which "airport system" (e.g., basics [sleep, food, routine], activity levels, thoughts, support or mood strategies) feels strongest in your life right now?
- Which one could benefit from extra attention or new strategies?
- How might using ACCEPTS as your manual help you bring more balance, compassion and purpose to recovery?

Summary

Depression after brain injury can feel like a prolonged storm in the skies above your control tower. The clouds may reduce visibility, the winds may force flights off course and the control tower may feel overwhelmed by the weight of traffic waiting to land. Yet, even in these conditions, airports do not shut down; instead, they adapt.

This chapter has shown that the strategies for navigating depression are like the control tower's essential operating procedures and building blocks. Attending to your basic needs is like switching on the runway lights. Managing activity levels creates a safe flight schedule that keeps planes moving. Learning strategies to compensate for cognitive challenges provides updated programmes for the radar and communication systems to work efficiently again. Working with gloomy thoughts, through your CRM, mindfulness and gratitude, ensures that the control tower does not overreact to distorted signals but instead, keeps guiding traffic with perspective and balance.

The aim is not to clear the skies entirely or guarantee perfect conditions. Storms are part of life after brain injury, just as they are part of aviation. What matters is having the support systems and compassionate mindset that allow the control tower to function safely and meaningfully, even when the weather is difficult.

With time, practice and support, your control tower can grow stronger and more confident. The planes may land more slowly, and the routes may sometimes need to change, but your airport continues to run, guiding you towards connection, purpose and a meaningful life (see Chapter 2: *Flowing Forward: Compassionate Resilient adaptation to Brain Injury,* for further guidance on how to connect to a meaningful life).

2 Flowing Forward

Compassionate Resilient Adaptation to Brain Injury

Vicki Hall and Emma Nicholas

After a brain injury, life can feel like being swept into a river whose currents no longer flow the way you expect. Familiar landmarks are gone, and every stroke feels uncertain. At first, "survival mode" takes over; you thrash against the water, desperate to reclaim control. However, in time, you realise that this is your river now and escape is not possible. Gradually, the struggle softens. You see that whilst you cannot force the river to run backwards, you can take up the paddle and steer with its flow. Fighting the current only exhausts you, but working with it helps you move forward, discover new directions and find steadier waters. True resilience lies not in resisting the river, but in learning to move with it, guided by courage, compassion and flexibility.

This chapter introduces the Compassionate Resilient Mind (CRM), i.e., a mindset that blends compassion and resilience to guide your journey of acceptance and adaptation. A CRM helps you step out of "survival mode", where fear and self-criticism dominate, and into a state of balance where acceptance, persistence and meaningful action can thrive.

Through the lens of CRM, you will explore strategies, reflective exercises and values-based goal setting that support you in navigating your river. As you begin to navigate your river with greater purpose, using compassion and resilience as your compass, opportunities for growth and adaptation become clearer. Along your journey of personal evolution, self-awareness and flexibility can gradually develop, opening up new pathways that take you towards what matters most.

"Survival Mode": When the River Turns Rough

As you journey down the river of life after brain injury, your mind carries an inbuilt alarm system that constantly scans for threats. When it perceives a threat, it instantly sounds the alarm and throws you into "survival mode", as though the river has suddenly turned into dangerous rapids. After brain injury, this survival alarm can become over-sensitive and triggered by changes in the current or shifts in the weather (e.g., pain, fatigue, memory slips). For example:

- Losses may feel like side streams drying up (e.g., loss of a work role or parenting role).
- Limitations, such as mobility or memory problems become new boulders blocking the channel.
- Symptoms like fatigue can create more turbulent conditions.
- Pain can feel like heavy rain falling, making every stroke harder.
- Difficult emotions rise and fall like stormy gusts of wind, easily mistaken for danger.

DOI: 10.4324/9781003464655-2

In these moments, you may find yourself swept into survival reactions:

- **Fight**: Battling against your symptoms and pushing them away, like thrashing against the current. The fight drains your energy, leaving you exhausted and no closer to the shore.
- **Flight**: This can feel like paddling frantically to escape from difficult experiences, driven by anxiety and avoidance.
- **Freeze**: This can feel like shutting down, drifting powerless as if the boat will not move, leaving you mentally "stuck" and unable to get started.

These automatic reactions are driven by the "Gatekeeper" (the "survival mode" part of your mind), who assumes danger is ahead and rushes out to protect you (see Appendix 8: *Unlocking Adaptation: A Practical Guide to the Compassionate Resilient Mind*). This happens instantly, often outside of your awareness, before you can even grip the paddle or steer rationally with wise intentions. Sometimes the alarm system, which signals threat or danger misfires, mistaking ordinary discomfort, uncertainty or pressure for danger and the mind can get stuck in this "survival mode".

When the "Gatekeeper" (the "survival mode") appears, the river narrows. The flow of thought is squeezed tight (e.g., you get sucked into rigid thinking), prioritising protection over exploration. The mind clings rigidly to what it knows, like gripping onto the rocks on the bank, afraid to release and move forward. This makes learning and adaptation harder, even when calmer waters lie just beyond. This narrowed focus clings to signs of threat (e.g., rocks in the way or catastrophic thoughts like "I'm always no good") to prepare you for the worst-case scenario (a "better safe than sorry" strategy), but it can do this even in calm waters, which leaves you exhausted and unable to notice calmer waters just beyond.

When the waters of discomfort rise, the "Gatekeeper" throws up barriers to block the current or prevent it from getting in, resisting its force at all costs. Signs that the "Gatekeeper" may be in charge include when you notice that you:

- **Experience Thoughts that Urge Avoidance**: Steering you away from certain waters, like avoiding social gatherings because you fear that your symptoms will be exposed (e.g., you may lose track of conversations).
- **Pretend Obstacles Do Not Exist**: Minimising symptoms (e.g., thinking that you can walk further than you can) or denying memory slips, leaving you unprepared when you hit them again.
- **Battle Symptoms Head-on**: Pushing through a full day without breaks despite fatigue, exhausting yourself against the current.
- **Impose Rigid Rules**: Such as "I must be perfect" or "I can't make mistakes," narrowing your channels and restricting your ability to adapt.
- **Deny, Minimise or Distort Symptoms**: Like pretending the water is calm when fog makes the way unclear or the current pulls you sideways. Thoughts, such as "It only happens because I'm tired" or "That didn't really happen," are ways of looking away from the rocks instead of navigating around them. At other times, the mind may catastrophise normal slips or difficult moments, interpreting small waves as overwhelming storms.
- **Rigidly Focus on Failure or Catastrophe**: Like staring only at the largest, darkest boulder, whilst the storm rages and concluding there is no way through. Statements, such as "There's no hope" or "This makes me a failure" keep you stuck in the roughest waters.

- **Resist the Use of Strategies**: This is like throwing away your paddle or map during a downpour because using them feels like weakness. Thoughts, such as "I don't need a planner," "Asking for help means I'm weak" or "I'll just do nothing because nothing helps," leave you drifting without tools, making the river even harder to manage.
- **Disown Symptoms or Blame Others**: Like insisting another passenger is rocking the boat when in fact the headwind or current is strong. For example, "It's my boyfriend's fault I forget things."

Though meant to protect, the "Gatekeeper's" rigid walls narrow flow and flexibility. Left unchecked, they heighten turbulence, increase emotional reactivity and pull you further away from meaningful adaptation. To begin softening resistance in your own journey, it can be helpful to firstly bring into your awareness patterns of thinking and behaving that support or block adaptation (see Appendix 6: *From Resistance to Acceptance: Opening the Door to Adaptation*; Appendix 8: *Unlocking Adaptation: A Practical Guide to the Compassionate Resilient Mind*); then explore the pros and cons of moving away from resistance towards acceptance (see Appendix 6: *From Resistance to Acceptance: Opening the Door to Adaptation*). This reflection can show you how letting go of the "Gatekeeper's" resistance may feel risky but can also free you from exhaustion, allowing you to travel again with the current's energy.

NOTE: Sometimes after a brain injury, a person may not have awareness of their symptoms, not due to psychological denial, but due to damage to part of the brain, which prevents them from being able to monitor their symptoms (see Chapter 12: *Executive Skills after Brain Injury: A Compassionate Guide to Planning, Problem-Solving, and Self-Control,* for further guidance on this).

A Compassionate Resilient Mindset (CRM): Learning the Way of Water

The "Gatekeeper" is rigid like rock (i.e., hard, resistant and unyielding). In contrast, the CRM is flexible like water, flowing, adaptive and able to gradually reshape challenges. Neither rock nor water alone defines the river. Rock without water remains unyielding; water without rock has no direction. In the same way, challenges and resistance shape your journey, whilst the qualities of the CRM give you the ability to adapt, flow and discover new routes towards balance, identity and purpose.

Below, each water-like quality of the CRM (the ACCEPTS qualities) shows how flexibility can soften the "Gatekeeper's" rigid, rock-like mindset and help you move forward along the river.

ACCEPTS Qualities—The Rock of Resistance (Gatekeeper) and the Water of Resilience (CRM)

A—Awareness and Acceptance

- **The "Gatekeeper" (Rigid Rock Mindset)**: Blocks awareness by responding immediately before you have time to stop, think and reflect. Blocks flow by denying the river's turbulence ("This isn't happening"), avoiding reminders of symptoms (e.g., not trying things in case you fail), or catastrophising ("This is unbearable, it makes me an idiot"). May focus rigidly on uncomfortable experiences (e.g., painful thought or memory slips). Like staring only at the rocks, these reactions keep you thrashing or frozen, unable to see the wider current.

- **CRM (Flexible Water Mindset)**: Softens resistance by noticing the water's movement (i.e., noticing inner experiences, such as pain, fatigue or memory slips) without harsh judgement. It says, "This is hard, but I can float." Able to shift awareness between past and present and between internal (e.g., fatigue, pain, uncomfortable thoughts) and external experiences (e.g., what you can see and hear). This creates space where you can see the wider current without judgement and adaptation can begin to grow.

C—Cognitive Flexibility

- **The "Gatekeeper" (Rigid Rock Mindset)**: Clings rigidly to one channel, stuck in all-or-nothing thinking ("If I can't do it the old way, it's not worth doing at all"). Like refusing to leave a blocked stream, it prevents exploration. Focuses rigidly on perceived threats (e.g., internal events, such as unwanted thoughts, feelings and sensations).
- **CRM (Flexible Water Mindset)**: Flows around obstacles, considering alternative perspectives and balancing past and present; problems and possibilities. It says, "Maybe there's another way or maybe there's another interpretation." This softening reopens the river's course, allowing you to find new directions and opening the door to adaptation.

C—Compassion

- **The "Gatekeeper" (Rigid Rock Mindset)**: Fills the waters with self-criticism ("You should cope better") or resentment towards others, fuelling shame and defensiveness. These inner currents are not the problem in themselves, but the "Gatekeeper" urges you to act quickly causing you to get caught up and pushed around by your thoughts and feelings. As a result, they can sweep you away from meaningful destinations which connect you to what matters most.
- **CRM (Flexible Water Mindset)**: Invites you to pause, reflect and notice the currents without being swept away. With kindness, it softens judgement: "I'm struggling, but that's human." Like a calm pool, compassion allows rest, perspective and renewed strength to move forward in line with your values.

E—Effort with Balance (Compassionate Persistence)

- **The "Gatekeeper" (Rigid Rock Mindset)**: Pushes extremes, either forcing the boat endlessly against the current or giving up entirely. Both lead to exhaustion, hopelessness or capsizing.
- **CRM (Flexible Water Mindset)**: Encourages steady paddling with rest, saying, "Stroke, pause, stroke." It says, "I can take this step, then pause, then try again." This rhythm supports sustainable progress downstream.

P—Purposeful Action

- **The "Gatekeeper" (Rigid Rock Mindset)**: Reacts automatically, like being swept helplessly by rapids, driven by fear or rigid rules, bypassing choice.
- **CRM (Flexible Water Mindset)**: Pauses to steer by values, asking, "What really matters here?" This creates room for intentional movement, ensuring each stroke of the paddle aligns with direction and purpose.

T—Tools and Strategies

- **The "Gatekeeper" (Rigid Rock Mindset)**: Rejects paddles, maps or companions. It says, "I don't need a planner," "If I don't try, I won't fail." Treating tools as a weakness leaves you drifting without support. In other cases, the "Gatekeeper" may cling too rigidly to strategies or routines, becoming fearful of coping without them. This can make it harder to adapt flexibly when conditions change or when familiar supports are unavailable.
- **CRM (Flexible Water Mindset)**: Uses tools and structures when needed as waypoints across the river: "Using support helps me move forward." Strategies become allies, guiding you safely around obstacles.

S—Self-Reflection/Self as Context

- **The "Gatekeeper" (Rigid Rock Mindset)**: Avoids looking at the river altogether or fixates only on failures, fuelling self-criticism. This is like being swept inside the rapids, unable to step back and see the journey clearly. Mistakes become your identity, keeping you stuck in circular currents.
- **CRM (Flexible Water Mindset)**: Pauses at still pools to reflect with compassion: "Yes, I slipped, but what can I learn from that?" From the steady seat in the boat, you notice the river's twists and your own reactions without being swept away. This is self-as-context: the observing part of you that holds experiences without judgement, turning mistakes into teachers, rather than definitions, and guiding you more wisely downstream.

By approaching adversity with the CRM's water-like qualities, Brain Injury Survivors (BISs) can discover their inner capacity to cope, adapt and grow not by avoiding the rough waters, but by learning to flow with them. In this way, discomfort itself becomes part of the current that builds resilience and personal growth when embraced with compassion and flexibility (see Appendix 8: *Unlocking Adaptation: A Practical Guide to the Compassionate Resilient Mind*, Part 2, for further narrative metaphors).

The CRM can be trained and strengthened after brain injury, offering opportunities for post-traumatic growth; creating space for a renewed sense of self, carried downstream with both strength of mind and compassion.

Also for further help in cultivating a CRM, see:

- Appendix 8: *Unlocking Adaptation: A Practical Guide to the Compassionate Resilient Mind*—practical exercises for becoming aware of resistance and strengthening compassionate, resilient responses.
- Appendix 7: *Navigating Mind Influencers: Guidelines for Adaptive Thinking*—guidance for becoming aware of unhelpful thoughts that block adaptation or connection to what is meaningful to you and developing a compassionate, resilient thinking style.
- Appendix 9a: *Martial Arts Metaphor, Metaphors for a Compassionate Resilient Mind*—for a further metaphor to explain the importance of yielding, rather than resisting and an exercise to help adapt, rather than resist.
- Other chapters in this book for symptom-specific tools and strategies (such as those on memory, sleep and pain), each explored through the lens of the CRM.

Navigating Identity Change: Looking Upstream and Downstream

Following a brain injury, it is common to feel caught between two stretches of your river: the waters behind you and those ahead. The difference between the "old you" and the "new you" can be magnified by what is known as the "good old days" bias. It is like gazing upstream with rose-tinted glasses, remembering the river before the rapids as smoother, gentler and easier than it really was. In contrast, the waters you are in now may feel harsher and more difficult, making the challenges of the present seem overwhelming.

When your focus stays fixed upstream, it not only stirs grief, sadness, depression or shame, but it also makes the waters ahead harder to read. By believing the past was far calmer than it really was, the present seems stormier, and you lose sight of the real currents and opportunities directly in front of you. This distortion that makes today's river appear more treacherous than it really is, sharpens the contrast between the "old me" you long for and the "current me" you struggle with. That gap can trigger the brain's alarm system, summoning the "Gatekeeper," who narrows the channel and churns the waters into turbulence. Emotional reactivity rises, rigid thinking takes over and resistance to adaptation sets in. If this pattern of looking backwards becomes exaggerated or stuck, it can form a whirlpool of emotional resistance, spinning you in circles and making it harder to accept and adapt to your current course.

Learning to notice and gently question or soften this "good old days" bias is like lifting your gaze from the receding current behind you to the new stretches of river unfolding ahead. By developing a compassionate understanding of your evolving self, you calm the waters; the river opens up again, creating space for flexibility, realistic self-appraisal, and purposeful adaptation (see Appendix 13: *Rose-Tinted Reflections: Navigating the Good Old Days Bias*).

To help re-orientate yourself to the stretch of river you now float on, one practical strategy is to compare how you lived your values before your injury with how you live them now. This is like checking your compass along the river, noticing not only where channels have closed, but also where new side streams of meaning may have appeared (see Appendix 2: *Your Inner Compass: Exploring Values after Brain Injury*, for a worksheet to guide this exercise). Through this reflection, you may discover that, whilst some values may no longer be met in the same way as before, other values have grown stronger. For instance, someone may no longer work in the same role, yet find they are living their value of resilience more fully by overcoming adversity or, in enduring hardship and pain, you may have deepened your compassion and empathy. Through this process, you may discover that, although the river's course has changed, it can still carry you to meaningful and even richer landscapes downstream - a process often described as post-traumatic growth.

Creating a New Meaningful Life and Goal Setting: Finding Your Compass and Waypoints

When living with limitations or symptoms after a brain injury, you may find that some stretches of your river are no longer passable. Certain channels that once carried you forward may now be blocked, and some roles you used to sail through may have shifted or even dried up. This can be an emotionally difficult realisation, like watching parts of the river you once knew vanish from the map. Yet, this moment also creates an opportunity: a chance to redraw your map, re-evaluate your course and rebuild a life that still feels rich and meaningful. The river may look different than before, but it can still carry you towards landscapes that matter if you navigate it with compassion and resilience.

A meaningful life is one where you travel through activities and relationships that matter to you. What makes the river meaningful will look different for everyone and your new journey may not resemble the one upstream, but it can still be fulfilling, alive and aligned with who you are.

Values as Your Compass

We find meaning by living in line with our values. These values act as your internal compass, steady and reliable, guiding your choices even when the current shifts. For help identifying values, see Appendix 2: *Your Inner Compass: Exploring Values after Brain Injury.* By clarifying what truly matters, you can begin to set values-based goals that act as waypoints along the riverbank; guide your steering and prevent you from getting swept away by the currents (i.e., difficult thoughts, feelings and sensations; see Appendix 3: *Turning Values into Action: Setting SMART Goals*). These waypoints help you reconnect with parts of your pre-injury identity or, if needed, begin shaping a new sense of self that is flexible, grounded and capable of navigating changing currents.

Steady Strokes towards What Matters

Sometimes, acting on your goals feels like paddling against a strong headwind. The "Gatekeeper" urges you to wait until you "feel ready" or until the waters are perfectly calm. Procrastination is like circling endlessly in a stagnant pool, missing the chance to move downstream.

Procrastination does not only happen when the water feels rough, overwhelming or when a storm hits. It can also occur when the stretch of river ahead looks dull or repetitive, for example, doing rehabilitation exercises or college work. In these moments, it is tempting to steer towards side streams that feel easier or more enjoyable in the moment, like checking your phone, watching TV or avoiding the task altogether. The risks are that these detours may pull you further off course, leaving your meaningful journey stalled and waiting for the "perfect moment" often means missing opportunities to move towards what is useful and meaningful.

Instead of letting the "Gatekeeper" keep you stuck or distracted, it therefore helps to notice the urge to delay and choose to take a stroke anyway, guided by your compass of values. You do not need to feel motivated or confident before you act, often it is the act of dipping your paddle into the water that gets the boat moving again. Accepting that you may not feel like doing something but still choosing to do it because it matters is a powerful step towards growth. Motivational statements can be like wind in your sail and reviewing the pros and cons of waiting versus moving forward can help you steer back into the current (see Appendix 11: *Turning Procrastination into Meaningful Action*). With each small stroke, you build momentum, carrying yourself steadily towards what matters most.

Steady Strokes through the Storm: Loosening Fear and Perfectionism

Goal setting can also stall when fears of failure rise, or when perfectionism insists the river must be navigated flawlessly. These fears can feel like stormy weather that makes the waters rough, convincing you not to try until conditions are perfect. For help loosening perfectionism, see Chapter 5: *Living Beyond Anxiety* and Appendix 11: *From Perfectionism to Progress: A Compassionate Resilient Mind Exercise.* These exercises shift the focus away from flawless performance and towards gentle persistence. Instead of setting a rigid outcome like, "I must paddle (or walk) 20 metres today," you can set a compassionate goal, such as, "Today I'll show persistence by taking a few strokes (or steps) and resting as needed." (See Appendix 10: *Acceptance and Resilience Goals: Choosing Growth over Perfection.*) Such goals are like steady paddle strokes that carry you forward through the storm; instead of waiting for calm waters, you learn to navigate the waves with resilience and compassion.

Holding the Paddle: Choosing Presence Over Automatic Pilot

As well as moving forward, meaningful travel is also about learning to pause and take in where you are on the river. If you are always waiting until you reach the next bend to feel "good enough," you risk missing the important moments happening right now.

Mindfulness is like taking your boat off "automatic pilot" and choosing to hold the paddle yourself. Instead of being swept wherever the current or rapids pull you, driven by the "Gatekeeper's" survival reactions, you pause, steady the boat and notice the water and banks around you without judgement. In that space, your CRM can guide the journey, helping you steer with purpose, rather than being dragged by the loudest wave or swirl (i.e., you can pause, reflect and make wise intentional responses, rather than letting your thoughts, feelings or sensations pull you around without purpose). Mindfulness also enables you to purposefully shift your awareness between past and present and between internal (e.g., fatigue, pain, uncomfortable thoughts) and external experiences (e.g., what you can see and hear). This creates space where you can see the wider current without judgement and adaptation can begin to grow, providing the first step towards purposeful action and regaining a sense of control over your river. For guidance on mindfulness, see Appendix 14: *Switching Off Automatic Pilot: The Art of Mindfulness.*

Gratitude can also help you shift your gaze from obstacles to resources by noticing the efforts, small victories and quiet joys already present along the way. It is like pausing to appreciate the sunlight reflecting on the water or the calm pools where the river slows enough for you to rest, helping you to replenish your energy (see Appendix 5: *Shifting Focus: Building Resilience through Gratitude*). In this way, goal setting becomes less about forcing yourself through rapids or demanding perfection, and more about steering steadily with your compass of values and flowing forward in a way that is sustainable, compassionate and deeply meaningful.

Pulling It All Together: River Survival Guide

Guide principle	Description	Self-reflection prompt
Know the river	Life has changed; the goal is not to go upstream but to travel forward.	"In what ways am I still trying to fight upstream?", "How could I focus instead on moving forward with what's here now?"
Watch for rocks (the "Gatekeeper")	Notice when you are avoiding, denying or fighting the current.	"What 'rocks' (avoidance, denial, catastrophising) do I notice in my river today?", "How do they affect my journey?"

(*Continued*)

Guide principle	Description	Self-reflection prompt
Use water skills (CRM)	Flow like water: flexible, compassionate, steady.	"Where could I soften or flow around an obstacle instead of resisting it?", "How can I bring compassion into this challenge?"
Carry a compass (values)	Let your values guide your direction when the river bends.	"Which of my values can guide me through today's twists and turns?", "Am I steering towards what matters most?"
Waypoints across the river (goals)	Choose small, achievable steps that keep you moving in the right direction.	"What is one small, realistic step I can take this week that aligns with my values?"
Learn to paddle through the storm (procrastination and perfectionism)	Do not wait for perfect conditions; practise taking steady strokes even in rough weather.	"Where am I waiting for things to be 'perfect' before I act?", "What small stroke forward could I take anyway?"
Rest in calm pools	Pause for compassion, gratitude and reflection.	"Have I given myself permission to pause and rest?", "What would a compassionate break look like for me today?"
Flow forward	This is still your river; with resilience and compassion, you can shape a meaningful life.	"How can I remind myself that this is my river?", "What does flowing forward with resilience and meaning look like right now?"

Flowing Onwards: A Closing Vignette

By the end of this journey, the river may still twist and surge, but it no longer feels like an enemy to be fought. The rocks, rapids and bends are part of its nature and part of yours. You have learnt to take up the paddle, to steer with the current, rather than against it and to use its flow to carry you forward. There may still be moments of turbulence and stretches of calm, but both belong to the same river. With your CRM as your guide, you can meet each turn with awareness, persistence and kindness. The river has changed, but it is still yours to travel. As you flow onward, with resilience and compassion as your compass, you may come to notice that even in unfamiliar waters, new possibilities for meaning, connection, and fulfilment can begin to emerge.

3 Riding Emotional Waves

Navigating Emotionalism after Brain Injury

Vicki Hall

A Compassionate Resilient Mind (CRM) does not fight emotional waves; it learns to surf them, knowing they will rise, crest and fall. The power lies not in stopping emotion, but in moving with it.

What Is Emotionalism?

Emotionalism is a common change after brain injury, particularly following a stroke. It describes sudden and uncontrollable episodes of laughing or crying that feel much stronger, longer or less appropriate than the situation seems to warrant. Importantly, the strength of the outward reaction often does not match the inner emotional state. For example, someone may cry intensely but only feel mildly sad.

Typical signs of emotionalism include:

- Sudden, brief episodes of laughing or crying, sometimes without a clear trigger, or as an exaggerated response to one.
- Emotions that feel difficult to control and may not reflect what you are truly feeling inside.
- Having emotions "close to the surface," meaning that small things can trigger tears or laughter that would not have done so before the injury.
- Rapid switches between crying and laughing.

This phenomenon is usually called emotionalism, though other terms include emotional lability, pathological laughing and/or crying and pseudo-bulbar affect. It most often occurs in the early weeks after injury and often improves with time. If symptoms continue, medication, such as antidepressants may sometimes be prescribed.

Emotionalism is thought to arise when areas of the brain that regulate the motor patterns associated with laughing and crying are damaged. It is not the same as depression, though the two conditions can sometimes occur together. Importantly, episodes of emotionalism do not mean that someone is "losing control," extremely distressed or at risk of harm. What tends to cause the most disruption is not the episodes themselves but the way they are interpreted and responded to by both the person and others.

Many people find emotionalism difficult because they worry about what others might think, fear that they are "losing control" or misinterpret it as a sign of deeper distress. These worries can add further anxiety, which in turn, can make episodes more frequent or intense.

DOI: 10.4324/9781003464655-3

How a CRM Can Help

The CRM is built on core "ACCEPTS" qualities, a set of flexible skills that can be applied when emotionalism arises:

- **A—Awareness and Acceptance**: Notice and name episodes as they happen (e.g., "hello wave I'm ready to ride you") and allow them to pass without resistance or harsh judgement.
- **C—Cognitive Flexibility**: Step back from catastrophic or self-critical thoughts about the wave of emotion, shifting towards more compassionate and balanced interpretations.
- **C—Compassion for Self and Others**: Offer yourself the same patience you would extend to a close friend. Share understanding with others, so they can respond with support, rather than confusion.
- **E—Effort with Balance (Compassionate Persistence)**: Keep participating in life's activities even if episodes occur, balancing courage with gentleness.
- **P—Purposeful Action**: Choose actions guided by your values, rather than fear or avoidance, so your life remains meaningful and connected.
- **T—Tools and Strategies (Adaptation through Self-Awareness)**: Identify and prepare for triggers, such as fatigue, stress or overstimulating environments, using self-awareness to guide supportive strategies.
- **S—Self-Reflection**: Learn from each episode, noting what helps, what hinders and how you can adapt next time, so you gradually develop a personal toolkit of resilience.

Each section ahead explores how the ACCEPTS qualities can be applied to help you build confidence in navigating emotional waves with resilience and self-kindness.

Awareness and Acceptance

Emotionalism is a brain-based response, which is not harmful or a sign that you are losing control or highly distressed, so the challenge is often not the emotional response itself, but the way the mind reacts to it. A frequent response to emotionalism is self-criticism, embarrassment, or a strong pull towards avoidance or suppression. The latter are attempts to regain control that can unintentionally intensify distress and tighten the struggle.

CRM encourages a different approach. Meeting emotional surges with kindness, acceptance and understanding helps soften the internal battle and reduces the threat response. When emotionalism is allowed, rather than judged or resisted, its intensity often eases, and greater flexibility becomes possible, creating space to respond with awareness and purpose, rather than react automatically.

Like a martial artist who softens around an incoming force, rather than resisting it head-on (see Appendix 9a: *Martial Arts Metaphor, Metaphors for a Compassionate Resilient Mind*) or a surfer who learns to ride the wave, rather than trying to block it, emotional adaptation sometimes means gently meeting the display of emotionalism, rather than battling directly against it or running away from it. When you approach emotion with openness, rather than tension, it often becomes more pliable, its intensity softens, and its hold loosens. Like a wave, it rises, crests and eventually falls.

Use mindfulness or relaxation techniques (see Appendix 14: *Switching off Automatic Pilot: The Art of Mindfulness* and Appendix 16: *Relaxation Skills: Finding Calm and Balance*) to help you stay grounded when an emotional wave rises. The more calmly you can observe it, the less influence it is likely to have over you. See Appendix 8: Part 2.1: *Unlocking Adaptation: A Practical Guide to the Compassionate Resilient Mind*, which provides metaphors and reflections to help you understand how riding the wave of emotions, rather than suppressing them, can be helpful.

Cognitive Flexibility

You may experience unhelpful thoughts like "Everyone's staring" or "I must be going mad." You may worry that everyone is focusing on you and the display of emotions, and this may cause you to inwardly focus on yourself. This, in turn, may magnify your feelings and may exacerbate the emotions. It may therefore help to try and shift your focus on your surroundings using "the mindfulness of things technique" below.

Mindfulness of Things Exercise

> Without touching an object, first explore it visually. Imagine that you are describing the object to someone who cannot see it:
>
> > What colours does it have?
> > Does it have patterns?
> > What shape is it?
> > How many edges does it have?
> > Is it rough, smooth or bumpy?
> > Does it look heavy or light?
> > Is it straight or curved?
> > Is it shiny or dull?
> > How tall or wide is it?
> > Does it look soft or hard?
> > What else can you see about it?
> > Now move on to another object in the room and do the same thing.

You may have catastrophic thoughts about the display of emotions, which may cause you to worry about it and therefore magnify your emotions. Examples of catastrophic thoughts may include "If I have this emotional outburst people will think I'm crazy and won't want anything to do with me"; "If I have an emotional outburst, it may mean that I'm having a breakdown." It may therefore help to examine the helpfulness and credibility of these thoughts using adaptive thinking and instead, develop more compassionate, resilient responses (see Appendix 7: *Navigating Mind Influencers: Guidelines for Adaptive Thinking*). You could also think about behavioural strategies to address your anxieties (e.g., if you are worried that others will think you are crazy, explain to them why you are acting in this way).

Compassion for Self and Others

CRM encourages you to respond to your episodes with compassion as you would to a close friend: "It's okay. This will pass. I'm doing my best."

If explaining your symptoms to others is difficult, you can share this chapter or use a pre-prepared message card (see Figure 3.1). This helps reduce feelings of embarrassment and encourages mutual understanding.

I have a had a stroke
Sometimes I appear to laugh or cry uncontrollably but I don't always feel these feelings inside.
If you ignore it then it usually will pass and get better
Thanks for your patience.

Figure 3.1 Message Card.

Effort with Balance (Compassionate Persistence)

The CRM fosters resilience, encouraging you to stay engaged in life, even when episodes happen. Courage is not about stopping emotionalism; it is about staying with the moment and trusting yourself to move through it.

If an episode happens mid-conversation, try continuing with what you were doing. Or, gently reassure others: "It's okay, just ignore it, it passes." This sends a message to others (and yourself) that these moments are not something to worry about, and they should ignore it too.

Purposeful Action

It is important not to build your life around avoiding emotionalism at all costs. The constant effort to fight or suppress difficult feelings can be draining and over time, it may lead you to withdraw from experiences that provide you with meaning and pleasure. As the Unwelcome Guest metaphor (see Appendix 9b: *Metaphors for a Compassionate Resilient Mind*) reminds us, emotions may arrive without invitation, but that does not mean you have to let them control your life.

Purposeful action means making choices that are guided by your values or what is meaningful to you, rather than letting fear or the urge to avoid discomfort guide your choices. The CRM encourages this kind of flexible courage. It helps you notice your thoughts and feelings without being ruled by them and to respond with compassion, rather than criticism. In these moments, it can help to gently coach yourself with CRM-based prompts, such as:

- "What would be more meaningful right now: hiding from life or taking one small step towards it?"
- "You don't have to stay the whole time. Just go and let's see what happens."
- "It's okay if an episode happens. I don't need to fear it or fight it. This is part of my brain injury, not a sign that I'm broken. I'll let the emotions rise and fall. I don't have to run or hide."

Purposeful action may look like:

- **Choosing When and How to Engage Socially:** Sometimes purposeful action means choosing to attend a gathering, go to a café or talk to a friend despite fear, but with preparation. This might include having a plan for how to respond if emotionalism occurs, choosing a quieter environment, or bringing a trusted support person.
- **Choosing Rest or Redirection Intentionally:** On some days, purposeful action might mean pausing, resting or removing yourself from a situation, not out of avoidance or fear, but because you are tuning into what your mind and body need in that moment.

Tools and Strategies (Adaptation through Self-Awareness)

Building self-awareness around your personal triggers is key. It helps you anticipate difficult moments, plan ahead and respond more deliberately and compassionately with strategies.

Emotionalism can sometimes be triggered by indirect factors, such as fatigue, which may reduce your capacity to regulate feelings. It may also be influenced by specific environments or people, for instance, interactions that feel stressful or overstimulating. In some cases, noisy or overcrowded spaces may directly heighten your emotional reactivity and may be worth limiting where possible. See Chapter 8: *Pacing with Purpose: A Compassionate Guide to Navigating Fatigue*, for how to navigate fatigue and oversensitivity to stimulation.

Self-Reflection

After an episode, take time to reflect: "What helped?, What didn't?, What might I try next time?" This builds insight, confidence and self-trust. You could keep a journal of strategies that work for you and share reflections with a loved one, therapist or support staff.

How Can Other People Help?

Emotionalism can be confusing not only for you but also for those around you. Family and friends may interpret crying as deep sadness or assume you are distressed when you are not. This can lead to awkwardness, worry or misunderstanding. Here is how others can support you:

- **Educate with Kindness**: Help others understand that emotionalism is a brain-based symptom, not a sign that you are emotionally overwhelmed. If explaining feels difficult, consider sharing this chapter or using written explanations.
- **Give Guidance, Not Control**: Let people know how you would like them to respond when an episode happens. For example: "Just carry on talking to me like normal, it usually passes." Some people may find it helpful to distract or shift the topic, but only if that is what you find useful.
- **Clarify Emotional Meaning**: If you are genuinely upset or in need of support, let others know so they do not confuse it with emotionalism.

- **Normalise the Moment**: The less people react with panic or concern, the quicker the emotional episode often settles. Encourage them to follow your lead, offering quiet support without unnecessary attention.

By creating shared understanding, you invite others into your adaptation in a way that is respectful, empowering and compassionate for you, your family and friends.

Key Takeaway Points

- Emotional episodes may not reflect your true feelings and often settle on their own.
- Trying to fight or suppress emotionalism can increase distress; responding with acceptance and compassion is often more helpful.
- A CRM supports flexibility, self-kindness and continued engagement with life.
- The ACCEPTS framework offers practical ways to ride emotional waves and reduce shame, fear and avoidance.
- With understanding, preparation, and support, emotionalism can become manageable and need not limit a meaningful, values-led life.

4 Finding Calm in the Storm

Anger, Irritability and Compassion

Vicki Hall

After a brain injury, anger can feel like a ship being swept away by a storm. With resilience and compassion as your compass, you can purposefully take charge of the sails, and navigate your way towards destinations connected to what matters most.

Why Anger Feels Stronger after Brain Injury

It is common to be more angry or irritable following brain injury. This may be because you are dealing with a range of new stressors, such as forgetfulness, fatigue, pain or difficulty expressing yourself. These challenges can build up and make you more likely to react quickly or feel like you have a "short fuse."

A helpful analogy is the "leaky bucket." At the start of the day, your emotional bucket may be empty, but as frustrations accumulate (e.g., word finding difficulties, dealing with noise, managing pain) your bucket begins to fill. When your bucket starts to get full, even a small trigger can lead to strong feelings of anger. Taking time to "empty the bucket" through rest and self-awareness can increase your ability to cope.

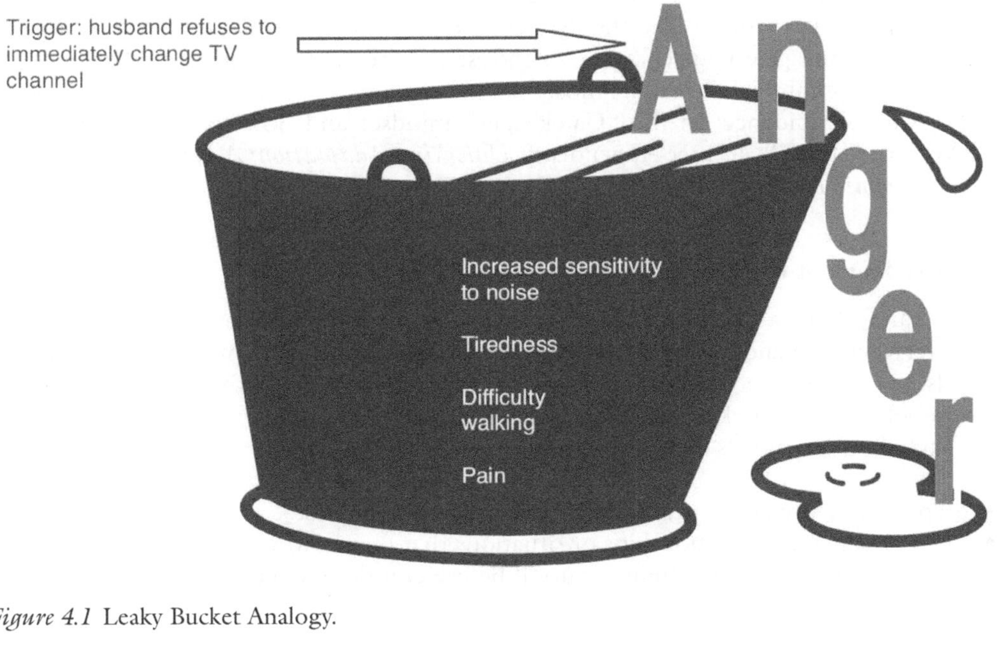

Figure 4.1 Leaky Bucket Analogy.

DOI: 10.4324/9781003464655-4

Why Is It Harder to Stop Myself from Venting My Anger?

After a brain injury, some individuals can experience more explosive anger, causing them to have anger outbursts, including shouting, swearing, throwing things or reacting too quickly. This may be because the parts of the brain responsible for inhibiting impulses (the "stop-think button" in your brain) and reflecting before reacting have been affected. Your "leaky bucket" can also contribute to this reaction. The Compassionate Resilient Mind (CRM), the reflecting part of your mind, invites you to meet these moments with understanding, rather than criticism.

How Anger Hijacks the Brain

When anger rises, your brain may flip into "survival mode". This is when the "Gatekeeper" mindset often steps in, which is a way of thinking shaped by the survival system. The "Gatekeeper's" role is to protect you, but its tools are rigid rules, harsh criticism and black-and-white thinking. It reacts quickly, assuming danger or disrespect; pushing you to fight back before you have had time to reflect.

The "Gatekeeper's" messages might sound like:

- "They're disrespecting you, fight back!"
- "You're weak if you back down."
- "You need to get control by shouting louder."
- "Do something quickly, let them know you're angry."

Although these messages may feel convincing, they can trap you in cycles of blame, tension and frustration. You may find yourself reacting harshly or defensively, even when the situation does not truly call for it. This is where "Eve Olve" (your CRM voice) can sometimes step in. "Eve Olve" represents resilience paired with compassion. She reminds you that, even when anger rises, it usually does not mean that you are in real danger. You do not have to react automatically like the "Gatekeeper" urges you to. Instead, you can pause, take a breath and give yourself space to choose how to respond, in a way that is aligned with your values and what matters most.

For further guidance on the "Gatekeeper" mindset and how to respond with your CRM voice ("Eve Olve"), see Appendix 8: *Unlocking Adaptation: A Practical Guide to the Compassionate Resilient Mind*.

Identify Signs of the Storm

Anger can feel like a storm. If you only notice when it starts to crash down on you it can feel overwhelming and harder to navigate. By recognising the early warning signs, the first clouds, the shift in the wind, you have more chance to respond with your CRM, and take action before the "Gatekeeper" takes control.

Catching these signals early allows you to:

- Step back before anger peaks when your choices are widest.
- Prevent damage to relationships or situations that matter to you.
- Protect your energy by calming yourself before emotions spiral.

- Stay aligned with your values choosing responses that reflect who you want to be, rather than just how the "Gatekeeper" wants you to react.

Signs that your anger is building can include:

- Raised voice
- Muscle tension
- Faster breathing
- Racing heart
- Feeling hot or flushed

Catching Early Warning Signs

When you sense one of these warning signs, pause and name the emotion you are experiencing. This gives your brain a moment to slow down and reduces the intensity of the reaction. For example:

- "I notice my heart is racing, I think I'm feeling frustrated."
- "My voice is getting louder, this feels like anger building."
- "I feel heat in my face, I'm starting to feel upset."

By putting words to the emotion, you move from the reactive parts of your mind (the "Gatekeeper") to the reflective parts ("Eve Olve" and the CRM). This small step strengthens your "mental brakes" and helps you regain self-control. Once you have noticed and named the emotion, take a compassionate stance:

- Remind yourself: "This is my brain reacting quickly. I can choose what happens next."
- Use a calming action, such as slowing your breathing, stepping out of the room or grounding yourself with a soothing phrase.

With practice, noticing, naming and responding with compassion helps you step back from the "Gatekeeper's" rigid assumptions and act from "Eve Olve's" wisdom instead. Over time, this skill gives you greater choice and control in how you navigate anger.

You can also use compassion to soothe this survival system and help restore balance. For example:

- **Self-soothing**: Talk to yourself as you would a friend. "It's okay to feel angry. This is hard, but I can calm myself."
- **Grounding**: Place your hand on your chest, breathe slowly, relax your shoulders.
- **Imagery**: Picture "Eve Olve" wrapping the angry part of you in reassurance, or steadying your "ship in the storm."

Plan for the Storm

Planning for the storm means putting supports in place before anger reaches its peak. Just as you would close the windows and secure the house when you see dark clouds gathering, you can prepare yourself when you notice the first emotional signs building. One important way of planning is to work out what triggers your anger so you can navigate it. To help you work out your triggers, use an anger diary (see Appendix 17: *Anger Diary*) to note:

- What triggered your anger directly
- What happened earlier that day that may have increased your propensity for anger (fatigue, pain, overstimulation)

This can help you:

- Avoid or manage known triggers (e.g., shopping in quieter environments)
- Address indirect factors (e.g., rest if fatigued, use pain relief if needed)
- Plan for conversations or interactions when you feel more resourced

It may also help to express needs more clearly and assertively when calm. For example: "When I feel ignored, I get frustrated. I need to feel heard." If you find it difficult expressing your needs assertively, the assertiveness strategies from Chapter 13*: Communicating with Assertiveness and Compassion after Brain Injury* may be helpful.

When you notice the triggers or early warning signs of anger, think about how "Eve Olve" might guide you; for example, she may say: "The "Gatekeeper" wants you to react now, but you can plan ahead so you can respond when you feel stronger and calmer."

To help you plan for your "storms," so that you can successfully navigate them, you may find it helpful to work with the story and reflective questions in Appendix 18: *A Narrative about Riding the Rage Storm*. This appendix uses the metaphor of a storm at sea to illustrate how anger can build like sudden weather and how the "Gatekeeper" may panic and make things worse. With "Eve Olve's" guidance, the storm becomes something you can recognise, ride through and recover from without losing your dignity. The appendix also includes the Ride the Rage Storm Worksheet, which helps you:

- Identify your own "storm signals."
- Build an "anchor" phrase or strategy to steady yourself.
- Practise using "Eve Olve's" compassionate voice, instead of the "Gatekeeper's" panic.

You can return to Appendix 18 whenever you want to practise these skills more actively. Also see Appendix 20: *Taming the Dragon: A CRM Relaxation Script for Anger and Embitterment*, for a guided imagery exercise to help you understand your anger more clearly and plan how to manage it differently in the future. By relating to your "inner dragon" (i.e., anger) with curiosity and compassion, you can begin to see what lies beneath the fire, recognise what matters most to you and prepare ways of responding that feel calmer, safer and more in line with your values.

Practise Adaptive Thinking Skills

Separating Facts from Opinions

Rigid thinking makes anger feel justified. It can therefore help to distinguish between:

- **Facts**: Things that can be proven ("She closed the door").
- **Opinions**: Assumptions, beliefs or labels ("She slammed it to annoy me" / "He's an idiot").

For more detailed guidance on separating fact and opinion, see Appendix 7: *Navigating Mind Influencers: Guidelines for Adaptive Thinking.*

Pausing and Thinking before Responding

Ask:

- "Could there be another explanation?"
- "Would acting on this thought help or harm me right now?"
- "Is my urge to respond with the 'Gatekeeper' mindset and could I think of an alternative 'Eve Olve'/CRM response?"

Worked Example 1:

- **Situation**: Someone cuts in front of you in a queue.
- **The "Gatekeeper"**: "They think you're weak, show them you're not!"
- **"Eve Olve"/CRM**: "Thank you 'Gatekeeper' for trying to protect me but I'm not in danger. Maybe they didn't see me, they're in a hurry or they may be being selfish, but if I show them that I'm angry it could start an argument. It makes sense to just let it go."

Worked Example 2:

- **Situation**: You are in a team meeting at work. You share an idea you have been working on, but another colleague quickly interrupts and talks over you, pushing their own view instead.
- **The "Gatekeeper"**: "You're not being respected, fight back!"
- **"Eve Olve"**: "Thank you 'Gatekeeper' for trying to protect me but I can stand up for myself without losing control. Calm is my strength. If I show I'm angry it looks like I've lost control and I'll lose respect."

For further guidance, see:

- Appendix 8: *Unlocking Adaptation: A Practical Guide to the Compassionate Resilient Mind.*
- Appendix 18: *A Narrative about Riding the Rage Storm: When the Fire Takes Over.*
- Appendix 7: *Navigating Mind Influencers: Guidelines for Adaptive Thinking.*

Check Your "Leaky Bucket"

Sometimes, anger is not about the trigger, but about what has already filled your bucket. Ask:

- "Am I tired, in pain or overloaded?"
- "Is this anger really about now, or is it about build-up?"

For more detailed guidance on navigating symptoms that can fill up your bucket, such as pain and fatigue, see other chapters in this book.

Gently Redirect from the Trigger

It is natural to find yourself getting caught up in angry ruminations (thinking over and over); this is often the "Gatekeeper" at work, trying to protect you by keeping your focus on the perceived threat. However, this protective stance can also intensify anger and keep you stuck. When you notice this happening, try not to judge yourself. Instead, kindly acknowledge the "Gatekeeper's" effort to keep you safe, and then gently guide your attention elsewhere. Practising letting go in this way, and using mindfulness to ground yourself, can help ease the intensity of anger (see Appendix 14: *Switching off Automatic Pilot: The Art of Mindfulness*, for further guidance on mindfulness).

Values-Based Action

Anger often pulls you away from the kind of person you want to be. Values-based action brings you back on track.

Ask:

- "What matters most here: respect, fairness, connection, dignity?"
- "How can I act in a way that reflects my values, even whilst angry?"

Worked Example

- **Situation**: A friend forgets to call you back.
- **The "Gatekeeper"**: "They don't care about you, drop them!"
- **"Eve Olve"**: "Thank you, 'Gatekeeper', I know you're trying to protect me from being hurt, but my friend matters to me, and forgetting doesn't always mean not caring. I can stand up for myself by asking why they didn't call back, and check in calmly so I understand what happened. This way, I protect the friendship that's important to me, whilst also respecting my own needs."

Use the Traffic Light System

You have already learnt how anger can build like a storm, how the "Gatekeeper" reacts quickly with rigid rules and how "Eve Olve" offers a calmer, wiser alternative. The traffic light system pulls these ideas together into a simple map you can use to notice where you are in the cycle of anger and what actions will help most.

Strategies for Each Zone

Red Zone: The Storm Has Hit

In the red zone, anger has taken over. You might be shouting, swearing, shaking or completely overwhelmed. This is when the "Gatekeeper" is fully in control, pushing you to fight back without reflection. Your "mental brakes" are not working as they once did.

What to do:

- Remove yourself from the situation immediately.
- Use physical tension-release methods: e.g., a brisk walk, punching a pillow, squeezing a stress toy.

- Try calming your body (using techniques from Appendix 14: *Switching Off Automatic Pilot: The Art of Mindfulness*, for guidance on how to use mindfulness; Appendix 16: *Relaxation Skills: Finding Calm and Balance*, for guidance on how to use relaxation techniques).
- Return only once you feel calm again (green zone).

Amber Zone: Storm Clouds Gathering

The amber zone is the warning stage. You may notice faster breathing, a racing heart, muscle tension or rising irritation. This is when the "Gatekeeper" is getting louder, trying to push you into action. But you still have the chance to pause, slow down and listen for "Eve Olve's" steadying voice.

What to do:

- Say: "I need a break, we can talk later."
- Use relaxation techniques or mindfulness to slow down in the moment (see Appendix 14*: Switching Off Automatic Pilot: The Art of Mindfulness and* Appendix 16*: Relaxation Skills: Finding Calm and Balance*).
- If possible, use pre-planned signals or agreements, so that others know that you need space.
- To help you calm down once you have walked away, use the compassionate resilient relaxation script for anger (see Appendix 20: *Taming the Dragon: A CRM Relaxation Script for Anger and Embitterment*). This script also helps you reflect on whether the anger is based on assumptions or unmet needs, alongside creating a space for calm.

Green Zone: Calm, Reflective, In Control

Once anger has eased and you have moved into the green zone, this is the best time to pause and reflect on the situation that made you angry. Reflection is not about criticising or judging yourself it is about learning. By looking back with curiosity, rather than blame, you can understand what triggered your anger, what was happening underneath it and how you might handle similar situations differently in the future. This kind of reflection strengthens your CRM, helping you protect yourself, live by your values and move forward with more balance.

What to do:

- Use Appendix 7*: Navigating Mind Influencers: Guidelines for Adaptive Thinking* (Table 7.1) to check if your thoughts were fact-based or emotionally skewed.
- Explore what the anger was really about, was there hurt, fear, shame or frustration underneath? (see Appendix 20: *Taming the Dragon: A CRM Relaxation Script for Anger and Embitterment*).
- Use the "practise adaptive thinking" section of this chapter to apply adaptive thinking strategies to anger.
- Prepare for future situations by imagining how "Eve Olve" (your CRM) would respond (see Appendix 18: *A Narrative about Riding the Rage Storm: When the Fire Takes Over* to help with this reflection).

Once calm, consider re-engaging with the person or situation using assertiveness strategies from Chapter 13: *Communicating with Compassion and Assertiveness after Brain Injury.*

Pulling It Together: Sailor's Storm Survival Guide

Spot the Clouds Early: Just as sailors watch the horizon, notice the first signs of rising anger (e.g., faster breathing, tense muscles and a louder voice). Early detection gives you more options to act wisely.

Drop Your Anchor: When the storm builds, ground yourself with calming actions; slow breathing, repeating an anchor phrase, such as "Calm is my strength." This steadies your ship and keeps you from drifting into outbursts.

Check Your Compass: The "Gatekeeper" may shout orders to fight back and respond immediately, but pause and consult your inner compass - "Eve Olve" / your CRM. Ask: "What action keeps me aligned with who I want to be?"

Adjust Your Sails: You cannot always control the wind, but you can set your sails. Step back, choose calmer words or delay a heated conversation until the seas settle. Adaptive actions steer you towards safer waters.

Ride Out the Storm: If the storm hits hard, protect yourself and others; remove yourself from the situation, release tension physically and return only once calm. No sailor battles a storm by force; survival comes from wise navigation.

Chart the Course Ahead: After the storm, reflect with curiosity, not criticism. What triggered the tempest? What mattered most beneath the anger? Each reflection helps you learn, adapt and strengthen your CRM for the voyages ahead.

Final Thought: Reframing Anger with Compassion

Anger is a human response, rather than a flaw; it is a sign that something matters and can reflect frustration, hurt or unmet needs. The goal is not to eliminate anger, but to develop the ability to hold it with greater flexibility and compassion, helping you stay connected to what matters most, rather than being pulled around by the anger itself. The CRM supports you in:

- Noticing and naming your emotional state
- Adapting your response based on what is meaningful to you
- Learning and adapting after an outburst

Use your traffic light system, your appendices and your inner "Eve Olve" (your CRM) to steer you back towards clarity, control and self-respect.

5 Living Beyond Anxiety

A Compassionate, Resilient Approach

Vicki Hall

Crossing the Bridge and Meeting the "Gatekeeper"

Imagine that you are standing before a bridge that leads to the places and people that matter to you most: independence, friendships, meaningful activities and adaptation. After a brain injury, this bridge can feel shaky and uncertain. Just as you prepare to cross, a guard (the "Gatekeeper") steps forward. It is the "Gatekeeper's" job to keep you safe, so it warns you of every possible danger: "Don't step forward, the bridge might collapse!", "Turn back, people will laugh if you stumble."

At first, listening to the "Gatekeeper" feels reassuring. It seems to know the risks and obeying it gives short-term relief. However, its voice is not only cautious, but also critical. It tells you, "You'll never manage this" or "You're not as strong as you used to be. You're not good enough." Sometimes, it compares you to others: "They would cross without stumbling, why can't you?" The "Gatekeeper's" intention is to be protective, but its words chip away at your confidence and self-worth. Each time you retreat, the bridge feels more frightening and the world on the other side grows further away.

With "Eve Olve" beside You: Moving Beyond Fear after Brain Injury

After a brain injury, it is natural for fears to arise, such as:

- Fear that the incident that caused the injury will happen again ("I may get knocked over by a car").
- Fear of being seen as foolish if you make a mistake ("I'm too scared to speak in case I muddle my words").
- Fear of being judged in public because of visible or invisible difficulties ("People will stare and pity me").

These fears can trigger the body's fight-or-flight response, a survival system designed to protect you. Symptoms, such as a racing heart, dizziness or tense muscles were once vital for escaping real danger, but after brain injury, this system can become overactive and misinterpret ordinary situations as threats. In this state, the "Gatekeeper" (a "survival" mindset, whose intention is to protect, and triggered by threat and discomfort) grows louder, shouting rigid rules and enforcing safety behaviours, such as "don't go out", "keep quiet", "hide your difficulties". Whilst comforting at first, these strategies keep fears alive and gradually shrink your world. One of the "Gatekeeper's" sharpest tools is criticism: pointing out flaws, predicting failure and insisting you are "not ready." From the

DOI: 10.4324/9781003464655-5

"Gatekeeper's" perspective, convincing you to avoid risk is protection; the effect, however, is shame, self-doubt and low self-worth.

It helps to remember that even the "Gatekeeper's" harshest words are fear in disguise, for example, fear that you might stumble, be judged or feel pain again. When you can see its warnings as misguided protection, rather than absolute truth, you create space to respond differently. A helpful first step in breaking this cycle is naming and noticing "Gatekeeper" thoughts. For example, saying to yourself, "I notice my 'Gatekeeper' is telling me I'll make a fool of myself," creates space between the thought and your response. This simple act weakens the "Gatekeeper's" grip and opens the door to another way forward.

You do not have to face the "Gatekeeper" alone. Alongside the "Gatekeeper," another figure can appear: an ally who sees your strengths, your values and your courage. This is "Eve Olve," symbolising your Compassionate Resilient Mind (CRM). The CRM does not fight or silence the "Gatekeeper"; it acknowledges the "Gatekeeper's" efforts with kindness, and gently offers alternatives. Where the "Gatekeeper" brings criticism and avoidance, the CRM brings compassion, flexibility and adaptive thinking. With this support, you can step onto the bridge again, not recklessly, but wisely and gently, discovering that it is stronger than it first seemed.

Through mindfulness, self-awareness and compassionate reflection, you can learn to step out of automatic "survival mode" and into a way of being that supports growth, resilience and adaptation. Over time, the "Gatekeeper's" warnings grow quieter, and your confidence grows stronger. The bridge may always sway a little, but with your CRM as your guiding compass, it becomes a pathway back to the life you want to live.

Fears about Being Knocked Over

If your brain injury was caused by a road traffic accident, it is understandable that you will worry about this happening again. The "Gatekeeper" may try and protect you by telling you, "Don't go out" or "Avoid crossing the road," but the more you avoid similar situations, the harder it becomes to face them.

The best way to navigate your fear is to face it. You can do this gradually in a way that feels safe by using a technique called "systematic desensitisation" (see Appendix 21: *Courage in Motion: Practising Safe Exposure*). This approach incorporates the CRM, because it embodies the dual qualities of courage and care, using resilience to face your fears step-by-step, and compassion to approach the process gently, at your own pace. Rather than avoiding what you fear or overwhelming yourself, this method builds strength gradually through safe and consistent exposure.

Sometimes it can feel very difficult to take the first step towards facing your fear, especially when the "Gatekeeper" is urging you to stay in the safety of avoidance. In those moments, it can help to bring in your CRM (symbolised by "Eve Olve") to respond with flexibility and care (see Appendix 8: *Unlocking Adaptation: A Practical Guide to the Compassionate Resilient Mind*).

For example, if the "Gatekeeper" says, "Don't go out. It's too dangerous. Stay inside where nothing can hurt you." "Eve Olve" may gently reply:

- "Thank you, 'Gatekeeper.' I know you're trying to keep me safe, but I also know that I can take sensible steps to protect myself, whilst still living my life."
- "Even if I feel anxious, I can still choose actions that matter to me, like being independent and enjoying the outdoors."

Social Anxiety and Fear of Judgement

After a brain injury, it is common to feel more sensitive about what others think. You might worry that people will see you as foolish if you make a mistake or notice your difficulties. This fear of negative evaluation is often called social anxiety. The following can help with this:

Redirecting Your Focus: From Self to Others

When social anxiety shows up, your attention often turns inward, for example, you may find yourself intensely focusing on your thoughts, your body, your feelings of anxiety or imagined judgements. This inward focus is the "Gatekeeper's" way of trying to protect you, but it can heighten self-consciousness and make situations feel overwhelming.

When attention is pulled inward, you may lose touch with what is actually happening around you and miss supportive cues from another person, such as a smile, a nod or a warm tone of voice. This may cause you to rely on harsh assumptions (e.g., "They must think I'm stupid because I couldn't find my words") that are not grounded in reality. By gently shifting focus outward with curiosity and compassion, you can tune into others, for example:

- Facial expressions
- Body language
- Tone of voice
- The actual words being said

This outward focus softens worry-driven assumptions, and keeps you in the present moment, noticing what is going on around you. Mindfulness can support this shift by helping you notice when attention drifts inward, and gently guiding it back outward. Over time, mindfulness strengthens flexibility, builds self-awareness and helps move you out of "survival mode" into a calmer, more compassionate state of mind (see Appendix 14: *Switching off Automatic Pilot: The Art of Mindfulness*).

With practice, you may become better at:

- Catching anxious self-focus early
- Reconnecting with the present moment
- Noticing that people often respond more positively than you assume

Facing Fear with Compassion

To protect you from a fear of socialising, the "Gatekeeper" may encourage safety behaviours, such as avoiding eye contact or only going out with close friends. Whilst these ease anxiety in the moment, they can prevent you from discovering that you can cope without them and, in the long run, they maintain anxiety. By noticing the "Gatekeeper's" protective efforts with kindness, you can begin to gently loosen reliance on safety behaviours and experiment with new ways of responding. One helpful approach is to start with the least feared situations first (e.g., talking to a close friend, whilst making eye contact), then gradually work your way towards more challenging ones (e.g., meeting a group of friends in a pub, whilst making eye contact). This step-by-step method allows you to build confidence slowly and safely, proving to yourself that you can cope at each stage. Each small step, taken with courage and compassion, strengthens resilience and flexibility, helping you live more fully in line with what matters to you. See Appendix 21: *Courage in Motion:*

Practising Safe Exposure, for guidance on how to face fears gradually and gently, whilst softening reliance on safety behaviours.

Practising CRM Thinking

Uncomfortable thoughts often fuel social anxiety. For instance, you might think: "If I can't follow a conversation, no one will want to be my friend." When these thoughts show up, they can feel very convincing, but with the support of your CRM, you can take a different approach. The CRM helps you notice thoughts without judgement, reflect on whether they are truly grounded in evidence and respond with more flexible, compassionate alternatives, whilst keeping your actions aligned with what matters to you (see Appendix 7: *Navigating Mind Influencers: Guidelines for Adaptive Thinking*).

At times, the "Gatekeeper" may appear with messages designed to protect you by encouraging avoidance. For example, it might say, "Don't meet up with your friends, they may not want to speak to you." If this happens, you can turn to "Eve Olve," who embodies the flexible, compassionate voice of your CRM.

"Eve Olve" might respond by saying:

- "Thank you, 'Gatekeeper,' I know you're trying to protect me from rejection, but friendships matter to me and the best way to keep them is to spend time with my friends."
- "Even if conversations feel hard at times, I can still connect and enjoy being with people who care about me."
- "I don't need to be perfect to be accepted. I can bring my real self to my friends and let them meet me where I am."
- "I can take things step by step; even a short meet-up is a way of building confidence."

For further guidance, see Appendix 7: *Navigating Mind Influencers: Guidelines for Adaptive Thinking and Appendix 8: Unlocking Adaptation: A Practical Guide to the Compassionate Resilient Mind.*

Fears about Making Mistakes or Appearing "Different"

After a brain injury, it is common to feel anxious about making mistakes in everyday tasks, such as cooking, speaking or remembering things. These worries often stem from real changes in thinking skills or physical abilities, and it can feel distressing to struggle in situations that once felt easy. It is also natural to worry about what others might think. You may fear being judged or misunderstood. These concerns can trigger self-criticism, shame and/ or denial, and make it harder to accept or adapt to your difficulties. You can try the following to help:

Responding with a CRM

Everyone makes mistakes. A CRM ("Eve Olve") views mistakes not as failures, but as opportunities to:

- Learn what helps, what does not, and adapt
- Fine-tune strategies
- Build emotional resilience

The CRM responds with curiosity, rather than criticism, creating an inner environment where it feels safe to reflect, learn and adjust. A well-developed CRM has the flexibility to consider different perspectives, adapt to uncertainty and respond effectively to life's challenges. You can begin to retrain your mind by practising how you respond to mistakes. When you notice an error, pause and ask:

> How would my CRM ("Eve Olve") respond right now?

For further help in responding with a CRM see also:

- Appendix 10: *Acceptance and Resilience Goals: Choosing Growth over Perfection*
- Appendix 7: *Navigating Mind Influencers: Guidelines for Adaptive Thinking*
- Appendix 8: *Unlocking Adaptation: A Practical Guide to the CRM*
- Appendix 6: *From Resistance to Acceptance: Opening the Door to Adaptation*

Normalising Mistakes: A Perspective-Shifting Exercise

After a brain injury, you may feel highly self-conscious about errors, fearing they reveal your difficulties or define you as "defective." However, everyone makes mistakes as they are part of being human.

Over the next few days, try this:

- Notice when others make slips or action errors, such as forgetting a word, losing track or misplacing something.
- Observe how they handle making the mistake, for example, do they ignore it, laugh it off, ask for help?
- Pay attention to how others react, for example, do they notice it?; are they critical or understanding?

This is not about judging others, but about retraining your mind to see that mistakes are ordinary and manageable. You may discover that:

- Mistakes do not define worth
- Others are not as focused on your errors as you fear
- Support strategies are common and smart, not shameful

Facing the Fear of Mistakes

The "Gatekeeper" may step in to protect you from mistakes by encouraging you to avoid situations or tasks where you may make a mistake, but this often keeps you stuck, fuels anxiety and limits growth and adaptation. It also stops you from connecting to what matters in life, and from getting on with your life. Facing fears gently and gradually can help you build confidence and flexibility. The following may help you to do this:

- **Graded Exposure**: Start small, with tasks you know you can manage, then gradually stretch towards more challenging ones (see Appendix 21: *Courage in Motion*).
- **Test Your Fears**: Try a harmless mistake (e.g., send a message with a minor error) and notice the outcome.

- **Learn by Watching**: If you are not ready yourself, observe a friend making a small mistake and see how others respond.
- **Practice Coping**: Work with a therapist or trusted person to rehearse strategies for real-life "action errors" (e.g., catching the wrong bus, getting lost).

If the "Gatekeeper" shows up telling you not to try, you can say, "Thank you, 'Gatekeeper', for trying to protect me. I know you want to keep me safe, but I also know It's safe enough to try. I'm going to give this a go." You can also try creating your own CRM statements (see Appendix 8: *Unlocking Adaptation: A Practical Guide to the Compassionate Resilient Mind*, for further guidance on CRM statements). See Appendix 36: *The CRM Guide for Navigating Cognitive Symptoms with ACCEPTS*, for guidance on how to respond to slips and cognitive errors with a CRM.

Reframing Perfectionism

Perfectionism can make adapting after a brain injury especially hard, and fuel fears about your symptoms showing up (e.g., memory slips, not being able to find the right words). The drive to "get everything right" may feel like strength, but it often leads to fear of failure, harsh self-criticism and difficulty moving forward. What can sometimes help is to reframe goals from external achievement to internal achievements based on values. For example:

- Instead of: "I must cook a meal without mistakes."
- Try: "I'll cook a meal, and if I forget a step, I'll respond with flexibility and self-compassion."

It may also help to reflect on long-held beliefs about perfectionism, such as:

- "If I don't meet high standards, I'm not worthwhile."
- "Perfectionism is what's helped me succeed."

Ask yourself:

- "Do these beliefs support my well-being or hold me back?"
- "Do they make it harder to adapt or cope?"
- "Could I pursue meaningful goals with care and purpose, rather than pressure and fear?"

For further guidance, see Appendix 12: *From Perfectionism to Progress: A Compassionate Resilient Mind Exercise.*

Watch Out for the "Good Old Days" Bias

After a brain injury, it is easy to compare yourself to an idealised version of who you were before, believing:

- "I never made mistakes before."
- "Now I always forget things."

This "good old days" bias paints the past in rose-tinted tones and the present in gloom, and is likely to make you think that your symptoms are worse than they actually are. In reality, everyone has made mistakes before. Memory slips are part of being human, not just part of brain injury. See Appendix 13: *Rose-Tinted Reflections: Navigating the Good Old Days Bias,* for strategies to restore a more balanced view of yourself.

Skills Learning with Compassion

Sometimes, social anxiety stems from genuine communication difficulties after brain injury. Chapter 13: *Communicating with Assertiveness and Compassion after Brain Injury,* offers strategies to strengthen communication skills. From a CRM perspective, the goal is not to eliminate all mistakes, because everyone makes slips at times. Instead the goal is to support yourself with practical tools that increase confidence and adaptability. A CRM accepts that errors will happen and responds with compassion and purposeful strategies, rather than harsh self-judgement.

In some cases, social anxiety may come from perceiving your communication skills as worse than they really are. Practising skills, seeking feedback and building supportive strategies can help you gain a more balanced view of your abilities (for more support with this, see Chapter 13: *Communicating with Assertiveness and Compassion after Brain Injury*).

Use Your CRM to Live Beyond Fear

Fear is a natural part of being human, especially after brain injury. However, using all your energy to avoid fear or to fight against it directly, often backfires, intensifying the very discomfort you are trying to escape (see Appendix 9a: *Martial Arts Metaphor, Metaphors for a Compassionate Resilient Mind*). Your CRM offers a more balanced and empowering way to face fear. It invites you to meet fear with courage, kindness and purposeful action through the tools and strategies outlined in this chapter. For example, your compassionate side helps you approach fear gently and patiently, accepting that it is okay to take small, manageable steps (e.g., through the Appendix 21: *Courage in Motion: Practising Safe Exposure* guidelines). At the same time, your resilient side provides the strength to stay present with fear long enough to reduce its hold on you.

Your CRM ("Eve Olve") provides encouragement by telling you:

> "By gently guiding yourself to face your fears using courage and kindness, your CRM grows stronger, helping you navigate towards what matters most".

Whilst facing your fears is important for growth and adaptation, dwelling on them excessively can be limiting. If you spend all your time trying to keep fear away, it can start to dominate your life. The Unwelcome Guest metaphor from *Acceptance and Commitment Therapy* (see Appendix 9b) reminds us that we cannot always stop fear from showing up, but we do not have to let it run our lives. An excessive focus on fear, such as constant worry or over-controlling your environment, can make the fear feel larger and more powerful. However, when you accept its presence and choose to live your life anyway, the fear fades into the background; it becomes more tolerable, more manageable and far less defining. Your CRM ("Eve Olve") can enable you to do this by helping you shift your focus from fear itself, to what truly matters: staying engaged with what is important to you in life and growing through challenges, rather than avoiding them.

Summary

Anxiety after brain injury is a common and understandable part of recovery, but it does not have to control your life. By learning to recognise the "Gatekeeper's" voice as fear trying to keep you safe and turning instead, to the support of your CRM ("Eve Olve"), you can meet worries with kindness, courage and flexibility. The guidance in this chapter is designed to help you navigate anxiety at your own pace. Anxiety may still show up, but with practice you can soften its grip, rebuild confidence and keep moving towards a life filled with connection, resilience and meaning.

6 The Weight of Injustice

Finding Freedom through Compassion

Emma Nicholas

Buddha has said: "Holding on to anger is like grasping a hot coal with the intent of throwing it at someone else; you are the one who gets burned." Injustice experience, also known as "embitterment," is a prolonged emotional response that is caused by perceived injustice or mistreatment. Embitterment is an emotion that most people will recognise. It is most often experienced when people feel they have been treated unfairly, or they feel they are the victim of some injustice (e.g., dismissal at work, they have been the victim of a road traffic accident or an assault). People may also feel embittered if they experience a loss of some kind (e.g., relationship, bereavement, physical functional ability), and they feel that they cannot cope with the loss or the situation. Embitterment often includes feelings of resentment, a need for distress or harm done to be recognised, and a desire for revenge against the person or persons that have done you wrong.

It is unsurprising that people who have acquired a brain injury because of an accident, assault or medical negligence, may experience the emotion of embitterment. Others may experience embitterment because they have suffered a brain injury and this itself feels unjust or unfair.

Reclaiming Strength and Meaning after Injustice

This chapter invites you to explore these powerful emotional experiences through the lens of the Compassionate Resilient Mind (CRM). The CRM is not about denying or suppressing distress. Rather, it offers a framework for responding to adversity in ways that support well-being and long-term adaptation. A CRM is grounded in values of compassion and resilience. It fosters the capacity to stay present with suffering, whilst responding in a way that promotes healing, meaning and personal growth.

Shifting from a threat-based mindset to CRM mode involves developing skills that enable you to:

- Acknowledge the reality of injustice without allowing it to define your ongoing experience.
- Redirect psychological energy towards constructive, value-driven action, rather than cyclical blame or revenge-focused thinking.
- Engage in the process of forgiveness as a self-directed strategy for emotional relief, aimed at reducing the psychological burden associated with unresolved anger and rumination. The focus is not on condoning the actions of others, but on facilitating one's own recovery and psychological flexibility.

DOI: 10.4324/9781003464655-6

- Maintain behaviour that is consistent with personally held values, even in the presence of strong emotional impulses towards withdrawal, aggression or disengagement. This supports adaptive self-regulation and the ability to act in line with what matters most.

Forgiveness, in this context, is not an act of forgetting, nor is it an endorsement of harm. It is a deliberate act of releasing oneself from the emotional entrapment of past injuries in order to reclaim agency and invest in a future shaped by values, rather than by pain.

The CRM offers a pathway through embitterment, not by minimising the injustice, but by empowering you to respond with flexibility, meaning and purpose. In doing so, it becomes possible to re-engage with life as it is now, and to rebuild a future with integrity, clarity and strength.

What Is Embitterment and Why Can It Happen?

It is normal to feel some "bitterness" if you have been adversely affected by something. Such bitterness is often characterised by feelings of anger, shame, humiliation, hostility and disappointment. These feelings are usually transient and pass with time.

People experiencing embitterment may have ongoing recurrent thoughts about what has happened to them. They may ruminate on these thoughts, which serves to exacerbate their feelings and experience of the perceived injustice that has been done to them.

Embitterment is related to core beliefs about the world and expectations of the way that things should and/or should not happen (e.g., bad things should not happen to good people). When a negative event occurs, which conflicts with your core beliefs (e.g., you believe that you are a good person and you sustain a brain injury), then this can lead to feelings of helplessness, resentment and embitterment. This means that there are no set criteria for the negative event needed to trigger embitterment. All individuals have different core beliefs, and something perceived as minor to one person can feel enormous to another. Some people may also be naturally predisposed to experience situations as being unjust.

A brain injury can be a life-changing event with serious consequences for the Brain Injury Survivor (BIS). Such an unexpected and unwanted change can result in core beliefs (e.g., the world is safe, the world is a fair place) being challenged. Of course, there is a period of adjustment for anyone following such an injury and this is normal. With embitterment, strong feelings about the injustice continue, become chronic and impact the person's well-being and recovery.

Importantly, the person suffering with embitterment strongly believes that their suffering is caused by the actions or inaction of another person/s. They may lack insight into how their strong feelings of blame perpetuate their own difficulties and distress. They may fantasise about revenge against the person/s they believe are responsible for their situation or distress. Such fantasies may even result in them feeling better for a short period, but in the long-term, they are likely to make them feel worse and prolong their embitterment.

People experiencing embitterment may wish for others to recognise their suffering and the cause of their suffering. This can lead to them declining help, which may resolve their suffering, because then their suffering would no longer be seen. Following a brain injury, this can be a barrier to engaging in important rehabilitation, which may restore function or teach compensatory strategies, thus prolonging their difficulties and missing opportunities for recovery. In turn, this ongoing nature of problems can reinforce the embitterment perspective.

How Do I Know If I Am Experiencing Significant Problems with Embitterment?

At its most severe, embitterment may be considered as Post-Traumatic Embitterment Disorder (PTED) (Linden et al. 2008).

For a diagnosis of PTED, you must have experienced a (1) negative life event, (2) which you believe has caused your current difficulties, and (3) experience the symptoms below for a period of at least three months, (4) resulting in impaired function in daily life. (5) These symptoms must not be part of a pre-existing mental health condition.

The symptoms include:

- Feeling that you are a victim and helpless to cope with the event or the cause of the event.
- Blaming yourself for the event, for not preventing it, or for not being able to cope with it.
- Repeated intrusive memories of the event. You may think that it is important not to forget what has happened to you.
- Having thoughts that it no longer matters how you are recovering. You may even feel some uncertainty about whether you want to recover.
- You may have suicidal thoughts, or talk about suicide, or aggression towards others.
- You may also experience feelings of unhappiness, unease, aggression and low mood, which can resemble depression.
- You may experience physical (somatic) symptoms, such as loss of appetite, sleep disturbances and pain.
- You may experience phobic feelings about the event or situation.
- You may feel negative and low in motivation, or unwilling to engage in some activities.
- Your mood may be changeable when you are distracted from thoughts of the event and what has happened to you. You may even smile when thinking about revenge.

Recognising embitterment through the lens of a CRM helps reduce shame and blame. These symptoms are signs of distress, not character flaws. Compassionate awareness helps us recognise that embitterment is an emotional signal that something painful and meaningful has happened, something that deserves care and healing.

What Is the Difference between PTED and PTSD?

Post-Traumatic Stress Disorder (PTSD) and PTED share some similar characteristics. They both include intrusive thoughts, avoiding places or situations linked to the trigger event, low mood and suicidal ideation. The difference between these two conditions is the event that triggered them and the emotions underpinning the symptoms. For a diagnosis of PTSD, exposure to a significant life-threatening event is necessary. In PTED, the triggering event, whilst distressing for the individual, is often considered a "normal" event, for instance, a divorce or bereavement. With regard to emotions, in PTSD, symptoms are caused by panic or anxiety, whereas in PTED, the underlying emotions are embitterment, injustice, fantasies of revenge and aggression (Linden et al. 2008).

What Are the Consequences of Embitterment?

Psychological Consequences

- A person with embitterment or PTED, may experience symptoms of low mood and depression, anxiety or issues with anger.
- Relationships may be strained by the constant rumination over the harm done to them. This can lead to a breakdown of relationships and social isolation, which can serve to further increase the embitterment.

Rehabilitation Consequences

- The desire of the person with embitterment to maintain their negative situation in order to have their suffering witnessed, could be problematic in engaging with rehabilitation to improve their symptoms.
- Following a brain injury, rehabilitation is important to restore function where possible, and to learn adaptive skills and strategies to respond to those symptoms (e.g., use of memory aids). Failing to engage in support provided to address these issues in a timely manner, may limit or reduce recovery potential.

Litigation

If you have been injured due to the actions or inaction of someone else (e.g., car accident, medical negligence), then you may be participating in litigation. Litigation seeks to redress the harm done to a BIS by suing the party responsible for the injury. This process can include access to private rehabilitation resources (e.g., private psychology, occupational therapy or physiotherapy clinicians).

Litigation could be a factor in exacerbating or maintaining the experience of embitterment or PTED for several reasons:

- Litigation can take years to settle. This delay in having reparation for your difficulties or distress can itself be a factor in embitterment. Furthermore, it can impact engagement with rehabilitation as the person may wish their symptoms to continue in order to exact maximum compensation that they feel is commensurate with their experience of being harmed.
- The litigation process can create an adversarial situation between the injured party and the defendant, which could also impact the development and/or maintenance of embitterment. The injured party may continue to feel like a helpless victim within the larger context of litigation.
- Litigation demands that the injured party be assessed by both legal sides, which leads to having to recount your triggering event and how it has affected you multiple times to expert witnesses. This may reinforce and maintain feelings of embitterment and victimhood.
- As litigation involves attributing blame for the negative event, where this is unclear, the victim themselves may come under scrutiny for their role in the event. This may leave the injured party feeling embittered about the litigation process in addition to the triggering event.

Through the CRM, we learn to balance necessary advocacy (e.g., legal justice) with inner healing. The CRM invites you to ask: "How can I participate in this process without it dominating my identity or delaying my recovery?"

Brain Injury Interaction with Embitterment

A brain injury can result in changes to thinking skills, which may also interact with the development and experience of embitterment. A CRM sees these difficulties, not as personal failures, but as consequences of injury. It helps you approach these challenges with kindness, resilience, adaptation and skill-building, rather than self-criticism. Below are some of these changes and ways in which you can adapt to them:

- **Difficulty with Flexibility of Thought**: Sometimes, as a result of a brain injury, it can be more difficult to access higher-order cognitive skills, such as problem-solving and taking alternative perspectives. People may find that they become stuck in their way of thinking about the triggering event, which could maintain embitterment (see Appendix 7: *Navigating Mind Influencers: Guidelines for Adaptive Thinking*, for how to navigate this).
- **Difficulty with Emotions**: People can experience changes in their mood or temperament following a brain injury. Anger and irritability can be common consequences. Being angry about what has happened could lead to or maintain embitterment (for further help, see Chapter 4: *Finding Calm in the Storm: Anger, Irritability, and Compassion*; Appendix 7: *Navigating Mind Influencers: Guidelines for Adaptive Thinking*, for adaptive thinking guidelines; Appendix 20: *Taming the Dragon: A CRM Relaxation Script for Anger and Embitterment* and Appendix 8: *Unlocking Adaptation: A Practical Guide to the Compassionate Resilient Mind*, for navigating embitterment with a CRM).

How Can I Overcome Embitterment?

Embitterment is not a sign of weakness, but a sign of suffering that has not been heard. A CRM acknowledges this pain, whilst encouraging courageous steps towards healing. It asks: "How can I be kind to myself, whilst still moving forward? How can I restore purpose, even when things feel unfair?"

There are several strategies and interventions that can be applied to reducing the symptoms and impact of embitterment or PTED outlined below. You can set time aside to work through these steps by yourself, or you may benefit from help from a therapist or support worker to help you through the process.

Identify and Understand the Trigger for Your Feelings of Embitterment

In order to address and work through feelings of embitterment, it is first necessary to understand what exactly has triggered these thoughts and emotions.

- Clearly identify the trigger for your feelings of embitterment. This may be the event or situation in which you sustained your brain injury, or it could be related to how you were treated after your injury. It may be something else.
- What was it about this situation that feels so painful?

- What beliefs or values does it transgress? Examples may include: "I was involved in a hit and run. People should not drive off and leave someone on the road." "I was hit in a fight, which caused a brain injury. I must be respected and it's wrong for them to hit and disrespect me." "The world should be a fair place with everyone respecting others' rights and feelings."
- Reflect on how both the trigger event and your feelings about it have led to you feeling embittered.

Acceptance of How You Are Feeling

To start to work on difficult thoughts and feelings, it is important to first accept them. This includes thoughts and feelings that you may find challenging to accept, for example, thoughts of revenge, feelings of anger and hatred.

Noticing, naming and allowing these thoughts and feelings to come and go is an important part of overcoming the difficulties they pose. Show compassion: speak kindly to yourself, offering compassion and understanding, rather than criticism. Accept and welcome your feelings with compassion, rather than fighting them. Nurturing self-compassion allows you to regain control over how you respond to this situation and how you choose to express your feelings. (For further help, see Appendix 14: *Switching off Automatic Pilot: The Art of Mindfulness* and Appendix 20: *Taming the Dragon: A CRM Relaxation Script for Anger and Embitterment*).

Consider the Pros and Cons of Continuing to Feel Embittered

Embitterment keeps you trapped in the past, thinking about the triggering event or person who harmed you. Ask yourself who benefits from your feelings of embitterment and who is harmed?

- "Is the other person negatively impacted by my feelings?"
- "Am I being negatively impacted?"
- "Am I being punished by being harmed twice? First by the event that harmed me, and second by my feelings of embitterment?"
- "Is it fair for me to be punished by my experience of embitterment in addition to the way I've already been harmed? Especially if the other person is unaware and unaffected by my anger and feelings of embitterment."

You can use the pros and cons of the embitterment worksheet in Appendix 23: *Pros and Cons of Remaining Embittered,* to help you to consider what holding onto your sense of injustice and feeling embittered is costing you.

Some costs of continued embitterment:

- Embitterment requires you to maintain the hurt/injury that has been done to you, to show others how you have suffered. This can impact your recovery progress. Following a brain injury, it is important to have rehabilitation in a timely manner to ensure you have the best outcome possible. Delay in rehabilitation can prolong symptoms and may mean that recovery potential is reduced.
- The negative focus of embitterment can impact your relationships with others.
- Embitterment may lead you to feel low in mood. You may feel helpless and hopeless.

- You may experience physical symptoms, such as pain, poor sleep and reduced appetite associated with your feelings of embitterment.

Navigating Intrusive Thoughts

Intrusive thoughts ("mind influencers") can be a symptom of embitterment. Such thoughts are often unhelpful and may contribute to maintaining the injustice experience. For example, you may find that you experience thoughts about what has happened to you, how it is unfair, or how your life has been changed. You might also have thoughts about revenge and unpleasant things happening to the person who harmed you. These thoughts may initially make you feel better, but their negative content will only serve to increase your embitterment over time.

Intrusive thoughts can take you away from the things you value and can make you feel low in mood, anxious or angry. Learning strategies to respond to these thoughts can be a way to help you regain control over your experience and move you towards the things that are important to you.

Outlined below are ways that you can learn more adaptive ways to respond to the intrusive thoughts:

Adaptive Thinking

An important part of managing intrusive thoughts is assessing their credibility. We see things from our own side, from our own perspective. It can help to consider how this situation might look from the perspective of others and to develop CRM-based thoughts. See adaptive thinking guidelines (Appendix 7: *Navigating Mind Influencers: Guidelines for Adaptive Thinking*), for how to manage this.

Disempowering Unhelpful Thoughts about Injustice

In the case of an injustice experience, it sometimes is not useful to challenge the credibility of these thoughts, as in reality, sometimes people or situations can be unfair, unjust, inconsiderate or just nasty. There is nothing we can do about it; we cannot change it or make it better. These experiences can be particularly hard if they transgress rigid rules for living: "People should respect me; people should be considerate" and can cause angry thoughts "How dare they; I want revenge." You may also find yourself replaying the same story about the injustice. If these angry thoughts become "mind influencers" and you overly focus on them, and they dominate your emotions, you may find it useful to develop strategies to disempower these unhelpful thoughts (see Appendix 7: *Navigating Mind Influencers: Guidelines for Adaptive Thinking*) in order to regain control of your life.

Consider an Alternative Perspective

Whilst it is understandable to feel like a victim in a situation where you have been harmed, this can be a disempowering and unhelpful position to maintain. Such a position can serve to reinforce your feelings of embitterment and anger. Instead of taking on a victim role, think about how you can respond to your feelings of embitterment and anger with compassion and resilience (see Appendix 20: *Taming the Dragon: A CRM Relaxation Script for Anger and Embitterment*).

Embitterment can also make you feel angry towards your symptoms, which can make you fight your symptoms, instead of responding to them with compassion and resilience. You may not be able to change the past, but you can change your interpretation of it and how you respond to it going forwards. For example, focussing on how you are working to overcome your difficulties (e.g., by reading this book!), or recognising your strengths and resilience in the face of adversity.

- Ask yourself:
  - "What lessons have I learnt about myself from this experience that can empower me moving forward?"
  - "What would it look like if I became the hero in this story, rather than the victim? What difference would this make to my life?"
- Use the guidelines in Appendix 7: *Navigating Mind Influencers: Guidelines for Adaptive Thinking.*
- Use the therapeutic letter exercise (Appendix 22: *Therapeutic Letter for Forgiveness and Healing Courage in Motion: Practising Safe Exposure*).

It can be helpful to work on considering a different perspective with regard to the person or situation that caused your difficulties. Our actions are influenced by our lived experiences, emotions, understanding and difficulties. This is also true of the person who harmed you. This does not excuse the harm done, but having some understanding of this can be helpful for you in how you understand the situation. This, in turn, can change your feelings about what has happened.

It can feel challenging, but trying to understand the perspective of the person who triggered your embitterment can help you move forward. You may want to consider:

- How would they describe the triggering event or situation?
- What might have influenced their behaviour?
- Was it their intention to harm you?
- Have they also been affected by this in any way?
- Have there been any misunderstandings or miscommunications around the situation? (e.g., hearsay or gossip).

Mindfulness

The nature of embitterment is to focus on the event or person who harmed you in the past, and the suffering that you experience as a result. Embitterment requires this focus on the past, the other person and the suffering to be maintained, resulting in feeling negative and getting in the way of present-day relationships, treatment and activities. It can therefore be useful to change the focus of your mind to being in the present.

(See mindfulness exercises in Appendix 14: *Switching Off Automatic Pilot: The Art of Mindfulness.*)

Forgiveness

Forgiveness is the act of letting go of the emotional burden of resentment that is experienced after the triggering event. Part of forgiveness is the acceptance of what has happened to you. Forgiveness then provides an opportunity to act in accordance with your values and choosing how to respond and promote your own well-being (see Appendix 2: *Your Inner Compass: Exploring Values after Brain Injury*). Forgiveness is a gift to ourselves, to let go of hurt and move forward with our lives.

Forgiveness is not about forgetting what has happened, or condoning or excusing the behaviour or action that caused harm. Forgiveness is not for the benefit of the perpetrator of harm. It means making peace with what happened as an act of compassion towards yourself. Letting go of resentment can be an act of power and dignity. It gives you space to live in alignment with your values, instead of your pain.

Some ways that forgiveness can benefit you:

- Letting go of chronic resentment or anger can lead to a reduction in stress, anxiety and can lead to improved mood.
- It makes space for you to be able to access and accept help for your injuries or any difficulties that you have experienced as a result of the trigger event.
- You may find that physical symptoms, such as pain, poor sleep, blood pressure and heart rate improve after forgiveness.
- Forgiveness can improve your relationships with other people that you care about.
- You may develop increased self-compassion as you learn to focus on your own well-being, instead of anger towards the person who harmed you.
- You can use the pros and cons of the forgiveness worksheet in Appendix 24: *Pros and Cons of Forgiveness* to help you consider how letting go of embitterment and moving towards forgiveness may benefit you.

Therapeutic Letter Writing

Writing a therapeutic letter that you will never send can be a helpful way to process and let go of feelings of embitterment, and move towards forgiveness. You can write this letter to the person who harmed you, or you can write it to yourself, or perhaps separate letters to both yourself and the perpetrator. This is a practice of self-compassionate expression. You can release feelings without needing the other person to understand or validate them. It is a symbolic act of reclaiming your narrative and your power.

How to write a therapeutic letter:

- Describe the event or situation that harmed you. Write about how you experienced the event and the way that you have been affected by it.
- Express how you feel about what has happened, including how you continue to be affected by the event.
- State your forgiveness and explain why you are forgiving them (e.g., "To allow me to move forward with my life, I want to let go of my negative feelings, and so, I forgive you").
- Write about how you hope your life will improve now that you have let go of the event. What are your best hopes for the future?

Once you have completed your letter, you can choose what you would like to do with it. Choices include, keeping it for your future reference to remind you why you chose to forgive, or you can destroy it; for example, you could tear it up into tiny pieces or burn it (ensure you do this safely).

You can use the therapeutic letter template as a guide to help you (see template in Appendix 22: *Therapeutic Letter for Forgiveness and Healing*).

Healing and Post-Traumatic Growth

Events, such as acquiring a brain injury can be life-changing. Whilst this may be difficult to process and accept, and can result in embitterment, it is also an opportunity for post-traumatic growth. You have the power to choose where you place your attention and focus your energy.

Redirect your energy and attention away from the past and how you have been harmed, and focus on growth. What do you need to heal and nurture yourself? Can you use this painful experience to develop resilience and become a wiser, stronger person?

- **Self-Compassion**: Give yourself permission to recover and let go of embitterment. Self-compassion can provide the strength needed to move beyond embitterment to adapt and rebuild your life.
- **Gratitude**: Shift your attention away from the things that you have lost and towards what you still have. Even in difficult times, there are always things to be grateful for—whether it is the love of others, your own resilience, or lessons learnt about yourself. Look for the little moments of happiness and connection to others. Perhaps start a gratitude practice (see Appendix 5: *Shifting Focus: Building Resilience through Gratitude*).
- **Engage in Rehabilitation**: Seek specialist rehabilitation to help you to overcome any emotional, cognitive or physical difficulties that you experience as a result of your brain injury. You may be offered this as part of your litigation. Otherwise, seek advice from your doctor.
- **Purposeful Action**: Take positive steps to rebuild your life and relationships. Moving your attention away from the person who harmed you and focussing on your own recovery, is the best course of action. Reviewing what is important to you after your brain injury can be a helpful way to get started on taking back your control and rebuilding your life (see Values and goals in Appendix 2: *Your Inner Compass: Exploring Values after Brain Injury* and Appendix 3: *Turning Values into Action: Setting SMART Goals*).

Accepting the Unwanted Feelings Beneath the Embitterment

Beneath your anger or embitterment, there may be feelings of hurt, loss or shame. Anger can sometimes be a way of fighting directly against these unwanted feelings to get rid of them. However, fighting directly against these feelings can sometimes be counterproductive and sometimes, we can gain more control by embracing the unwanted feelings, which can then allow us to tame them and let go of them (see Appendix 9a, the martial arts metaphor, to help you understand this concept; see the *Resilient Compassionate Relaxation Exercise for anger*, Appendix 8: Narrative 2.3, *Unlocking Adaptation: A Practical Guide to the Compassionate Resilient Mind*, for application of strategies aligned with this concept).

Summary

It is normal to go through a period of adjustment where you may perceive your brain injury acquisition as unjust. Embitterment or PTED can develop when these feelings become chronic and interfere with your recovery and quality of life. Symptoms associated with embitterment include, depressed mood, feelings of hopelessness or helplessness and needing your suffering to be witnessed. Physical symptoms can accompany this emotional condition, including pain, poor sleep and reduced appetite. Engagement with important neuro-rehabilitation may also be affected, which in turn, negatively influences the outcome of recovery from brain injury.

Letting go of embitterment and moving towards forgiveness, can ease the emotional burden and allow you to rebuild a meaningful life.

Reference

Linden, M., Baumann, K., Rotter, M., & Schippan, B. (2008). Posttraumatic embitterment disorder in comparison to other mental disorders. *Psychotherapy and Psychosomatics*, *77*(1), 50–56.

7 Resting with Resilience

A Compassionate Guide to Sleep

Vicki Hall

A Compassionate Resilient Mind (CRM) cannot command sleep, but it can choose how to meet the night, with compassionate and calm guidance, instead of struggle.

The Rhythm of the Tide

Sleep after brain injury is often unpredictable, like the ebb and flow of the sea. Some nights, the tide of sleep rises smoothly, carrying you into rest with little effort. Other nights, the water seems to retreat, leaving you stranded on the shore, awake and restless. You cannot command the ocean to come in, no matter how hard you try because the tide has its own rhythm. However, you can prepare your shoreline. You can smooth the sands, clear away waste and create conditions that welcome the tide when it comes.

After brain injury, many factors can disturb the natural rhythm of your sleep, such as changes in the brain's clock, stress, pain, fatigue or disrupted routines. This can feel overwhelming, but your CRM can act like a wise sailor who understands the sea. Instead of fighting the water, the CRM helps you notice its patterns, work with them and find calm, even when the tide is low.

This chapter invites you to stop battling against sleeplessness and begin tending to the shoreline with compassion and resilience. By learning simple strategies, you can create the best conditions for rest and soften your struggle with the night and give sleep the best chance to return in its own time.

How Can a Brain Injury Affect Sleep?

After a brain injury, the natural tide of sleep can become unsettled, as if the moon's steady pull has been disrupted. Instead of a smooth rhythm of rising and falling, the water may come in too late, too early or not at all. Several factors can disturb this tide:

- **Changes in the Brain's Clock**: The part of your brain that regulates alertness and body rhythms may have been affected, or hormone imbalances may have shifted the natural pull of the tide.
- **Other Symptoms Acting Like Stormy Weather**: Anxiety, low mood and pain can churn the waters, keeping you restless, instead of letting you drift into sleep.
- **Reduced Daytime Activity**: If your days are quieter or less active, there is less natural ebb and flow, making the tide weaker at night.
- **Loss of Routine**: Without the structure of work or regular activities, the shoreline becomes less predictable, and the tide of sleep may struggle to find its way in.

DOI: 10.4324/9781003464655-7

- **Medications**: Some prescribed medications can act like currents, interfering with the natural rhythm of rest.

When the tide of sleep is disturbed, the next day can feel like walking on heavy, waterlogged sand. You may feel more tired, find it harder to complete everyday tasks, and notice your mood and thinking skills are affected.

The good news is that, like any coastline, the rhythm can often be gently restored. By tending to your shoreline through daily routines, environmental changes and compassionate ways of meeting the night, you can encourage the tide to return more regularly.

What Can I Do to Help Myself Sleep?

Just as you cannot command the tide to rise on demand, you cannot force yourself to sleep. However, you can shape the shoreline by setting the conditions that allow the tide of rest to come in more smoothly. The following strategies can help you prepare the shore, so that when sleep does arrive, it finds a calm and welcoming place to settle.

Balance Your Daytime Rhythm—Setting the Tide in Motion

The pull of the tide begins long before it reaches the shore. How you spend your day shapes how sleep will come at night. Make sure you have a balanced and calm rhythm by:

- **Pacing Your Activities**: Avoid both over-exertion and long inactivity. Like a balanced tide, steady rhythms of effort and rest make it easier for sleep to flow in later (see Appendix 28: *Breaking Out of the Boom-Bust Cycle – Pacing Activities*).
- **Creating a Calming Pre-sleep Tide**: Allow at least an hour to gently wind down before bed. You could try a warm bath, light reading or quiet relaxation. Avoid strenuous activity that stirs the waves.

Choose Fuel Wisely—What You Add to the Water

What you consume during the day can ripple into the night. Try to:

- Avoid alcohol and nicotine in the evenings. These substances may feel calming at first, but often disturb the natural tide of deep sleep.
- Limit caffeine and energy drinks in the second half of the day as they can act like a false current, pushing back the tide.
- Avoid large meals close to bedtime, whilst ensuring you do not go to bed hungry.
- Limit fluids in the evening to reduce sleep disruptions.
- Reduce stimulation by avoiding heavy exercise and reducing blue light for at least two hours before bed, so the waters can settle.

Keep a Consistent Routine—Honouring the Rhythm of the Tide

The sea follows a rhythm, and your body responds best when it does too. To stabilise your rhythm:

- Go to bed and rise at the same times every day, even after poor sleep.
- Use an alarm clock to help you rise with the tide each morning.

- Plan a meaningful morning activity to encourage you out of bed.
- Avoid long daytime naps. If you must nap, set an alarm for 15–30 minutes.
- If you have a tendency to drift off too early in the evening, keep yourself gently active. Try to avoid "passive currents," like long stretches of TV.

Shape Your Shoreline—Preparing a Safe Harbour for Sleep

Sleep comes more easily when your environment welcomes it. Prepare your environment by:

- Ensuring your bed is comfortable and supportive.
- Keeping the room dark, cool and quiet (use blackout curtains, earplugs if needed).
- Removing TVs, computers and phones from the bedroom, so the space is a harbour for sleep only, not a busy port full of distractions.

Navigate Thoughts and Feelings—Calming the Inner Waves

At night, the waves of frustration, anxiety or hopelessness can churn most strongly, keeping you from drifting into rest. Your CRM can act like a wise lighthouse, steadying the shore with calm light. To steady your mind:

- **Allow Room for Difficulty**: If you accept that, in this moment, you cannot sleep, without rigidly trying to make yourself sleep, this can help to reduce pressure. A compassionate mindset gives you space to rest, even if sleep does not come immediately.
- **Use CRM ("Eve Olve") Statements to Steady the Waters**: You can meet unhelpful "threat-based/Gatekeeper" thoughts with CRM ("Eve Olve") responses (see Appendix 8: *Unlocking Adaptation: A Practical Guide to the Compassionate Resilient Mind*). "Eve Olve" can also help you manage discomfort when the sea feels restless during a wakeful night. Example "Eve Olve" statements include:
  - "Even when sleep doesn't come, you can respond with compassion, rather than frustration."
  - "You may not be able to control the tide, but you can choose how you float with it."
  - "Resting your body and quieting your mind is still valuable, even without perfect sleep."
  - "Sleep isn't something you can command or force, but you can choose to rest kindly."

- **Practice Mindful Acceptance**: If ruminating thoughts are keeping you awake, observe them like passing waves, rising and falling, without trying to chase or push them away. Then, gently redirect your attention to the steady rhythm of your breath or the sensations of your body relaxing (see Appendix 14: *Switching off Automatic Pilot: The Art of Mindfulness*, and Appendix 16: *Relaxation Skills: Finding Calm and Balance*). This strengthens purposeful control of attention, a key quality of the CRM.
- **Work Gently with Unhelpful Beliefs**: You might notice catastrophic thoughts like: "If I don't sleep, I'll have a breakdown" or "I won't be able to cope tomorrow." These are like storm warnings that intensify anxiety. Using CRM principles, you can meet them with curiosity, rather than fear. Ask yourself: "Is this wave (thought) carrying me anywhere helpful?, Is there a more helpful wave (thought) I can follow instead?, Is this a credible thought?" (See Appendix 7: *Navigating Mind Influencers: Guidelines*

for Adaptive Thinking.) Adaptive thinking strategies are best practised in the daytime, rather than at night. If practised at night they may fuel ruminations. At nighttime mindfulness strategies are more helpful.

- **Focus on Rest, Not Perfection**: From a CRM perspective, resting on the shore is still restorative, even if sleep feels distant. Try shifting your mindset to: "I'm giving my body and mind space to recharge, even if I'm not fully asleep." This self-soothing approach reduces stress and improves your chances of drifting off naturally.
- **Avoid Clock-watching**: Watching the clock is like staring at the horizon, demanding the tide to rise. Your perception of time at night can be distorted, and you may be drifting in and out of light sleep without realising.
- **Avoid Self-criticism**: Judging yourself for being awake (for example, having thoughts like "Why can't I just sleep like everyone else?") can feed a cycle of stormy waters. A CRM approach involves noticing these harsh inner voices and choosing kinder alternatives, such as: "This is difficult, but I'm doing my best to ride the waves with patience."
- **Write Down Your Worries and Release Them**: If your thoughts are about things you need to remember for tomorrow, jot them down (like setting adrift a note in a bottle), so you can let them go for the night. If they return, use mindful redirection techniques (Appendix 14: *Switching off Automatic Pilot: The Art of Mindfulness*) with a compassionate inner voice to bring your focus back to calmer waters.

Managing Nightmares—Weathering the Night Storms

Nightmares can feel like a sudden storm rising, pulling you into frightening waters. Your CRM can help you steady the boat until the storm passes through the following:

- **Acknowledge the Distress without Blame**: Nightmares can make you feel frightened, overwhelmed or even ashamed. It may help to remind yourself that nightmares are a natural response to a traumatic event, not a personal failing. A compassionate mind allows you to say, "This is scary, but it's not my fault. I can steady myself until the waves pass."
- **Reclaim Control by Rewriting the Ending**: Just as sailors can adjust their course when the wind changes, you can reshape the ending of a nightmare (rescripting). Imagine bringing in a wise, strong or comforting version of yourself who helps calm the storm or guide the dream safely to shore. This can restore a sense of safety and self-control.
- **Ground Yourself in the Present**: After a nightmare, your body may still feel caught in the swell of waves. Use grounding techniques to bring yourself back to the here and now: look around your room and name what you see. Remind yourself: "I'm safe. This is my bedroom. The storm has passed." Speaking kindly and reassuringly to yourself acts like an anchor dropping into steady ground.
- **Use Relaxation to Soothe Your System**: Nightmares can stir the waters of the nervous system, leaving you restless and unable to drift back to sleep. Use the relaxation exercises from Appendix 16: *Relaxation Skills: Finding Calm and Balance,* to calm your body. Visualise a safe harbour or gently tense and release your muscles. Let your body hear the message: "It's okay to relax now; the sea is settling."
- **If Nightmares Persist, Seek Support**: A CRM perspective values asking for help as a sign of strength, not weakness. If the storms of nightmares continue to cause distress or are linked to trauma, talk to a clinician or therapist. You do not have to sail through rough seas alone.

Conclusion—Navigating the Tide

Sleep after brain injury can feel unpredictable, like the ocean's tide, sometimes calm and steady, sometimes rough and resistant. You cannot order the sea to rise, nor can you force sleep to come. However, you can learn to navigate the tide by preparing the shorelines, tending to your rhythms and meeting sleeplessness with patience, acceptance and restful compassion. By pacing your days, choosing fuel wisely, creating a safe harbour for rest, and working gently with thoughts and emotions, you encourage the tide to return in its own time.

8 Pacing with Purpose

A Compassionate Guide to Navigating Fatigue

Vicki Hall

A Bridge in the Fog

Imagine standing at the edge of a long bridge. On the other side lies the life you want to live with independence, connection and activities that give you meaning. The bridge is shrouded in a heavy fog called fatigue. Some days the fog is light and you can just about see the way forward. Other days, it rolls in thick and heavy, making every step uncertain and slowing your progress. At times, it even feels as if the bridge vanishes altogether, leaving you stranded and cut off from the world you long to reach.

Fatigue after brain injury can be like this fog, unpredictable, overwhelming and difficult for others to see or understand. It can cloud your thinking, dull your motivation and magnify other challenges. Sometimes, it descends suddenly, stopping you in your tracks, whilst at other times, it creeps in slowly until you realise you can no longer see the path clearly.

When faced with the fog, some people push forward blindly, only to then collapse in exhaustion. Others turn back, fearing the shrouded bridge and believe that the other side is out of reach forever. Both responses are understandable, but neither allows you to travel the bridge in a sustainable way.

This chapter invites you to approach fatigue differently, not as an enemy to battle or an obstacle to fear, but as a signal to be understood and navigated with compassion and resilience. Just as a wise traveller pauses to gauge the fog, adjust their pace and use guiding lights to keep their bearings, you too can learn strategies to move forward steadily, even when fatigue lingers. With the support of your Compassionate Resilient Mind (CRM), you can learn to cross the bridge at your own pace, step by step, finding ways to live meaningfully beyond fatigue.

How Can I Respond to My Fatigue?

Recognise the Signs of Fatigue

Sometimes, people may not notice when they are getting tired. This may be because they are so focused on getting through their day that they do not pay attention to the signs of fatigue. For example, if a person runs a marathon, they sometimes do not notice how exhausted they are until the end of the race. Ignoring the signs of fatigue is often not useful because, to navigate fatigue, you need to pace yourself and recognise when you need to slow down or take a break (e.g., if you were running a marathon and sprinted from the beginning, you would soon run out of steam and would not be able to complete

DOI: 10.4324/9781003464655-8

it). Sometimes, people's minds may also be shut off to recognising fatigue for a range of reasons, including because they see it as a sign of weakness, or believe that it is better to ignore it.

Rather than seeing fatigue as a weakness or something to fight against, it is useful to approach fatigue with compassionate curiosity "What's my fatigue telling me?", so that you can adapt to it and work around it. The first step is mindful recognition (i.e., paying attention to the early warning signs of fatigue without judgement). People may experience observable signs of tiredness that tell them they are becoming fatigued (e.g., slurred speech, heavy legs). A CRM encourages you to view these signs as signals for self-care, rather than weakness. See Appendix 25: *Recognising Signs of Fatigue*, to help you identify these signs; this self-reflective journaling or the "fatigue recognition" worksheet is a way to check in with yourself, honouring your body's limits as a form of inner strength that can help you identify when you need to take a break. When you need a break, relaxation may help you to recuperate your energy levels (see Appendix 16: *Relaxation Skills: Finding Calm and Balance*, for guidelines on relaxation).

Recognise If You Are in a "Boom–Bust" Cycle

Fatigue can sometimes be maintained by a "boom–bust" cycle. This means that when you have "good days," you will do too much, and on "bad days," you will do nothing or very little. This causes problems because:

- If you push yourself too hard, you are likely to have more "bad days" and thus, gradually be able to do less. You may also feel you need to do more on the "good days" to make up for the "bad days".
- If you do too little, this is likely to have a negative impact on your mood, making you feel more sluggish and more tired. This means you may find it difficult to kick-start yourself back into action. Furthermore, if you do not do much, you may also have a tendency to focus on your symptoms of tiredness.
- If you do too little, this will not help you maintain strength and stamina, which in turn, will mean that you will tire more easily.

Plan Your Day around Your Fatigue Levels (Pace Yourself)

A CRM encourages you to develop adaptive, balanced routines that support consistent energy use and emotional regulation. Adaptive pacing is a response to fluctuating energy levels, rooted in acceptance and strategic self-kindness through the complementary values of compassion and resilience:

- **Compassion** is the voice inside that notices your limits without criticism. It is the friend who offers a seat when you are tired, who reassures you it is okay to rest, and who reminds you that your worth is not measured by productivity, but by who you are. It helps you keep going.
- **Resilience**, on the other hand, is the strength that rises when you are ready. It is the part of you that says, "You've got this," not by pushing you past breaking point, but by helping you move forward one small step at a time, even on your hardest days.

To break out of the "boom–bust" cycle, it can help to plan activity levels around fatigue.

To plan activities around fatigue, it may help to:

I Write an activity diary and record your fatigue ratings after each activity (see Appendix 26: *Fatigue Diary: Tracking Patterns to Support Adaptive Pacing*).

II Use the activity diary to identify direct and indirect triggers to your fatigue, which may include:

   a The times of day when your fatigue is at its worst.
   b Activity levels: if you are doing too much or too little, which is making you tired.
   c Environmental factors: if there is anything going on around you that has made you more tired (e.g., noise, crowds, bright lights).
   d Types of activities that make you the most tired: this may include physical (e.g., walking, doing sports) versus cognitive activities (e.g., playing computer games, doing work, concentrating, driving), social activities (e.g., socialising/talking) and/or activities that you find emotionally difficult.

III Plan activities and tasks for the times of the day when you have the most energy, and make sure you take breaks at the times you feel tired. Many people find that alertness is at its best between 08:00 and 12:00, and from 18:00 to 20:00, although this may vary according to the individual.

IV Plan your day around the scenarios and situations you have identified that make you feel tired; for example, going to the shops when it is less busy. Make sure you take a break after you have engaged in an activity that you know makes you tired.

V Alternate between different types of activities (i.e., fatiguing and non-fatiguing activities; see Appendix 28: *Breaking Out of the "Boom-Bust" Cycle – Pacing Activities*, for guidelines to manage activity pacing).

VI Break out of the "boom–bust" cycle by pacing your activities (see Appendix 28: *Breaking Out of the "Boom–Bust Cycle": Pacing Activities*, for activity-pacing guidelines).

VII Try and think of alternative ways that you could do activities to preserve energy, or alternative activities that you could do (see Appendix 27: *Evaluating Beliefs about Fatigue and Initiating Compassionate-Resilient Change*, Worksheet 27.5).

VIII Write a list with the following headings to prioritise tasks:

   a Things that are very important to me and I really want to do or have to do (importance of tasks 8–10/10; 10 being the most important task ever).
   b Things that are moderately important/desirable (4–7/10 important).
   c Things that are of minor importance (1–3/10 importance).
   d Things that I can delegate to other people.

CRM tips: Use your fatigue diary to plan in alignment with your values and energy rhythms, rather than rigid expectations. Choose when and how to do activities based on what matters to you most, rather than what you "should" be doing. Prioritising is not just about achieving external outcomes, it is about letting your values guide your choices, even when fatigue is present.

Build Activities within Your Day May Help Renew Energy Levels Including

- Graded exercise (e.g., going for a walk), but do not set unrealistic goals. Physical activity has been shown to improve the symptoms of fatigue in medical conditions, including

chronic fatigue. If you have a physiotherapist, they may be able to help set goals. Do not plan vigorous exercise late in the evening as this can interfere with sleep.
- Going out and getting fresh air.
- Leisure activities may increase your energy levels by providing pleasure (e.g., doing yoga, seeing friends, listening to music). Plan out how and when you will do them to ensure that you will start doing them again.
- Relaxation or mindfulness (e.g., see Appendix 14: *Switching off Automatic Pilot: The Art of Mindfulness*, and Appendix 16: *Relaxation Skills: Finding Calm and Balance*).

Purposeful activity, such as graded exercise, and/or leisure activities, which provide a sense of mastery and pleasure, supports emotional resilience. Choosing these activities from a place of self-compassion and intention helps rebuild energy and mood. Reconnecting with life-enhancing experiences (like nature, music or gentle movement) can also foster resilience by grounding you in what feels nourishing and alive.

Reduce the Demands Placed on You

It may help to consider:

- Are people putting pressure on you to do tasks? Can you say no? See Chapter 13: *Communicating with Assertiveness and Compassion after Brain Injury*, for strategies to navigate problems with assertiveness.
- How could you do tasks in a more energy-preserving manner? (e.g., could you ask for help for parts of the task? Could you take breaks or do part of the task? Could you do the task for shorter periods? Could you take your time?).
- Could the environment in which you undertake the task be less demanding on your energy levels (e.g., would you feel less fatigued if you did the shopping at times when the supermarket was quieter)?

Use Naps More Effectively

Naps can sometimes be refreshing and restore energy, but they can sometimes also make you feel more tired and interfere with your sleep cycle. It may therefore be better to limit or avoid napping. If you do nap, then it is important to consider the following:

1. Make sure you do not nap for too long; otherwise, it can disrupt your sleep routine. Brief naps (15–30 minutes) are also more effective than long naps. Set an alarm.
2. Try to take a nap in your bed.
3. The best time to take a nap may vary from person to person, but naps later in the afternoon should be avoided (e.g., past 3 pm) as they may disrupt your sleep at night.

Plan naps as a wise and deliberate strategy, not as a retreat from fatigue, but as an engagement with it in order to empower you to keep going later.

Softening Resistance to Fatigue

Sometimes, people may not want to pace themselves because of the beliefs that they have about fatigue. These beliefs can be driven by the "Gatekeeper" mindset (see Appendix 8: *Unlocking Adaptation: A Practical Guide to the Compassionate Resilient Mind*), which is more likely to be triggered when you are worried about fatigue. The "Gatekeeper" is like a strict guard standing at the door of your mind. It believes it is protecting you, but it does so with rigid rules and harsh judgements, and it does not allow much flexibility, for example, the "Gatekeeper" may demand that either you push on no matter what or you hold back completely. This all-or-nothing approach may feel protective, but it often traps you in patterns that make fatigue worse, rather than better.

When it comes to fatigue, the "Gatekeeper's" rules may sound like:

- "I must push through tiredness or nothing will get done."
- "Resting means I'm weak."
- "If I accept fatigue, it means the brain injury has beaten me."
- "The only way I can cope is to do as little as possible."

These rules can make it difficult to pace yourself or accept your limits. The CRM offers another way. Like "Eve Olve", the adaptive CRM thinking steps past the "Gatekeeper's" rigid guard rules and thoughts, and brings in curiosity, flexibility and purposeful action aligned with what matters most to you. Instead of asking, "Am I weak if I rest?", CRM reframes the question: "Will resting help me achieve more over the day and help me to connect to what matters most?"

By recognising the "Gatekeeper's" rules and then reviewing how helpful they really are (see Appendix 27: *Evaluating Beliefs About Fatigue and Initiating Compassionate-Resilient Change*), you can begin to loosen their grip. With the guidance of Appendix 7: *Navigating Mind Influencers: Guidelines for Adaptive Thinking*, and Appendix 8: *Unlocking Adaptation: A Practical Guide to the Compassionate Resilient Mind*, you can learn to unlock more compassionate, realistic and supportive responses that soften resistance, make space for pacing, and help you navigate fatigue in a way that sustains your energy and well-being.

Identifying and Caring for Vulnerability Factors

Identify factors, which will make you more prone to fatigue (e.g., anxiety, anger, poor sleep). See the relevant chapters in this book for ways to provide support for these factors. Treat your emotional vulnerabilities, not as flaws, but as parts of your inner world that need care, understanding and support.

Make Wise Choices about Substances

Making choices about alcohol, caffeine and drugs can reflect a compassionate commitment to your long-term well-being. It is not about restriction; it is about supporting your recovery. Consider the following:

- Do you drink much alcohol? Alcohol can exacerbate fatigue; therefore, try and reduce alcohol intake.
- Caffeine offers a "quick fix" for tiredness, but in the long run, it makes you more tired. It can therefore help to gradually cut out all caffeinated drinks (including energy drinks, coffee, tea and cola) over a three-week period. As an experiment, try to stay off caffeine for a month to see if this helps you feel less tired. It is possible that avoiding caffeine will give you headaches. If this happens, try to very gradually reduce the amount of caffeine that you drink.

- Do you take substances that can affect fatigue (e.g., cocaine, cannabis)? If so, you may need to seek help to stop your intake of them.

Build the Basics

Establishing regular routines, good nutrition and light exercise can serve as daily anchors of resilience. Each small act of care can contribute to rebuilding your energy (see Appendix 1: *Building the Basics for Recovery and Adaptation,* for purposeful action to rebuild energy and navigate fatigue).

Controlled Steps in Stimulating Environments

After a brain injury, some people find busy or noisy places, like supermarkets, cafés or buses, much more tiring than before. If you are sensitive to sound, light or movement, these environments can quickly drain your energy. It is natural to want to avoid them altogether. Whilst avoiding can feel like a relief at first, over time, it may lead to:

- Becoming less able to tolerate everyday stimulation
- Feeling more isolated or cut off from others
- Losing confidence and independence in real-world activities

Graded exposure is a gentle, step-by-step way of re-introducing yourself to these environments. Instead of avoiding them completely, you take small, planned steps that gradually build your tolerance and confidence (see Appendix 21: *Courage in Motion: Practising Safe Exposure).*

Graded exposure can support you in navigating fatigue by:

- Preventing over-avoidance, which can actually make sensitivity and tiredness worse over time.
- Helping your brain and body learn that these places are not as threatening as they may first seem.
- Pairing exposure with calming strategies, so you teach your body to link calmness with environments that used to feel overwhelming.
- Giving you space to practise making space for some discomfort, whilst staying connected to what really matters to you, such as doing meaningful activities.

Bringing in your compassionate mind is essential. This means noticing your limits with kindness, not criticism. Everyone has a tolerance point, and compassion helps you recognise when you have reached yours. For some people, this may mean gradually returning to busier places. For others, it may mean recognising that highly stimulating environments will always be too draining and that is okay. In those cases, compassion involves adapting wisely: choosing quieter cafés, shopping at less busy times or designing your life in a way that reduces unnecessary overload. Think of graded exposure as building a bridge: each small step takes you a little closer to where you want to be, without exhausting yourself or shutting yourself off from the world.

Using Mindfulness to Redirect Attention and Broaden Awareness

Mindfulness is not simply about sitting still or trying to relax; it is an attentional skill that helps you take charge of where your mind goes. After brain injury, the ability to regulate attention can be compromised. Fatigue can become the dominant signal in your awareness, drawing your focus inward towards unpleasant sensations and exhausting thoughts. This narrowed focus can amplify the distress of fatigue, creating a loop where the more you attend to it, the more overpowering it feels. Mindfulness gives you a different option. Through regular mindfulness practice (see Appendix 14: *Switching off Automatic Pilot: The Art of Mindfulness*), you can train your mind to notice fatigue without becoming entangled in it. Rather than trying to suppress the experience, mindfulness supports you in accepting it gently, then redirecting your focus with purpose; broadening your awareness away from fatigue.

When practised consistently, mindfulness can help you:

- **Shift from Internal Sensations to External Awareness**: By deliberately noticing what is around you (e.g., sights, sounds, textures), you reduce your focus on fatigue-related discomfort. This can create space for more grounded, less overwhelming experiences.
- **Observe Thoughts without Being Pulled into Them**: For example, instead of automatically believing "I can't do this when I'm tired," you might note, "There's the thought that I can't do this when tired," with curiosity and distance.
- **Interrupt Automatic Reactions**: Mindfulness builds a pause between noticing fatigue and reacting to it. In that pause, you can choose a helpful response, such as taking a breath, changing posture or shifting attention.
- **Focus Attention on Values-Based Action**: Mindfulness helps anchor your attention on what you are doing now and why it matters to you. You become more able to keep doing something meaningful, even with fatigue present.

Practical Exercise

Try using a brief mindful grounding technique the next time you notice fatigue rising:

1. **Pause and Breathe.**
   Bring your awareness to your breath for just one full cycle of you breathing slowly in through your nose and slowly out through your mouth.
2. **Look around and Name Three Things You Can See.**
   Let your eyes rest gently on colours or shapes.
3. **Notice Two Things You Can Hear.**
   Notice sound coming in and out, like waves.
4. **Feel One Physical Sensation That Is Not Fatigue.**
   For example, feel the floor pressing up on your feet, the chair pressing up under you, or your hands resting.
5. **Remind Yourself:**
   "Fatigue is here, but it's not all of me. I can choose where to focus."

This mindful redirection does not ignore fatigue; it simply invites the mind to hold it more lightly, as one experience among many, rather than the whole story. You can imagine your fatigue as a post from a "body influencer" on your mind's social media feed (the mind being analogous to the internet, and the social media feed being analogous to your thoughts and sensations; see Appendix 7: *Navigating Mind Influencers: Guidelines for Adaptive Thinking*, for a full illustration of this metaphor). Just like with unhelpful thoughts, you do not have to "like," comment or follow the "body influencer." Instead, simply notice it and name it (e.g., "Ah, here's another post from Captain Foggy again") and gently scroll past. Let it be part of the background feed, but not the headline story.

Alternatively, think of fatigue like radio static or a slow internet connection interfering with your ability to tune into your day. It is there, fuzzing up the signal, but you do not need to fight it or give it your full attention. Imagine your CRM as a skilled broadcaster or a digital filter, one that can gently shift the dial, refocus the stream and amplify what really matters right now. You are not pretending the interference is not there; you are just choosing to tune in to a different channel or refresh your focus. With practise, this can reduce the mental grip that fatigue has on your attention, freeing up bandwidth for more purposeful, values-aligned responses (see Appendix 29: *Rebalancing the Volume: Highlighting What Matters, Softening the Noise of Pain and Fatigue*, for an exercise in how to facilitate this). With practise, mindfulness becomes a strength that helps you respond to fatigue with flexibility and purpose. It cultivates the qualities of the CRM: awareness, acceptance and purposeful action aligned with what truly matters to you.

Acceptance and Living Beyond Your Fatigue

To support your journey in living beyond fatigue, it helps to use metaphors, the Unwelcome Guest and the Martial Arts analogies (see Appendix 9: *Metaphors for a Compassionate Resilient Mind*). These metaphors highlight the importance of shifting away from a struggle-based mindset. Rather than fighting fatigue in an exhausting battle to eliminate it, these approaches invite you to accept its presence, respond with awareness and adapt with compassion (see also mindfulness practices in Appendix 14: *Switching off Automatic Pilot: The Art of Mindfulness*).

The unwelcome guest metaphor:

Imagine fatigue as an uninvited guest who shows up at your door for a party. If you devote all your energy to keeping them out (e.g., watching the door and standing guard), you become consumed by the effort and miss out on the party. Your attention narrows, your energy drains and your life revolves around trying to keep them out. Similarly, if you spend all your time trying to keep fatigue out, this intense focus can amplify its presence, making it feel even more overwhelming. Instead, what if you allowed the guest to be there without engaging in constant battle? By noticing fatigue without resistance, you create space to focus on what truly matters and get on with life despite it being there. Acceptance does not mean giving up; it means softening the grip of struggle, so you can re-engage with life. With time, you may discover that fatigue is more tolerable than you imagined, even if it is always there.

For further details, see Appendix 9b: *The Unwelcome Guest, Metaphors for a Compassionate Resilient Mind.*

The martial arts metaphor:

In martial arts particularly, practitioners learn not to oppose force with force. When an opponent pushes, the goal is not to resist head-on. Instead, you yield, flow and redirect the energy with skill and awareness. Pushing back only creates tension, intensifies the conflict and makes your opponent feel stronger and more immovable.

Fatigue is similar. The more you push against it, through overexertion, denial or harsh self-judgement, the more entrenched and powerful it can become. But when you respond like a martial artist, staying grounded, open and adaptable, you reduce internal resistance. You move with the fatigue, not against it.

By accepting its presence, pacing your energy and responding with flexibility, you regain a sense of control. This does not mean surrendering to fatigue; it means shifting your strength from forceful resistance to mindful adaptation. Your power lies in your capacity to adjust, respond wisely and live meaningfully alongside fatigue, not in defeating it.

For further details, see Appendix 9a: *Martial Arts Metaphor, Metaphors for a Compassionate Resilient Mind.*

Bringing It All Together: Crossing the Bridge through Fog

- **Fatigue Is Fog, Not Failure**: Treat signs of fatigue as signals to navigate with compassion and resilience, rather than an enemy to defeat.
- **Sense the Fog Early**: Notice physical, cognitive, emotional and behavioural signs (see Appendix 25: *Recognising the Signs of Fatigue*), and use brief relaxation strategies to steady yourself (see Appendix 16: *Relaxation Skills: Finding Calm and Balance*).
- **Avoid "Boom–Bust"**: Replace sprint–crash patterns with pacing: alternate demands with restoration and plan around your best-energy windows (Appendices 26–28: *Fatigue Diary: Tracking patterns to support adaptive pacing; Evaluating Beliefs About Fatigue and Initiating Compassionate-Resilient Change; Breaking Out of the Boom-Bust Cycle – Pacing Activities*).
- **Lighten the Load**: Reduce pressures, modify environments, ask for help and prioritise by values, not "should dos."
- **Refuel Wisely**: Use short, planned naps; choose restorative movement/leisure; make thoughtful choices about alcohol, caffeine and other substances.
- **Support the Terrain**: Address vulnerability factors (sleep, mood, anxiety, pain, sensory load) with targeted strategies in related chapters.
- **Work with Your Mind**: Notice "Gatekeeper" rules and navigate them; use mindfulness to widen attention and refocus on what matters (Appendix 14: *Switching off Automatic Pilot: The Art of Mindfulness* and Appendix 29: *Rebalancing the Volume: Highlighting What Matters, Softening the Noise of Pain and Fatigue*).
- **Keep Crossing with Acceptance**: Like a skilled martial artist, move with fatigue (i.e., pace, pause, proceed). You do not need to clear all fog to live a meaningful life beyond it.

9 Finding Strength and Compassion in Living Beyond Pain

Vicki Hall

Why Do People Experience Pain after a Brain Injury?

Living with pain after a brain injury can feel a little like setting out on a long walk with an unexpected weight in your rucksack. Sometimes, the weight is obvious, like when you have injured your head, face or another part of your body. Sometimes, it is less visible, such as when a stroke has changed the way the brain processes signals, so that even a gentle touch feels sharp and painful. In other cases, the weight comes from muscle tightness or weakness that makes movements harder. Medication can sometimes lighten the load, but it may not always take it away.

What is often overlooked is how much the way you carry "the weight" matters, i.e., thoughts, feelings and behaviours can all change how pain is felt, interpreted and responded to. This is where the values of compassion and resilience become your travelling companions.

Imagine yourself walking this path with two trusted friends by your side:

- Compassion is the friend with the backpack of snacks, reminding you to pause, to rest, to soften your steps and to speak kindly to yourself when the going is tough.
- Resilience is the steady voice beside you, pointing out the next foothold and saying, "Let's keep climbing when you're ready."

Together, they help you become a wise observer of your whole journey, noticing, not just the physical sensations of pain, but also the emotions, thoughts and patterns that shape the experience. With them by your side, you can learn to pace yourself, rest when needed and move forward again, even when pain feels heavy.

How Does Pain Affect Me?

When pain comes along on the journey, it does not just sit quietly in the background. Sometimes, it drains your energy like a leaky water bottle, leaving you tired, flat or low in mood. It can spill into your nights, disturbing sleep or cloud your days, making it harder to concentrate, remember things or solve problems. For help with these challenges, see Chapter 1: *Lighting the Way: Navigating Depression and Low Mood in Early Recovery*; Chapter 8: *Pacing with Purpose: A Compassionate Guide to Navigating Fatigue*; Chapter 7: *Resting with Resilience: A Compassionate Guide to Sleep*; Chapter 10, Catching the Slips: A Compassionate Resilient Guide to Remembering and Chapter 11, *The Compass of Attention:*

DOI: 10.4324/9781003464655-9

Guiding Learning with Resilience and Compassion and Chapter 12: *Executive Skills After Brain Injury: A Compassionate Guide to Planning, Problem-Solving, and Self-Control.*

Pain can also tug at your relationships and shrink the space you have for enjoyment. You may notice yourself doing less of the things you love, not because you do not want to, but because pain insists on slowing you down or stopping you. This is where the Compassionate Resilient Mind (CRM) makes a difference. With CRM, pain may still feel like an unwelcome presence in your life, but it does not have to become an enemy to battle. Instead, it can be understood as a difficult companion on life's journey. Compassion, courage and flexibility can help you navigate towards a meaningful life, broadening your awareness to life beyond your pain.

Understanding the "Pain Gate"

Sometimes, people can experience serious injuries, but feel little or no pain in the moment. A soldier, for example, may continue fighting despite being wounded, only realising the full extent of the injury once the danger has passed. Athletes can also keep running on an injury, barely noticing it until the race is finished and the adrenaline wears off.

At other times, pain can feel much worse, especially if you are tired, anxious or feeling low. One useful way of understanding this is the "pain gate" theory. You can imagine a gate in your nervous system that controls how many pain signals reach your brain (the "pain gate"). Now picture that this "pain gate" is controlled by a set of traffic lights:

- When the light is **green**, the "pain gate" swings open and pain signals rush through freely, making pain feel stronger.
- When the light shifts to **amber**, the "pain gate" partly narrows, so fewer signals get through.
- When the light is **red**, the "pain gate" closes more firmly, and only a small trickle of pain signals make it past.

Different factors act like signals that change the lights and affect whether the "pain gate" opens or closes:

- Stress, tension, low mood or inactivity keep the lights green and the "pain gate" wide open, allowing pain through.
- Relaxation, uplifting emotions, meaningful activity, and drawing on compassion and resilience switch the lights towards amber or red, helping the "pain gate" to narrow and reduce the flow.

The encouraging message is that you can influence these signals. You cannot stop every car from approaching the "pain gate", but you can change the way the traffic lights work, helping the "pain gate" to stay more restricted and making pain less overwhelming. The strategies below will show you how.

Relaxation

If your muscles are tense, this can either cause pain or make your existing pain worse. When pain is severe, people normally tense up. It is therefore important to learn to notice when your muscles are becoming tense, so that you can relax them. Relaxation may also help you to feel better generally when you are in pain by reducing your anxiety levels and broadening your awareness from the pain (see Appendix 16: *Relaxation Skills: Finding Calm and Balance*).

Broadening Awareness and Activity

When you are in pain your attentional focus can be narrowed onto this feeling as it is detected by the "Gatekeeper" (the "survival" part of your mind) as a threat. Your pain is likely to be magnified if you focus all your attention on it. Boredom can also lead to the "pain gates" opening. To restrict the gate, it may be important to broaden your awareness to other things. See Appendix 4: *Enjoyment and Achievement: Activities to Lift Mood and Motivation*, for guidelines for how to increase pleasurable activities and keep yourself active. Mindfulness can also help to broaden your awareness (*see Appendix 14: Switching off Automatic Pilot: The Art of Mindfulness and Appendix 15: Mindfulness for Chronic Pain: Meeting Discomfort with Compassion*).

Pacing Activities

The following are negative activity cycles:

- If you push yourself too hard, it is likely you will have more days in which your pain is very bad, and you will gradually be able to do less.
- If you do too little, this is likely to have a negative impact on your mood and lower your pain threshold.
- If you do too little, you will also not be maintaining your strength, stamina, and flexibility in your muscles. A lack of fitness may also make muscles and other tissues tight, meaning that they may tire easily when used or stretched. In the long run, the effect of this is that you may have more pain and feel less like doing any activity.

To restrict the "pain gate", it is therefore important to pace your activity levels (see Appendix 28: *Breaking Out of the "Boom-Bust" Cycle – Pacing Activities,* for activity pacing guidelines). If you have a physiotherapist, they may be able to help you do this.

Soften the Grip of Uncomfortable Thoughts and Feelings

Sometimes, the mind produces uncomfortable thoughts about pain, for example, anticipating that it will be bad, or worrying about how it might be in the future. These thoughts can stir up feelings, such as anxiety, frustration or anger, which in turn, can intensify the pain experience. Instead of trying to fight or eliminate these thoughts, it can be helpful to gently acknowledge them as they arise, and notice them for what they are: passing events in the mind, not absolute truths.

Bringing attention back to the present moment, one breath, one minute, one day at a time, can soften the impact of these thoughts. Practices, such as mindful awareness and acceptance (see Appendix 14: *Switching off Automatic Pilot: The Art of Mindfulness* and Appendix 15: *Mindfulness for Chronic Pain: Meeting Discomfort with Compassion*) support you to stay with the here and now, allowing pain to be present without resistance, whilst cultivating a more balanced and compassionate response.

When we become entangled with uncomfortable thoughts and feelings about pain, it can be easy to slip into seeing pain as an aggressor and ourselves as its victim. This can feel overwhelming and limiting. If you observe pain with mindful curiosity, as something distinct from your core self, you can change the relationship by moving away from an adversarial stance and towards a compassionate one. From this place of compassion, it becomes possible to approach pain with openness and resilience, rather than fear or struggle.

Empowering Helpful Value-Driven Thoughts Which Help You Live Beyond Pain

Uncomfortable thoughts about pain can be unhelpful as they can sometimes put you down and instil feelings of hopelessness about the future. The following may therefore be helpful:

- Detach from your uncomfortable thoughts by giving them a named voice (e.g., "Eeyore" voice). Acknowledge your uncomfortable thoughts by name when they come into your awareness.
- Now think about who you would like to help you to respond to this unhelpful voice. Think about what value system the person may have to help you counteract the unhelpful "doomsday" messages of "Eeyore" (e.g., compassion, strength, courage and wisdom). Name the voice (e.g., "Jedi").
- Now help "Eyore" by responding to him with your "Jedi" voice.

To connect with your helpful "Jedi" voice, remember the wisdom of your travelling companions, "Compassion" and "Resilience":

- **Pause before You Push**: When painful or difficult thoughts appear, it is not always helpful to fight them. With "Compassion" first acknowledge the adversity. Then, when you are ready, guide yourself forward with resilience.
- **Reframe Resilience**: Resilience is not about pretending the "rucksack" is not heavy; it is about finding ways to carry it. It is the quiet strength that helps you adapt, take steady steps and learn from challenges along the way.
- **The Compassion–Resilience Partnership:** Compassion gives you kindness and acceptance when you stumble; resilience gives you courage to rise and continue. Together, they balance rest with movement, gentleness with determination.
- **Listen for the Contrast**: The "Eeyore" voice speaks in hardship and hopelessness, whilst your CRM offers a language of courage, care and perspective. Notice how different they sound.
- **Respond with "Jedi" Wisdom**: Let your "Jedi" voice speak from the values compassion and resilience. Examples of the "Jedi" voice might be:
    - Focus on the path, not the fog ahead: "Live in the moment, instead of forecasting a painful future."
    - See adversity as a teacher: "Embrace challenges, they can help you grow stronger."
    - Travel steadily: "Don't give up. Keep going, one step at a time."
    - Be kind to yourself: "Don't beat yourself up, be your own travelling companion."

Some examples are listed in Table 9.1.

Table 9.1 Softening uncomfortable thoughts and feelings about pain

"Eeyore voice"	Response from "Jedi compassionate, resilient voice"
"My pain will keep getting worse."	"Hello, Eeyore. My name is Jedi. My values are compassion and resilience. I'll try and guide you towards a path that instils these values. Eeyore, I acknowledge and understand your pain. I know it's hard, but crystal ball gazing about future pain will take you away from the path of resilience. Accept the pain as it is now; take one day and one minute at a time. Stay in the here and now. This is what gives you strength of mind and helps you to develop resilience. A moment's reflection in the here and now is when your mind is the clearest and most focused."
"My family will leave me because I can't do anything."	"Eeyore, I know that at times, you may feel like you're a burden on others and that things are very difficult for you. It makes sense that you feel like this when you're struggling. When you say that you can't do anything, I'm wondering if you're being hard on yourself, which leads you away from the value of compassion. Be compassionate to yourself and recognise your strengths and what you can still do. Show resilience in the face of adversity by continuing to put one foot in front of the other, and make sure that you do things, however small. You can cope even if you're alone, if you show yourself compassion."
"The future is hopeless."	"Eeyore, it's okay to feel hopeless right now, but crystal ball gazing about future doom and gloom takes you away from the path of strength of mind and resilience. I understand that your pain may not get better. Accept the pain in the here and now, and focus on the present. This is how you can create strength of mind, which gives you resilience."
"I'm useless because I'm in pain all the time and there are times when I can't do things."	"Eeyore, I acknowledge that the pain hurts and it can make you feel useless, but it doesn't define you. It hurts to be in pain and to feel like you can't do what you want, but calling yourself useless is taking you away from the path of compassion and resilience, as it's putting yourself down and being unkind to yourself. Show respect and compassion for yourself by recognising what values and strengths you have. Show compassion by giving yourself permission to be kind to yourself. Don't beat yourself up when there are times that you need to take things easy and can't do things. It's okay to take a break at times, as this will restore your energy and give you strength of mind, so that you can respond to your pain with resilience. Your value isn't only about what you do, but also who you are."
"This is never going to get any better; therefore, I can't move on with my life. It's hopeless."	"It feels unbearable right now, and it's okay to feel overwhelmed by how things are. But Eeyore, life isn't about waiting for the storm to pass; it's about learning to dance in the rain (i.e., accepting pain, sadness and the great challenges that it presents, and nevertheless getting on with life). Accepting and facing adversity, whilst getting on with your life will take you on the path of resilience."

Acceptance and Living beyond Your Pain

Useful analogies to help you accept your pain and live beyond it are the "unwelcome guest" and "martial arts" metaphors (see Appendix 9a and 9b: *Metaphors for a Compassionate Resilient Mind*). These metaphors help you to realise that it is important not to avoid your pain by directly fighting against it and trying to get rid of it.

The "martial arts" metaphor illustrates that it is important to roll with an opponent's energy, rather than fighting it head-on and pushing against their resistance. The harder you push against your opponent's resistance, the more tension you will feel against yourself, and the more immovable your opponent will become. So, it is important not to fight your opponent with brute force; instead, you stay aware, flexible and open to the flow of energy; by adjusting and softening, you find the flow of least resistance. Similarly, the harder you battle against pain, or the harder you try to completely block it out, the worse you can make it. Instead, if you move with the pain by accepting it, pacing yourself and staying aware, you can make the experience more pliable, reduce tension and increase control over your experience. Your strength is in your ability to adapt and respond, not to overpower.

The "unwelcome guest" metaphor illustrates that if you focus on your pain all the time, and spend your life trying to control it by not letting it in, then you will not be able to get on with your life, and you are less likely to have control over it. An excessive focus on pain (e.g., by constantly worrying about it and fighting it) will also cause it to become magnified. If you learn to accept your pain and get on with life despite it, you may start to tolerate it better and realise it is not as bad as you believed.

Pulling It All Together: Traveller's Survival Guide

Living with chronic pain after brain injury can feel like setting out on a long journey with an unexpected weight in your rucksack. You may not be able to take the load away, but you can learn how to carry it more wisely. Here are your survival tips for the road ahead:

- **Pack Compassion**: Pause, rest and speak kindly to yourself when the path feels steep.
- **Carry Resilience**: Take steady steps, one at a time, and keep sight of what matters most to you.
- **Balance Your Pace**: Avoid sprinting and crashing; spread your energy, so the weight feels lighter.
- **Soften the Straps**: Relaxation, distraction and enjoyable activity cushion the burden.
- **Sort Your Supplies**: Notice unhelpful "Eeyore" thoughts, and counter them with your compassionate "Jedi" voice.
- **Travel with Acceptance**: Pain may be an unwelcome companion, but you do not have to fight it. Walk alongside it, adapting as you go.

With these tools, the weight in your rucksack may not disappear, but it can become easier to bear. Pain may still feel like an unwelcome guest in your life, but it no longer has to be the compass that directs your journey. With compassion, courage and resilience as your compass, life can still hold meaning and a connection to what matters most.

10 Catching the Slips

A Compassionate Resilient Guide to Remembering

Vicki Hall

The Control Tower: Navigating Memory and Attention after Brain Injury

Imagine your mind is like the control tower of a busy airport. Each plane in the sky represents something you care about or need to do today: for example, an appointment, a conversation, taking medication, remembering a name or completing a task. Your role in the control tower of the airport is to keep the flights running smoothly.

Memory slips happen when the flight plan goes off course. In this metaphor, memory slips might be planes that disappear from the radar altogether (forgetting an appointment), planes that circle endlessly in a holding pattern (you know there is something important, but cannot recall it at the right time), planes that land on the wrong runway (mixing up names or details), or a plane that touches down without its cargo (remembering you had something to do, but not the specifics).

Before your brain injury, the radar was crisp, the radios were clear, and you could guide planes to take off and land with ease. After your brain injury, the weather changed. Fog (fatigue) rolls in, crosswinds (pain or stress) force planes off course, and the radar blips (distractions) come and go. At the same time, the airspace has grown more complicated. Without the usual flight schedules and routines (like working hours or daily rhythms), planes begin arriving at irregular times. Some circle endlessly in holding patterns, whilst new traffic (e.g., medical appointments, treatment plans and unexpected demands) suddenly clutters the skies. It is not that you are careless or incapable; the conditions are simply more demanding, and the control tower needs new supports.

In this airport, external aids (e.g., calendars, alarms, pill boxes) are your runway lights and beacons. Habits and routines are your standard checklists and flight plans. Environmental tweaks (e.g., making sure there are no distractions, keeping everything ordered and in one place) are ground crew markers and clear signage that reduce confusion on the tarmac. Support from others is the coordinated team on the radios, helping sequence traffic. Metacognitive strategies are the "control tower view" itself, allowing you to step back to see the airspace, notice patterns and adjust the plan.

Your Compassionate Resilient Mind (CRM) is the calm co-controller who joins you in the control tower. It does not scold when a plane misses a slot; it steadies the process, helps you prioritise which planes must land first and guides you to pace traffic safely. Together, you learn to work with the weather, rather than fight it by lighting the runway, simplifying routes and landing one plane at a time.

This chapter invites you to become more intentional and proactive in how you support your brain to help navigate memory slips. You will be guided to build your own personal toolkit of strategies, your runway lights, checklists and co-pilots, to support your

DOI: 10.4324/9781003464655-10

autonomy and ongoing growth. You are not expected to remember everything. Instead, the goal is to find strategies that allow you to function with confidence and live in alignment with what is meaningful to you, even when memory is challenged.

Outlined below are examples of strategies to help ensure your airport is prepared, such as keeping the runways clear, the lights shining, and the control tower ready to guide each plane safely in (just as these tools help you remember and manage daily tasks).

General Strategies to Help with Forgetting Things (The 7 Rs)

1. Routine and Habits (Flight Plans and Checklists)

- Try to maintain a regular daily structure and pair tasks with established routines. For example, "After I brush my teeth, I'll take my medication."
- Build in the habit of double-checking, for example, checking hotel rooms before leaving to ensure that nothing is left behind.

2. Relationships (Ground Crew and Radio Support)

- Ask others to support your memory, but on your terms. Talk about how you would like to be reminded, so that help feels supportive, rather than controlling.
- Use shared calendars or diaries (e.g., Google Calendar) to stay connected with others around plans and appointments.
- CRM emphasises the value of kind collaboration. Asking others to communicate one task at a time can help reduce memory overload.

3. Restructuring the Environment (Clearing the Tarmac)

- Declutter to reduce visual and mental distraction.
- Keep important items (e.g., keys, phone) in consistent locations.
- Remove distractions in spaces where focus is required.

4. Readiness (Pre-Flight Briefing)

- Anticipate likely memory slips and plan ahead for them.
- Prioritise what you want to remember (the three most important planes).
- Be aware of high-risk times when you are more likely to forget (e.g., noisy environments).
- Readiness also includes setting clear goals and developing self-awareness (see Appendix 3: *Turning Values into Action: Setting SMART Goals*, for guidance on goal setting).
- In order to be ready, you need to be aware of memory slips, and this sometimes requires psychological acceptance (see Chapter 2: *Flowing Forward: Compassionate Resilient Adaptation after Brain Injury*, for help in facilitating this). Also see Chapter 12: *Executive Skills after Brain Injury: A Compassionate Guide to Planning, Problem-Solving and Self-Control, for guidance on problems with awareness caused by self-monitoring deficits.*

5. Reminders (Runway Lights and Beacons)

- Use reminders, such as alarms, notes, calendar alerts or digital assistants. Think of these not as crutches, but as tools of empowerment.
- Try labelled alarms (e.g., "Take medication now") and recurring notifications.

6. Reflect (Control Tower View and Debrief)

- Develop awareness of when, how and why memory slips happen.
- Reflection encourages problem-solving and strategy adjustment.
- Recognise that forgetting is human. CRM encourages responding to memory slips with gentleness, compassion and curiosity, not criticism. Reflection is not about blame or criticism, but learning.
- For help encouraging compassionate, resilient responses to memory slips, see:
    - Chapter 2: *Flowing Forward: Compassionate Resilient Adaptation after Brain Injury*
    - Appendix 6: *From Resistance to Acceptance: Opening the Door to Adaptation*
    - Appendix 7: *Navigating Mind Influencers: Guidelines for Adaptive Thinking*
    - Appendix 8: *Unlocking Adaptation: A Practical Guide to the Compassionate Resilient Mind*
    - Appendix 36: *Using the Compassionate Resilient Mind (CRM) to Navigate Cognitive Symptoms with ACCEPTS*

7. Renew Knowledge about Technology (Upgrading the Radar)

- Keep up to date with apps, gadgets and digital assistants that can support memory. If you struggle with technology, search for YouTube tutorials.
- Search the internet with queries like:
    - "Best apps for remembering appointments"
    - "Devices to help me to remember to lock doors"
    - "Best shared calendar tools"
- Smart devices (e.g., Amazon Echo, Google Home, Apple HomePod) can:
    - Set verbal reminders
    - Add items to shopping lists
    - Play alarms
    - Notify you of events

Strategies for Specific Types of Memory Slips

Everyone experiences memory slips now and then, but after a brain injury, these can feel more frequent or more disruptive. Below are examples of practical strategies for managing specific, common memory challenges. Think of these strategies as part of your pre-flight briefing: planning ahead, anticipating potential issues and putting structures in place, so your "airport" runs smoothly.

1. Forgetting Appointments
    - Record appointments immediately in a diary, phone or calendar.
    - If you use a paper diary, cross off each day at the same time every morning (e.g., before breakfast). If you use an electronic diary, use a different strategy (e.g., turn the activity green when it is completed).
    - If you are not near your diary, text or email yourself as a temporary reminder.
    - Check your calendar daily and use alarms to alert you in advance.
    - Keep your diary or calendar in an easy-to-access and consistent location.

2. Forgetting to Take Things with You When Going Out

   - Pack bags in advance and place them near the front door.
   - Create a checklist and post it near the exit (e.g., phone, keys, wallets).
   - Set an alarm before leaving the house to trigger a final check.
   - Use location-based reminders (e.g., geo-fencing technology).
   - Motion-activated voice players can offer auditory reminders as you leave.
   - Use visual signs (e.g., "Stop and Think" signs at the door).

3. Forgetting Items When Shopping

   - Make shopping lists and tick off items as you go.
   - Store the shopping list on your phone for accessibility.
   - Use apps like AnyList that can sync with household members or smart devices (e.g., Alexa).
   - Explore smart fridge technology that allows remote viewing of contents.
   - Set a reminder before leaving to check your list.

4. Forgetting to Do Things

   - Write notes and place them in visible locations.
   - Use your phone to record reminders, or send yourself texts or emails.
   - Keep a dedicated memory notebook or use notes apps.
   - Set regular reminders to review your to-do list.
   - Do tasks immediately when possible.
   - Use virtual assistants like Siri or Alexa to schedule prompts.

5 Forgetting If You Have Locked the Door

   - Place a sticky note on the door that says, "Lock Me."
   - Research smart locks or reminder technology (e.g., alerts, sensors, geo-fenced reminders).
   - Leave extra time when leaving the house, so you can check.
   - Make locking the door a consistent habit (e.g., lock it as soon as you enter).

6. Forgetting to Take Medication

   - Establish a daily routine for taking medication.
   - Place your medication near objects tied to your routine (e.g., toothbrush).
   - Use alarms or medication reminder apps. Pill boxes with timers can be helpful.

7. Forgetting What People Have Said

   - Take brief notes on your phone during or after conversations.
   - Keep a small notebook or digital notepad app with you.
   - Use a voice recorder for meetings or important discussions.

8. Losing Things

   - Keep your environment decluttered and organised.
   - Label containers and shelves.

- Use smart location trackers (e.g., Apple AirTag) for frequently lost items.
- Take a photo of where you park or store an item if you are worried about forgetting.
- Try visualising the last time you had the item.
- Assign each item a "home" and return it there after use (see table below for examples).

Important item	**Suggested home location**
Keys	Hook near the front door
Purse/wallet	Basket by kitchen counter
Phone	Bedside table or desk station
Glasses	Designated tray or shelf

9. Forgetting Why You Went into a Room

   - Pause and try to picture where you were and what you were thinking before you entered.
   - Retrace your steps physically or mentally to re-access the intention.

10. Forgetting to Turn the Oven Off

    - Place a sticky note near the kitchen exit saying, "Have I turned the oven off?"
    - Build a habit of saying aloud, "I'm turning the oven off now" when doing it.
    - Use a motion-activated voice prompt that activates and tells you to turn the oven off when you leave the kitchen to reinforce the habit.
    - Search online about current devices that support oven safety (e.g., smart shut-off plugs, auto-disconnect functions).
    - Set a timer that prompts you to check the oven.
    - Ensure you have a working smoke alarm.

The Control Tower View: Metacognitive Control

Metacognitive strategies (strategies enabling you to reflect on your mental processes) are like the control tower's bird's-eye view allowing you to step back to see the whole airspace. They help you notice slips, understand why they happen, and make small adjustments to keep things running smoothly.

These strategies strengthen CRM by nurturing the ACCEPTS qualities:

- **A—Awareness and Acceptance**
  Develop self-awareness by noticing slips as they happen, and meet them with acceptance, rather than judgement; recognising that they are normal parts of being human and opportunities for adaptation, not personal failures.
- **C—Cognitive Flexibility**
  Practise flexibility by adjusting your strategies as circumstances change, rather than getting stuck in rigid or self-critical patterns.
- **C—Compassion for Self and Others**
  Respond to slips with kindness, rather than harsh judgement, supporting yourself as you would a close friend.
- **E—Effort with Balance (Compassionate Persistence)**
  Keep engaging with strategies and goals, balancing persistence with gentleness, so slips become opportunities to adapt, rather than reasons to give up.

- **P—Purposeful Action**
  Stay guided by your values when setbacks occur, making choices that keep your life meaningful, rather than letting fear or avoidance take over.
- **T—Tools**
  Use tools and strategies to help you adapt or compensate.
- **S—Self Reflection**
  Identify triggers to slips (e.g., being tired or in a rush); what works to help you compensate and what doesn't, reflecting on what will help you to adjust next time.

See Appendix 36: *Using the Compassionate Resilient Mind (CRM) to Navigate Cognitive Symptoms with ACCEPTS,* for how to apply these qualities to memory slips.

Like flight plans that shift with the weather, memory tools are not fixed. A flexible mindset allows you to adapt to turbulence, such as:

- Emotional stress (turbulent skies)
- Fatigue or pain (low fuel)
- Competing demands (crowded skies)
- Rushing (too many planes at once)
- Overfamiliar tasks ("automatic pilot" without full attention)

Metacognitive tools help you pause, check your compass and gently re-adjust, so the control tower stays in control.

When "Automatic Pilot" Misfires

After a brain injury, the "control tower radar" that plans, directs and corrects can falter. Under pressure, you may slip into "automatic pilot," acting out of habit without awareness.

Common slips indicating that you have been operating on "automatic pilot" include:

- Forgetting why you walked into a room
- Forgetting where you parked your car
- Taking medication, then forgetting you did

The good news is that you can switch from "automatic pilot" to manual with simple strategies.

Switching to Manual

The following can help you switch from "automatic pilot" to manual:

1. Rushing, overload or stress increases errors. Slow down and ground yourself using mindfulness (see Appendix 14: *Switching off Automatic Pilot: The Art of Mindfulness*). This helps you notice distractions and purposefully direct your attention back to what matters.
2. Practising mindfulness in your everyday tasks can help you keep your attention focused where it matters (see Appendix 14: *Switching off Automatic Pilot: The Art of Mindfulness*).
3. Use regular alarms as "control tower radio check-ins." Ask: "Am I focused on my current flight path, or drifting?", and gently bring attention back when needed.

4. Keep a Memory Slip Tracker (Appendix 30: *Memory Slip Tracker Form*) as a flight log. Spot patterns, anticipate high-risk situations and plan better responses.
5. One plane, one runway: practise single-tasking and ask others not to overload you with instructions.
6. Broadcast your intentions, for example, "I'm locking the door now." Speaking aloud keeps attention engaged and prevents slips.
7. Repeat directions back, like confirming a flight clearance. This ensures accuracy and recall.

The Stop–Imagine–Go Method: A Quick In-Flight Checklist

Think of the SIG Method (Stop–Imagine–Go) as a simple cockpit checklist you run before take-off. Just as pilots pause to confirm settings before moving down the runway, you can use this method to bring your attention back on track, reduce slips and act with intention.

Step 1: Stop and Pause

Like a plane holding at the end of the runway before clearance, pause before starting a task. This moment helps you collect your focus and prevent rushing into "automatic pilot."

Step 2: Imagine

Visualise yourself completing the action. Speak the intention aloud, as if you are confirming a flight plan with the control tower:

- "I'm about to take my medication."
- "I'm locking the door now."

This mental rehearsal strengthens focus and primes memory.

Step 3: Go

Carry out the task with awareness, like a plane cleared for take-off. Stay mentally engaged until the "flight" is complete, then mentally tick it off the list. See below for the example of how the SIG method can be used to help you remember to take medication:

- **Stop**: "Pause before picking up my pills."
- **Imagine**: "I'm taking my medication now."
- **Go**: "Take the pills, then confirm: 'Done.'"

Using SIG helps prevent slips by slowing you down, sharpening awareness and keeping the control tower (your attentional system) in control.

Staying Engaged: When Tasks Feel Boring or Motivation Is Low

Planes are harder to land when the runway lights are dim. Similarly, attentional lapses often occur when tasks feel repetitive, dull or lack personal meaning. These slips are not signs of laziness or failure; they are normal responses to low motivation or overstimulation.

The key is to light up the runway with interest, variety and rewards. Below are strategies to stay focused when motivation is low:

- Identify high-risk tasks: Notice which activities cause your mind to wander (e.g., chores, admin or tasks that feel too easy).
- Minimise distractions: Clear the tarmac, put your phone out of reach and switch off notifications.
- Make tasks more interesting by:
    - Turning them into a challenge (e.g., "Can I empty the dishwasher in under 5 minutes?").
    - Using a timer to track speed and progress.
    - Playing favourite music, podcasts or audiobooks whilst working.
    - Trying gamification apps (e.g., Habitica, Do It Now) to turn tasks into achievements.
- Reward yourself: Build in small "refuelling stops" by treating yourself to rest, breaks or enjoyable activities after completing focused work.

Learning from Everyday Errors: Flight Debrief

Even the best-run airports experience the occasional delay or misstep, such as a misplaced bag, a late signal or a plane briefly off course. These are not failures, but reminders that the system is under pressure and needs an adjustment. In daily life after brain injury, attentional slips are the same: part of the natural turbulence of limited mental resources. By treating these slips as learning opportunities, you can refine your "flight plan" and strengthen your systems.

Use this table to record common attentional slips, note why they might have happened and explore strategies to keep your daily flights running smoothly. The final column is for your own notes. Track what worked best for you. If a strategy does not seem to work for you, that is okay, see it as useful feedback rather than failure. Sometimes, a strategy needs adapting, or a different one may be a better fit. Use the table again to reflect on why it did not work and what you might try instead. Sometimes, you may find that you have difficulty trying again or using strategies because of problems accepting your limitations, or emotional resistance to the use of strategies (see Appendix 36: *Using the Compassionate Resilient Mind (CRM) to Navigate Cognitive Symptoms with ACCEPTS* for further help with this).

Memory slip/ action error	*Why it happened (possible cause)*	*Strategy to try / adjustment*	*My notes (what worked for me? If it did not work, what could I do instead?)*
Lost handbag when out	Carrying two bags, forgot one	Tie handles together	This worked when I remembered to do it before leaving. If I forget, I could reduce to one bag only or use a cross-body bag that stays attached to me.
Left phone on table	Didn't think about phone safety	Keep phone in a case around neck / put it in bag straight away	The neck case helped when out, but I don't always like wearing it. A backup is to always put the phone straight into the same pocket after use.

(*Continued*)

Memory slip/ action error	*Why it happened (possible cause)*	*Strategy to try / adjustment*	*My notes (what worked for me? If it did not work, what could I do instead?)*
Lost bus pass	Dropped when boarding	Use a retractable holder	This strategy works well.
Drove off with bag on roof	Distracted, in a rush	Always place items directly in car	This helps if I stick to the rule.
Forgot to turn off bath taps	Left the room, got distracted	Stay nearby; put towel over shoulder	Staying nearby worked best. A backup could be setting a short timer when I turn the taps on.
Left house without bags	Forgot to stop and plan	Use "Stop and Think" sign at the door	The sign only sometimes works. A backup is a door checklist or one essential grab-bag.
Alarm for appointment	Alarm rang but no context	Use labelled alarms	Labelling helped.
Alarm for medication	Turned it off because busy	Use snooze / nagging alerts	Snooze works most of the time. Linking medication to a routine may help further.
Alarm to exercise	Ignored whilst gaming	Use procrastination guidelines and make gaming conditional on movement (Appendix 11)	This strategy works.

Be Realistic, Be Kind

No airport runs perfectly 24/7; minor delays and diversions happen. Likewise, even with strong systems in place, you will still experience memory slips and lapses of attention. That is part of being human. Instead of striving for perfection, ask yourself:

- How important is this slip?
- How often does it really happen?
- How much effort is worth putting into managing it?

These questions help you focus energy where it matters most, keeping your "flights" aligned with your values, rather than chasing unrealistic perfection.

Staying Intentional and Meaningful with a CRM

To reduce "automatic pilot" and stay mentally present, it helps to set clear intentions and align your actions with personal goals. Motivation rooted in what matters to you can help you practise attention in everyday life.

Use the *Goal Setting worksheet* (Appendix 3: *Turning Values into Action: Setting SMART Goals*) to clarify your focus and build habits that reflect the person you want to be.

Final Reflections: Rebuilding with Compassion and Adaptation

Memory slips and attentional lapses are not failures, they are part of being human, especially after brain injury. We all rely, to some extent, on systems, routines, reminders and structure to coordinate the demands of daily life. No airport could function safely without flight schedules, radar systems, checklists, communication procedures and air-traffic control. In the same way, the brain relies on routines, prompts and organised systems to keep daily life moving smoothly. After brain injury, these supports may need to be adapted, updated, and made more visible and intentional. What matters is not avoiding every slip, but how you respond. With your CRM as co-controller, you can steady the control tower, prioritise which planes to land and keep the skies manageable, even in turbulence. Every time you use a checklist, lean on a routine or pause to reflect, you are guiding planes safely down. These actions show resilience and wisdom, not weakness. With patience, adaptability and compassion, you can navigate the skies of daily life with confidence and hope.

11 The Compass of Attention

Guiding Learning with Resilience and Compassion

Vicki Hall

Navigating with a Wavering Compass

Imagine you are an explorer setting out on a journey across new and sometimes, unpredictable terrain. Before your brain injury, your compass of attention pointed steadily to your goals. You could concentrate on the path ahead, hold a map in mind, and steadily reach your destination. After a brain injury, the compass needle may feel less steady. Fatigue, pain or anxiety can act like magnetic fields pulling it off course. Distractions are like sudden storms that obscure the view. At times, you may feel as if the map has been misplaced, leaving you uncertain of the right direction.

However, a wavering compass does not mean the journey must stop. With the right tools, routines, support and mindset, you can chart a way forward. External aids become your landmarks, routines your reliable footpaths and supportive others, your fellow travellers. Metacognitive strategies are the vantage points where you step back, check your bearings and adjust your course. The Compassionate Resilient Mind (CRM) is the wise navigator who walks beside you. It steadies your hand on the compass, encourages flexible thinking when the trail changes, and offers kindness when you stumble or get lost. The goal is not to follow a perfect straight line, but to keep moving steadily, guided by values, towards a life that is both meaningful and fulfilling.

Common Challenges on the Path

After brain injury, difficulties with concentration and learning often arise because there is damage to the parts of the brain that help you to learn and concentrate. Some of the difficulties can also arise from the conditions that you are faced with, for example:

- The "compass" of attention is easily pulled off course by fatigue, pain or emotional stress.
- Motivation may dip when energy feels depleted.
- Environmental distractions act as a magnetic pull on the "compass" of your attention, scattering your focus like noisy "crosswinds".
- Cognitive resources may simply feel reduced, making learning more effortful.

These challenges are not signs of weakness. They are conditions of the terrain you are walking through. A compassionate explorer does not blame the hills for being steep, or the fog for rolling in. Instead, they adapt their route, rest when needed and keep adjusting the compass with patience and skill.

DOI: 10.4324/9781003464655-11

Keeping the Compass Steady: Concentrating for Prolonged Periods

In today's world, your "compass" of attention is constantly being pulled off course by competing signals, like magnetic fields disrupting the needle. Mobile phones, emails, social media, or even the sight of something tempting nearby can tug your focus in different directions. To walk steadily on your learning journey, it helps to reduce these pulls and create conditions where the compass can settle.

Clearing the Path of Distractions

Try the following to clear your path from distractions:

- Put your phone out of reach so you are not tempted to check it. Switch off notifications when working on the computer.
- Shut the blinds if your eyes wander out the window, or use earplugs/noise-cancelling headphones if noisy "crosswinds" are disrupting your focus.
- Move tempting objects (like a guitar or game console) out of sight, for example, you could place them high on a shelf, out of easy reach. Save them as rewards for completing a focused stretch of work, like resting at a waystation after a climb.
- Choose terrain that supports focus, for example, working on your bed is like setting camp on soft sand; you are likely to sink into sleep. A desk, library or quiet study spot provides a firmer trail.
- Keep supplies organised, as scattered materials are like branches blocking the path.

Travelling with Companions

Sometimes, it helps to have a fellow traveller on the journey. A "body double" or "study buddy" can act like a companion walking alongside you, keeping the pace steady. Simply having another person present can sometimes provide motivation and reduce the pull of distractions. If you are in a lecture or class and find focus slipping, use tools to record the journey; software that captures both audio and slides allows you to revisit the route later at your own pace.

Marking Waypoints with Breaks

Explorers know not to walk endlessly without stopping. Your concentration is similar: it works best when broken into short, intentional stretches with clear rest points.

- Work for about 30 minutes, then pause for a 10–15 minute break to refuel.
- Try the Pomodoro Technique: 25 minutes of focus, followed by a 5-minute break. Repeat this cycle. If this rhythm does not fit you, adjust the intervals until your compass feels stable.

Checking Your Bearings

Sometimes, your mind drifts without you noticing, like wandering off the trail without realising it. To counter this:

- Stop at intervals (e.g., every 10 minutes) to summarise what you have just read, heard or watched.

- When watching TV, try using subtitles to keep your mind anchored. Watching subtitles also provides more enriched encoding as it encourages words to be encoded through both your visual and auditory senses. Not everyone will benefit equally from this strategy as people differ in reading speed, language skills, and cognitive load capacity. For some, they may increase extraneous cognitive load and make attention harder, not easier.
- Use structured learning techniques like PQRST (which stands for Preview, Question, Read/ Review, Self-Recite and Test). This is a gentle way of keeping your mind on track, whilst reading or listening to something or watching TV. You briefly preview the material (Preview), ask yourself questions that you expect to be able to answer (Question), read or listen in short sections (Review), summarise the main ideas in your own words (Self-Recite), and then test yourself (Test) (see Appendix 31: *PQRST guidelines*).
- If the terrain feels dull, brighten it: use colourful pens, diagrams, flashcards or playful mnemonic devices to make the path more interesting.

Rewarding the Journey

Motivation often comes from knowing there is something good waiting at the next rest stop. Build in rewards for sustained focus:

- Allow yourself enjoyable activities (like social media or a favourite show) once you have completed a set period of focused work.
- Turn tasks into a points system: for example, award yourself one point for each email answered. When you reach ten points, cash them in for 30 minutes of something you enjoy.

These strategies do not just keep you on task, they help your compass stay steady, your pace sustainable and your journey more rewarding. With practice, concentration becomes less about fighting distractions and more about guiding yourself kindly, step by step, towards your destination.

Strengthening Learning and Memory: Marking the Trail

Learning new information after brain injury can feel like trying to follow a trail through misty terrain. Without markers, it is easy to lose your way or circle back in confusion. Memory strategies are like landmarks and signposts that guide you forward and make the path easier to retrace.

Simplify the Map

- Break material into short chunks – shorter stretches of trail are easier to manage.
- Group items by similarity (e.g., colour, meaning, starting letter) to cluster them like landmarks close together.
- Identify key words that serve as landmarks along the path, anchoring recall.

Make Landmarks Memorable

To prevent the compass needle drifting, give your landmarks colour, shape and story:

- **Dual Encoding**: Pair a visual marker with verbal information, like drawing both the map and writing the directions.

- **Elaboration**: Link new knowledge to familiar places on your journey.
- **Acronyms and Mnemonics**: Turn lists into signposts (e.g., turning the first letter of a chunk of information that you have to learn into a meaningful word or a meaningful sentence) or vivid story-images that stand out in the landscape.
- **Deep Processing**: Make the landmarks (i.e., things that you have to remember) playful or unusual; humour, exaggeration and creativity burn the trail more deeply into memory.

Examples of Landmarks in Practice

- **Memorise Roger's Birthday (27th December)**: Place the information that you want to remember beside the Christmas landmark—"Poor Roger, joint birthday and Christmas presents." This elaboration ties his date to a familiar festive marker.
- **Memorise PIN code 2814**: Imagine two travellers (2) who ate (8) one (1) biscuit with a fork (4). A silly, but vivid image becomes a memorable signpost.
- **Memorise Steps in a Task (Stop–Imagine–Go)**: Use the acronym SIG as a compass bearing. The single word acts as a cue to retrieve the whole sequence.
- **Memorise Colours of the Rainbow**: Use a sentence like, "Richard Of York Gave Battle In Vain." The phrase is a trail marker that unfolds into a full spectrum of colours.
- **Memorise The Ten Commandments**: Pick one keyword from each commandment, then build a story from their initials. The story becomes a narrative trail leading back to each principle.

Why Self-Made Landmarks Work Best

Whilst pre-made mnemonics exist, creating your own markers carves the path more deeply. When you invent an acronym, image or silly story, you are actively processing the material. It is like staking your own signpost into the ground. This makes recall more personal, more meaningful and more resilient. If you are stuck, you can always ask an Artificial Intelligence (AI) chatbot to generate ideas, but even then, try adapting them into your own landscape. The more the landmark reflects your imagination, the more meaningful it will be when you return to find your way.

Walking the Trail Again: Reinforcing Learning over Time

Explorers are aware that a single walk down a new trail may not be sufficient to remember the way. The more often you travel the path and revisit landmarks, the clearer and easier it becomes to follow. Memory works in the same way: each return strengthens the trail and makes recall more reliable.

Revisiting Landmarks

- Test yourself (e.g., check that you remember the mnemonics and the associated information) immediately after you have learnt the information. Then, gradually increase the time intervals at which you test yourself (spaced retrieval method).
- Ensure that you test yourself regularly over prolonged periods (e.g., every week or every day). This is called distributed learning.
- At regular intervals, expose yourself to the information that you need to learn. This is called spaced repetition strategy.

Avoiding Wrong Turns

Sometimes, when learning too much at once, mistakes can get "wired in" as part of the path, like wandering down a false trail and later confusing it with the right one. To prevent this:

- Learn in small, manageable chunks, so you do not mix up the terrain.
- Use errorless learning: master one step before moving on to the next, so that each stretch of the trail is solid before adding the next.

By revisiting the trail, testing yourself and strengthening each landmark over time, you carve a clearer route through the landscape of memory. Instead of constantly feeling lost in the fog, you begin to trust that the path will be there when you need it.

Checking the Compass: Reflective Learning and Metacognitive Strategies

Every traveller knows that it is not enough to keep moving; you must stop now and then, check your compass, and make sure you are still on course. This act of stepping back to review the map and adjust your direction is what metacognitive strategies provide. Metacognition means becoming aware of how you think, learn and remember, like climbing to a high vantage point to see the whole landscape. These strategies are central to the CRM because they encourage intentional choices, flexibility when the trail changes and kindness when you find yourself wandering.

Metacognitive strategies help you:

- **Plan the Journey**: Set realistic goals for distance, pace and rest stops.
- **Monitor Your Path**: Notice when attention has drifted off the trail.
- **Adjust the Route**: Change strategy when the terrain proves more difficult than expected.
- **Reflect on Conditions**: Learn which environments, tools or supports help you most, and which obstacles tend to block your way.

Practical Compass-Checking Tools

- **Plot the Route Ahead**: Create a weekly timetable with SMART goals (Specific, Measurable, Achievable, Realistic, Timed). Just as an explorer schedules supply stops, your timetable should include breaks and rewarding activities.
- **Plan for the Weather**: Study at times when your energy is higher and alternate "steeper climbs" (boring or difficult tasks) with easier or more interesting ones to keep your stamina.
- **Overestimate Distance**: Tasks usually take longer than expected, just as hikes look shorter on a map. By giving yourself extra time, you build confidence that you will reach the day's goal.
- **Prioritise Checkpoints**: Decide which tasks are the most important landmarks to reach and which can wait.
- **Use Recovery Tools**: If you stumble into procrastination, use the Procrastination Worksheet (Appendix 11: *Turning Procrastination into Meaningful Action*) as a guide to get back on track.

- **Navigate Cognitive Slips and Action Errors**: When slips, like losing track of where you are or forgetting occur, use the ACCEPTS framework (Appendix 36: *Using the Compassionate Resilient Mind (CRM) to Navigate Cognitive Symptoms with ACCEPTS*). This framework is especially useful at times when mistakes feel hard to accept, such as when self-criticism, frustration, or losing track leads you to want to withdraw, give up, or avoid the task. ACCEPTS helps turn setbacks into moments of awareness, compassion and purposeful action, so you can regain direction without harsh self-judgement.
- **Review and Adapt**: Regularly check whether your strategies are working. If a path proves too steep, do not judge yourself; adjust the plan, choose an easier route or pace yourself differently.

Extra Navigation Supports

If planning feels overwhelming, you do not have to plot the route alone. There are many apps and digital tools that can help you schedule tasks, track goals and remind you of deadlines. Think of them as digital maps and GPS devices that complement your compass. If you are unsure which to use, try searching online or asking an AI chatbot for "apps to help plan college work," and experiment until you find one that fits your terrain.

Summary: Walking with Your Compass

Learning and concentrating after a brain injury can feel like navigating unpredictable terrain with a compass that sometimes wavers. Distractions, fatigue and stress may pull the needle off course, and it is easy to feel lost or disheartened. Yet, with the right landmarks, signposts, routines and supports, the path becomes clearer and more manageable.

This is your compass toolkit:

Needle = Focus

- Reduce distractions (phone away, blinds closed, quiet space).
- Use routines to keep your compass steady.

Landmarks = Memory Aids

- Mnemonics, acronyms, vivid stories and visual imagery.
- Create your own for stronger recall.

Waypoints = Breaks

- Structure time with short focus periods and regular rests.
- Try the Pomodoro technique (25 minutes focus/5 minutes rest).

Trail Markers = Repetition

- Revisit material often (spaced retrieval and distributed learning).
- Use errorless learning to avoid walking on the wrong trail(familiarity with walking along the incorrect trail due to previous errors can pull you in the wrong direction).

Lookout Points = Metacognition

- Plan ahead with SMART goals.
- Monitor progress, reflect and adapt when needed.

Co-Navigator = CRM

- In charge of the whole plan, putting in place purposeful strategies and reflecting on what is needed.
- Responds to slips with patience and curiosity, not criticism.
- Keeps walking towards what matters, one step at a time.

Through using this toolkit, you are not fighting against your cognitive challenges; instead, you are learning to walk alongside them, using tools and supports to guide your way. This chapter aligns with the CRM**:** meeting cognitive challenges with self-reflection, strategies, flexible adaptability and kindness. By practising these qualities, you can rebuild confidence, adapt to challenges and continue learning in meaningful ways.

For further support, see:

- **Appendix 3**: *Turning Values into Action: Setting SMART Goals*
- **Appendix 11**: *Turning Procrastination into Meaningful Action*
- **Appendix 14**: *Switching off Automatic Pilot: The Art of Mindfulness*
- **Appendix 31**: *PQRST guidelines*
- **Appendix 36:** *Using the Compassionate Resilient Mind (CRM) to Navigate Cognitive Symptoms with ACCEPTS*

Together, these tools strengthen your ability to notice when your compass drifts, reorient yourself to what matters, and walk forward, step by step, towards growth, resilience, and renewed confidence in your learning journey. You do not need to walk in a perfect straight line. What matters is keeping your compass in hand, adjusting as you go, and continuing forward with resilience and compassion.

12 Executive Skills after Brain Injury

A Compassionate Guide to Planning, Problem-Solving and Self-Control

Vicki Hall

The Control Tower of the Brain

Imagine your mind as the control tower of a busy airport. Each plane in the sky represents a meaningful, purposeful action, things you need or want to do in your day-to-day life. Under clear skies, planes take off and land smoothly: you connect with loved ones, keep up routines, enjoy activities and make steady progress towards your goals.

But for this to happen, every department in the control tower plays a vital role:

- **Radar Systems Are Memory**: Tracking where each flight is, recalling past journeys and keeping records of what matters.
- **Air Traffic Radios Are Attention**: Tuning in to the right signals and guiding your focus where it needs to go.
- **Surveillance Screens Are Perception**: Showing what you see and hear in the present moment.
- **Ground Operations Are Movement**: Setting the rhythm, coordinating actions and driving life forward.

When these systems work together in harmony, the airport runs with purpose. Planes take off and land without chaos, and your mind stays aligned with your values and goals.

The Conductor of the Skies: Executive Skills

At the very centre sits the air traffic controller. This is your executive skills (mapping onto the frontal lobes of the brain). The controller does not fly a single plane but coordinates the departments and the whole airspace. They:

- Plan and sequence flights, for example: Deciding the order in which planes take off and land, and the steps needed to clear each runway.
- Problem solve, for example: Finding alternative routes when bad weather or traffic jams appear.
- Monitor errors, for example: Checking whether a plane has drifted off course or landed on the wrong runway.
- Make decisions, for example: Weighing up priorities when multiple planes need attention at once.

DOI: 10.4324/9781003464655-12

- Stay flexible, for example: Adjusting flight paths when unexpected planes arrive in the skies.
- Apply the brakes and hold off when needed, for example: Holding a flight in a holding pattern when it is not safe to land, preventing impulsive or risky movements.

Like a skilled conductor guiding an orchestra, the controller ensures each part of the system plays in harmony. After a brain injury, your executive skills (the air traffic controller of your brain) may not work as well, and the control tower may struggle. The radar may lose track of planes (memory slips). A flight may rush ahead without clearance (impulsivity). Radio chatter may drown out the air traffic making you lose sight of the bigger picture (rigid or repetitive thinking). The sequencing of flights may be muddled (planning difficulties) or decisions delayed (indecision). At times, some planes may be struggling, delayed or unable to fly as smoothly as before. At the same time, the control tower may also be finding it harder to coordinate the many moving parts of the airport. As communication, timing and prioritisation become disrupted, the whole system can begin to feel chaotic and out of rhythm.

Adapting the Control Tower

The good news is that airports adapt. Supports can strengthen the control tower's work:

External supports of the airport	*What It Does*	*Cognitive Support in Everyday Life*
Runway Lights & Beacons	Guide planes safely towards the correct runway	External aids, such as apps, phone reminders, alarms, calendars, and assistive technology that support planning and timing
Standard Flight Plans	Provide predictable routes and reduce decision load	Routines, habits, and structured frameworks that create reliable structure
Ground Crew Signage	Reduce confusion and prevent wrong turns	Environmental tweaks, such as decluttering, visual cues, and organised workspaces
Co-Controllers & Section Leaders	Step in when traffic is heavy or systems are overloaded	Family members, support workers, therapists, or technology acting as prosthetic controllers when cognitive load is high
Error-Monitoring Checklists & Flight Logs	Detect problems early and support learning	Structured monitoring tools, such as diaries, logs, review sheets, and checklists to notice slips, action errors, and progress

These supports do not replace the control tower, they extend its reach, allowing traffic to flow more safely and purposefully.

The Compassionate Co-Controller

Alongside the main controller sits your Compassionate Resilient Mind (CRM), a gentle co-controller who steadies the tempo and offers perspective when the skies grow crowded. Instead of criticising when a plane misses its slot, CRM helps you respond with flexibility and kindness. Its guidance can be remembered through the ACCEPTS qualities:

ACCEPTS Quality	*Executive Function Supported*	*Air Traffic Control Metaphor*	*Everyday Life Example*
A — Awareness & Acceptance	Self-monitoring, insight, emotional regulation	The control tower scans the whole airspace, noticing fog or delays without panic or blame.	You notice you are more tired today or have made action errors, without harsh judgement.
C — Cognitive Flexibility	Shifting your line of thinking, adaptive planning	When a runway closes, traffic is rerouted, rather than frozen in place.	If you keep forgetting medication when busy, you adapt your strategy by using labelled alarms, linking it to a routine or changing the timing.
C — Compassion	Error tolerance and emotional regulation	When a plane misses its slot, the co-controller reassures, rather than scolds.	You miss out a step in a recipe and kindly correct, rather than blame.
E — Effort with Balance (Compassionate Persistence)	Goal perseverance	Flights continue, but the control tower does not push traffic faster than conditions allow.	You work in short bursts with breaks, allowing reflection and preventing overload or shutdown.
P — Purposeful Action	Prioritisation, goal-directed behaviour	The control tower chooses which flight matters most right now.	You set goals alligned with what matters most.
T — Tools & Strategies	A range of executive functioning skills, such as problem-solving and planning aids	The airport relies on radar, checklists, and ground crew.	To guide tasks you can use routines, written plans, or structured frameworks to plan and problem solve.
S — Self-Reflection	Performance monitoring, learning from feedback	After landings, the contol tower reviews what worked and what needs adjusting.	You gently review the day and how you have performed in tasks, adjusting plans and strategies where necessary.

Within this framework, the CRM is not separate from executive functioning; instead, it operates as a stabilising co-controller that supports impaired frontal systems, enabling planning, inhibition, flexibility, and self-monitoring to function more effectively after brain injury. At the same time, it helps regulate the emotional responses that often arise when things go wrong, reducing self-criticism and threat, so thinking skills can re-engage. Through ACCEPTS, your CRM helps you work with the weather, rather than against it, steadying the process, keeping traffic safe and reminding you to land one plane at a time. See Appendix 36: *Using the Compassionate Resilient Mind (CRM) to Navigate Cognitive Symptoms with ACCEPTS,* for a worksheet showing how to respond to executive problems using these strategies alongside the key ACCEPTS qualities of the CRM.

Living with Purpose after Brain Injury

This chapter shows how to use practical supports, such as flight plans, checklists, co-pilots and error logs, to strengthen your control tower. The aim is not to create a perfect airspace, but to manage traffic in a way that keeps you flying towards what matters most.

Airports run safely and efficiently, not by chance, but through clear structures and well-rehearsed protocols. These systems ensure that, even under pressure or in challenging weather, traffic continues to flow. In the same way, using structured supports after brain injury provides stability and consistency, compensating for the demanding conditions your control tower may face. Over time, practising these strategies with compassion helps your responses become more automatic, placing fewer demands on the control tower itself. The more you engage in CRM-based thinking by pausing, noticing, adjusting and acting with purpose, the more resilient and confident your control tower becomes.

Each strategy in this chapter can be linked back to the control tower metaphor. For example:

- Goal-setting is like issuing flight schedules, so each plane has a clear slot.
- Checklists are the flight plans that keep tasks on course.
- Problem-solving frameworks are the rerouting procedures used when storms close a runway.

These are practical, everyday techniques that you can use to strengthen your control tower, steady your traffic and regain confidence in your skies.

Control Tower Strategies

Kick-Starting into Action and Staying on Track

You may have difficulty getting started on tasks and staying on track. This is like planes (things to do) queuing at the gate without take-off clearance. The controller needs to issue flight schedules and give the "green light." Examples of strategies to help you do this are below:

- Outline your goals for each week and month, and recognise what you need to do to achieve them (see Appendix 3: *Turning Values into Action: Setting SMART Goals*).
- Make activities that you want to do routine and habitual. You can tag new activities onto your existing routines in order to make them easier to intiate (e.g., after breakfast you could take your medication).
- Before you start any task, define what it is that you want to do, and define the task and the steps required. Whilst you are performing the task, check that you are on track and doing what you are supposed to be doing (see Appendix 3: *Worksheet A1.3—Your Step-by-Step Plan*).
- Start with small, achievable actions to build confidence and momentum.
- Make sure that every time you reach a goal, there is a reward (e.g., "after I have finished my homework, I can watch my favourite TV programme").
- Timetable activities and tasks for the day, and use an alarm system to remind you to do each of them.
- Pair tasks that you find difficult to motivate yourself to do (e.g., washing dishes) with something pleasurable (e.g., listening to music). Or pair them with something that you do routinely (e.g., practise mindfulness after you brush your teeth).
- If you find it hard to motivate yourself, it can sometimes help to have someone else present (e.g., go for a run with someone else, do a task with someone else there who can help).
- Check in with someone about your progress to keep you motivated.
- Consider whether you have an environment that is conducive to motivation (e.g., decluttered from distractions; light with a comfortable temperature).

- You may have poor motivation, which may not only be related to problems with executive functioning, but also be made worse by other factors, such as depression (see Chapter 1: *Lighting the Way: Navigating Depression and Low Mood in Early Recovery,* for advice on navigating low mood following brain injury), fatigue (see Chapter 8: *Pacing with Purpose: A Compassionate Guide to Navigating Fatigue*), perfectionistic standards (see Chapter 5: *Living Beyond Anxiety: A Compassionate, Resilient Approach*) or a tendency to procrastinate (see Appendix 11: *Turning Procrastination into Meaningful Action* for procrastination guidelines).
- To stay motivated it is also important to ensure your basic needs are in place (e.g., such as having an adequate routine, ensuring optimal energy levels through diet; see Appendix 1: *Building the Basics for Recovery and adaptation*).
- If you need to plan, remember, and organise college tasks, there may be software and apps that can help you. Ask Google or an Artificial Intelligence chatbot for advice on the latest devices.

Planning and Sequencing Tasks

When plans (tasks) do not have step-by-step instructions, they risk drifting. Breaking tasks into small steps and using templates or apps are like giving each pilot a precise route map. Examples of how to do this are below:

- Write down the steps in order.
- Follow each step and cross it off once completed.
- Use tools, like planning templates (Appendix 3: *Turning Values into Action: Setting SMART, Worksheet A1.3—Your Step-by-Step Plan*; see Appendix 33: *Guidelines for Planning Essays After Brain Injury*) or apps for mind-mapping and structuring essays.

Problem-Solving

Problem-solving can be essential to help work out solutions to new situations and problems that crop up, like a plane that has drifted off course and needs rerouting. Problem-solving frameworks help to define the problem, generate alternate routes, monitor progress and adapt if needed. Worksheets to keep these procedures systematic are outlined in Appendix 32: *Guidelines for problem-solving*.

Self-Awareness and Monitoring Errors

Radar systems help controllers spot flights drifting off course. After brain injury, these radar checks may fail. Using checklists, attention slip diaries, or mindfulness slows the process, so slips are noticed before planes stray too far off course. Outlined below is more detailed guidance:

- Before you do a task, plan it out in checklist form (see Appendix 3: *Turning Values into Action: Setting SMART Goals, Worksheet A1.3—Your Step-by-Step Plan*). If you complete a step successfully, tick it off; if you do not manage to complete it, try to work out the reasons why you have not been able to.
- Ask a friend or family member what things they think you may need help with.
- It may be useful to video yourself doing tasks, then watch the film and pay particular attention to the part(s) you struggled with.

- Address any perfectionistic standards or problem-avoiding tendencies you might have. Sometimes, self-awareness problems are caused by not being able to psychologically accept perceived weaknesses or failures. This is sometimes caused by perfectionistic standards and a psychological avoidance of accepting that you have problems (for help with perfectionism, see Chapter 5: *Living Beyond Anxiety: A Compassionate, Resilient Approach*; Appendix 12: *From Perfectionism to Progress: A Compassionate Resilient Mind Exercise*, and Appendix 10: *Acceptance and Resilience Goals: Choosing Growth Over Perfection*).
- Use task analysis checklists to assess your abilities and where you may have problems (see Chapter 5: *Facilitating Activities of Daily Living*, volume 2 of this book).
- Use attention slip diaries to monitor your cognitive errors (see Appendix 30: *Memory Slip Tracker Form*).
- The best way to monitor errors is to slow down what you are doing. If you are checking for errors in your work (e.g., an email or an essay), read the words aloud as this helps to slow you down.
- Use mindfulness to pay attention to what you are doing (see mindfulness guidelines, Appendix 14: *Switching off Automatic Pilot: The Art of Mindfulness*).
- After you have completed a task, or at intervals during a task (e.g., you could set an alarm to go off at intervals), pause and "stop, think." Ask yourself, "Does that look right?" "Have I made mistakes?" "Do I need to do anything differently?"

Changing Your Line of Thinking

After a brain injury, sometimes people may have problems shifting their line of thinking. This can be like planes endlessly circling without clear direction. Outlined below is detailed guidance for how to navigate this problem:

- If you find that you get stuck doing one kind of activity, try to make sure that there are plenty of things that interest you around (e.g., books, magazines, the television).
- If you find that you are obsessing on one topic, let others know and discuss with them how they could let you know when this happens, and direct your attention to something else.
- If your thoughts get stuck in ruminations, use mindfulness techniques to help redirect your attention from your thoughts to your surroundings (see Appendix 14: *Switching Off Automatic Pilot: The Art of Mindfulness*).
- If you have difficulty changing your line of thought because you are worrying about something or frustrated, the adaptive thinking guidelines may help (Appendix 7: *Navigating Mind Influencers: Guidelines for Adaptive Thinking*) may be useful.
- For help changing your line of thinking when trying to solve a problem, see Appendix 32: *Guidelines for Problem-Solving*.

Decision-Making

When multiple planes are circling low on fuel, the control tower must quickly, but wisely, decide which one to land first. Decision frameworks (see Appendix 34: *Structured Decision-Making Tool: Finding the Best Option for You*) act like air traffic priority rules by helping the controller weigh up fuel levels, runway safety and weather conditions, so choices are safe, balanced and values-driven.

Just as a controller avoids clearing a landing during turbulence, it can help to delay decisions when skies are stormy, for example, if you are tired, anxious or emotional. Waiting until conditions clear prevents rushed landings that might cause more problems later.

After a brain injury, some people find themselves hesitating even with simple decisions. This self-doubt is like a control tower that keeps planes circling unnecessarily. In these moments, motivational "clearance statements" can be useful, such as: "It's better to give clearance than leave planes circling forever" or "It's okay if my landings are not perfect; safe and steady is enough." Others may experience the opposite problem, for example, decisions being cleared too fast, without due checks. This impulsivity is like letting a plane land without fully inspecting the runway. For important decisions, try using the 24-hour rule (i.e., holding the flight in a safe pattern overnight before giving clearance). You can also invite a co-controller (friend, family member or therapist) to review the decision with you. Decision frameworks (Appendix 34: *Structured Decision-Making Tool: Finding the Best Option for You*) provide the structured checklists that keep the process grounded.

Acting before Thinking: Strengthening the "Mental Brakes"

In the control tower, one of the most important safety systems is the holding pattern. When a plane approaches too quickly, or when the runway is not clear, the controller signals the pilot to keep circling until conditions are safe. This is your brain's impulse control, i.e., the "mental brakes," which are located in the frontal lobes. After a brain injury, this holding system may weaken. Instead of keeping a flight circling, the control tower may clear it to land too soon. This can result in actions being taken on strong emotion or instinct, without considering long-term safety. Just as a rushed landing risks collisions, impulsive behaviours can lead to regret, risk or imbalance.

When Are the "Mental Brakes" Weaker?

Planes are most likely to be cleared too quickly when the control tower is under pressure, for example:

- Stormy weather is like strong emotions (e.g., anger, anxiety or excitement).
- Foggy conditions are like fatigue, pain or overstimulation that clouds judgement.
- Traffic overload (e.g., when you are stressed or have too many competing demands) switches you onto "automatic pilot," acting without awareness.

Strategies for Strengthening the Holding Pattern System

Like skilled air traffic controllers, you can train your control tower to keep planes circling until it is safe:

- **Spot Early Warning Lights (recognise triggers):** Notice when your skies are stormy. If you feel anxious, angry, embarrassed or overly excited, delay giving clearance. For example, if an email makes you angry, place that "plane" in a holding pattern with a 24-hour rule before replying.

- **Check Weather Conditions (Manage Fatigue and Pain)**: If you notice a pattern of impulsivity when tired or in pain, address those conditions first (see Chapter 8: *Pacing with Purpose: A Compassionate Guide to Navigating Fatigue* and Chapter 9: *Finding Strength and Compassion in Living Beyond Pain*). Clearer skies mean safer landings.
- **Use Your Co-controller (CRM)**: The CRM helps you hold planes steady with patience and perspective. If you feel an urge to act immediately, CRM says, "I see the plane, but let's circle until the runway is clear."
- **Practise Mindfulness (Interrupt "Automatic Pilot")**: Just as a control tower monitors every movement on the radar, mindfulness helps you slow down and pay attention to what you are doing (see Appendix 14: *Switching off Automatic Pilot: The Art of Mindfulness*). This gives you space to apply you "mental brakes" and respond with your CRM.

Navigating Noisy Passengers Who Urge You to Do Things

Sometimes, impulses feel like noisy passengers on a plane. They shout instructions about where you should land right now:

- "Land at the snack bar!"
- "Divert to social media!"
- "Touch down in anger - say it now!"

These voices can feel urgent and may tempt the plane to move off its planned flight path, i.e., the path aligned with your adaptation to your injury, your values, your longer term goals and what is meaningful to you. This is where the control tower (your executive system) acts as the safety check. If the plane starts to drift off course under pressure from noisy passengers, the control tower notices the diversion and buzzes through with a steady reminder:

> "Hold steady — this is not your landing spot. Stay aligned with your planned route".

The control tower's job is not to silence the passengers, but to keep guiding the plane back towards what truly matters.

Steps for navigating urges with the passenger and control tower metaphor:

1. **Notice the Voices**: Identify the "passenger" that is shouting for attention.
2. **Acknowledge the Turbulence**: Recognise the discomfort or pressure their voice brings.
3. **Remember Your Role as the Control Tower:** Passengers can make noise, but they do not decide where the plane lands.
4. **Send a Safety Check**: If the plane drifts towards an unplanned landing (i.e., it gets knocked off course by giving into an impulse), buzz back a reminder to return to course.
5. **Respond Calmly**: "I hear you, but we're staying on course for now."
6. **Refocus on Your Radar**: Bring attention back to the values and priorities that guide your chosen route.

By treating urges as passengers, rather than commands, and by listening to the control tower's steady safety checks, the plane stays on course. The passengers may stay noisy for a while, but if you remain steady, their voices eventually quieten, and the flight continues towards meaningful destinations. See Appendix 35: *Strengthening Your Mental Brakes with a Compassionate Resilient Mind (CRM)*, for a further worksheet to help you manage urges through "urge surfing."

Invite Co-Pilot Feedback

If you tend to "clear landings" too quickly in conversation (e.g., saying whatever is in your head without thinking about whether it is appropriate), invite trusted people to signal when you are being impulsive. Use the three guiding clearance checks before speaking:

- "Does this need to be said?"
- "Does it need to be said by me?"
- "Does it need to be said right now?"

Final Note

By strengthening your "mental brakes," you train your control tower to keep flights in safe holding patterns until conditions are right. With practise, impulsive planes are less likely to rush in unannounced, and your skies remain safer and more ordered.

Adapting the Tower: Quick-Reference Table

Airport function	*Cognitive skill*	*Practical strategies*
Flight schedules: issuing daily slots, so planes know when to land or take off	Goal setting and motivation	Outline weekly/monthly goals (Appendix 3: *Turning Values into Action: Setting SMART Goals*). Use timetables, alarms or activity pairing. Reward completed goals. Pair difficult tasks with routine ones. Do tasks with others for accountability.
Checklists and flight plans: providing pilots with a step-by-step route	Planning and sequencing	Break tasks into small steps. Write them down in order. Cross steps off once done. Use planning templates (Appendix 3: *Turning Values into Action: Setting SMART Goals, Worksheet A1.3—Your Step-by-Step Plan*) or mind-mapping apps.
Rerouting flights: finding safe alternatives when runways are blocked	Problem-solving	Use the 4-step process (define problem, generate solutions, monitor, adapt). Apply Appendix 32: *Guidelines for problem-solving,* worksheets for structure.
Radar monitoring: watching for flights drifting off course	Self-awareness and error checking	Use checklists and progress logs. Ask for feedback from others. Keep attention slip diaries (Appendix 30: *Memory Slip Tracker Form*). Slow down tasks; read aloud for error-checking. Use mindfulness (Appendix 14: *Switching off Automatic Pilot: The Art of Mindfulness*).
Flexible scheduling: reshuffling priorities when new traffic appears	Cognitive flexibility	Practise mindfulness to notice when stuck. Use adaptive thinking strategies to help you shift your line of thinking when stuck in a line of thought affecting mood (Appendix 7, *Navigating Mind Influencers: Guidelines for Adaptive Thinking*). Redirect attention with new activities or interests.
Landing clearance rules: deciding which plane lands first when multiple planes are circling and low on fuel	Decision-making	Apply decision frameworks (Appendix 34: *Structured Decision-Making Tool: Finding the Best Option for You*). Delay big decisions when tired or emotional (24-hour rule). Ask others for input. Use motivating self-statements to reduce self-doubt.

(Continued)

Airport function	*Cognitive skill*	*Practical strategies*
Holding patterns: keeping planes circling until it is safe to land	Impulse control ("mental brakes")	Recognise emotional triggers. Delay responses with a 24-hour rule. Practise urge surfing (Appendix 35: *Strengthening Your Mental Brakes with a Compassionate Resilient Mind (CRM)*). Use mindfulness to interrupt "automatic pilot." Seek gentle feedback from others if impulsive in speech.
Take-off clearance: giving the "green light" so planes leave the gate	Initiation (kick-starting into action)	Start with small, achievable steps. Build momentum with rewards. Tag activities to existing routines. Use alarms and schedules. Work alongside someone for support.

Final Reflections

Executive functions are the control tower of the brain, they guide, coordinate and prioritise the many tasks of daily life. After a brain injury, the control tower may be under strain: the radar may flicker, flights may go off course or planes may queue without clearance. Yet, as this chapter has shown, airports can adapt, and so can you.

By using structured supports (for example, flight schedules [goal setting frameworks], flight plans [planning and sequencing frameworks], rerouting procedures [problem-solving frameworks], radar checks [self-awareness], flexible scheduling [adaptive thinking strategies], landing priorities [decision-making frameworks], holding patterns [impulse control strategies] and take-off clearances [initiation strategies]), you may give your control tower the resources it needs to keep the skies safe and purposeful. These strategies extend the reach of your executive skills, helping you to manage traffic one plane at a time.

Importantly, your CRM is always alongside you in the control tower, offering perspective when skies are crowded, compassion when delays occur and encouragement when the work feels hard. Your CRM reminds you that the goal is not a perfectly ordered sky, but a meaningful and resilient journey.

Adaptation after brain injury is less about eliminating turbulence and more about learning how to guide flights through changing conditions. Each checklist used, each pause for awareness and each values-based decision may facilitate another safe landing that reinforces your control tower's strength. Over time, these small actions may accumulate, helping you to live with greater confidence, autonomy and alignment with what matters most.

Your skies may look different than before, but with practice, compassion and the right support, your airport can keep running and your flights can still reach meaningful destinations.

13 Communicating with Assertiveness and Compassion after Brain Injury

Vicki Hall

After a brain injury, many people find that communicating with others feels harder than it used to. This can happen for different reasons. Sometimes, it is linked to changes in thinking skills (such as concentration, memory or organising what you want to say). Sometimes, it is because of direct changes in the brain's language centres and sometimes, it is simply about confidence, for example, feeling less sure of yourself or finding it difficult to be assertive.

The good news is that there are practical things you can do to make communication easier and less stressful. In this chapter, you will find:

- Tips for improving listening, self-monitoring and conversation skills
- Guidance for building confidence through gentle assertiveness training
- Simple, step-by-step exercises you can try on your own or with a therapist

These tools are based on approaches from cognitive rehabilitation and from the umbrella of cognitive behavioural therapy models. They are also guided by the Compassionate Resilient Mind (CRM), which encourages you to meet challenges with flexibility, kindness and purpose.

A key idea in this mindset is that the aim is not to become a "perfect" communicator. Everyone, whether they have had a brain injury or not, sometimes forgets words, misreads social cues or struggles to find the right thing to say. What matters most is how you respond when these challenges happen. Instead of criticising yourself, your CRM encourages you to pause, notice what might help, and try again with curiosity and compassion.

The strategies in this chapter are here to help you feel more confident and connected. They are about giving yourself tools to build awareness, practise new skills, and grow at your own pace. Whether you are having everyday chats with friends and family; working your way through more complex social situations or picking yourself back up after a setback, these strategies are designed to support you in reconnecting with others in ways that feel meaningful and positive.

It is also important to remember that everyone's journey is different. Some people with more severe communication difficulties may need the support of a speech and language therapist.

Types of Communication Challenges and What Helps

Going Off on Tangents or Speaking Verbosely

After a brain injury, it can be difficult to organise and monitor speech, which may lead to going off topic, giving too much detail or saying a lot at once.

DOI: 10.4324/9781003464655-13

What Can You Do to Help?

- **Invite Feedback from Others**: Agree on a simple cue (e.g., raising a hand) that someone can use if you start going off track or giving too much detail.
- **Plan and Summarise before Speaking**: Think about your main points in advance, writing them down as bullet points if needed. Slow your pace and allow space for turn-taking.
- **Check in During Conversation**: Ask, "Are you following me?" or "Have I gone off on a tangent?" to stay aligned with your listener.
- **Read Non-verbal Cues**: Pay attention to facial expressions and body language to notice if someone seems confused or disengaged.
- **Pause and Reflect**: At intervals, ask yourself: "Is this relevant? What was my original point?"
- **Practise with Support**: Do conversation practice with a trusted friend or family member. Use strategies, such as:
    - Recording or videoing conversations to review when you went off track.
    - Setting a timer (e.g., every 1–2 mins) to pause and check: "Am I still on topic?"
    - Using conversation prompts (e.g., my morning routine, my favourite holiday, should all laws be eliminated?) to practise staying focused.
- **Track Progress**: Compare your own ratings of how often you go off topic with feedback from a trusted partner. Notice where strategies helped and where they could be used more effectively.
- **Practise Self-compassion**: Remember, it is normal for conversations to wander at times. Instead of aiming for perfect communication, focus on meaningful connection. If you notice yourself drifting off topic, gently ask, "Am I connecting? Am I being understood?" Approach slips with curiosity and kindness, rather than self-criticism. Over time, this compassionate awareness can strengthen your ability to monitor and adjust your speech, whilst staying true to your values of connection.

Difficulty Following What Others Are Saying

Sometimes, problems with concentration can make it hard to keep track of what someone else is saying.

What Can You Do to Help?

- **Be Open with Others**: Let them know this is a challenge for you. Ask them to slow down or keep to just a few sentences at a time. If it is important, invite them to check your understanding by asking you to repeat back what you have heard.
- **Use Active Listening Strategies**: Make eye contact, watch their mouth movements and reduce background distractions to stay focused.
- **Summarise as You Go**: At intervals, repeat back what you have understood (e.g., "So what you're saying is…"). This not only helps you check your understanding, but also shows the other person that you are listening.
- **Be Honest When You Lose Track**: It is okay to say, "Sorry, I lost you there, can you explain that again?" If you prefer not to draw attention to this, you can still stay engaged by picking up on a key point and asking for more detail (e.g., "You mentioned Katie, can you tell me more about that?").

- **Practise Concentration in Safe Settings**: Use TV programmes, podcasts or YouTube videos to practise listening. Pause at intervals and summarise what has been said, or do the same with a supportive conversation partner (for more guidance, see the PQRST techniques in Appendix 31: *PQRST guidelines*).
- **Compassionate Tip**: Remember, the aim is not perfect recall of every word, but maintaining connection and understanding. When you notice slips, respond with kindness, rather than frustration. Each time you pause, summarise or ask for clarification, you can strengthen your ability to stay engaged in ways that respect both yourself and others.

Building Communication Skills in Distracting Environments

It can be much harder to follow or join conversations when there is background noise or more than one person speaking. You can build up your tolerance gradually by starting in easier settings, and slowly increasing the level of distraction.

What Can You Do to Help?

- Start small: begin conversations in quiet, familiar settings.
- Add mild background noise (e.g., the television or soft music).
- Gradually increase difficulty by practising in busier settings, such as a café or pub.
- Only move to the next level once the current one feels manageable (difficulty rating around 0–3 out of 10).
- After each practice, rate how difficult it actually felt and compare it with your expectations.

Practice Table: Building Up Tolerance to Distractions

Level of distraction	*Predicted difficulty (0–10)*	*Actual difficulty after practice (0–10)*
At home, with no distractions, talking to one person		
At home with TV on, talking to one person		
In a quiet coffee shop, talking to one person		
In a busy coffee shop, talking to one person		
In a busy coffee shop, speaking to more than one person		

Word-Finding Difficulties

It is common to sometimes lose track of a word you want to say, especially after a brain injury. This does not mean you cannot communicate successfully, there are many ways to get your message across.

What Can You Do to Help?

- **Explain Around the Word**: If the exact word will not come, describe it in another way. For example, if you forget the word brush, you might say, "the thing you use to groom your hair," whilst pointing or using gestures.
- **Use All the Tools Available**: Gestures, pointing, drawing or using similar words can help others understand what you mean.
- **Focus on Connection, Not Perfection**: Everyone struggles to find words sometimes. What matters most is being understood, not saying everything "just right."

- **Practise Self-compassion**: When words do not come easily, take a breath and respond with patience and kindness towards yourself. Notice the effort you are making to stay connected, and value creativity in communication.

  Use this worksheet to practise different ways of communicating when a word does not come to mind.

Target word (the word I could not find)	*How I explained around it (gestures, description, drawing, etc.)*	*How well it worked (0–10)*

Anxiety about Communicating

Anxiety about communicating with others is common after a brain injury. Anxiety and communication difficulties often fuel each other. The more anxious you feel, the harder it becomes to think clearly, process information and concentrate. This can cause slips, such as word-finding problems or slurred speech more likely.

Anxiety also distorts perception. You may overestimate how often you make mistakes and underestimate your real strengths. Over time, this can lead to avoiding social situations, which maintains anxiety and creates further challenges, such as:

- Fewer opportunities to practise and build confidence.
- Missed chances to test the belief that you are "bad" at communicating.
- Less learning that mistakes can be coped with and that most people respond with patience, rather than judgement.

It is easy for the mind to catastrophise, imagining worst-case scenarios like, "I'll mess everything up" or "People will think I'm stupid." These fears can feel overwhelming and may stop you from engaging in conversations altogether.

A CRM Perspective

Your CRM offers a different approach. Instead of forcing yourself to "think positive" or suppress fears, your CRM encourages courage, curiosity, flexibility and self-compassion. You might ask yourself:

- "What if my fears are not completely accurate?"
- "What if confidence can grow gradually, even whilst uncertainty remains?"
- "Can I still act in line with my values, even if some of my fears come true?"

The goal is not to eliminate anxiety, but to build resilience and adaptation, to keep moving forward with compassion despite discomfort. For further guidance, see Appendix 7: *Navigating Mind Influencers: Guidelines for Adaptive Thinking* and Appendix 8: *Unlocking Adaptation: A Practical Guide to the Compassionate Resilient Mind.*

Graded Exposure: Facing Fears Gently

One effective strategy is graded exposure (i.e., facing feared situations step by step, whilst reflecting with compassion). This helps you gather real-life evidence of your ability to cope, instead of relying only on anxious predictions.

Caution: It is recommended to do this work with a therapist, who can help pace the steps safely and gently.

Steps for Supportive Exposure and Reflection

1. **Create a Hierarchy:** List situations where you fear your communication might go wrong.
2. **Rate Anticipated Anxiety** (0%–100%): Order situations from least to most distressing.
3. **Note Expected Mistakes**: Write down what you fear will happen (e.g., "I'll forget a word in every sentence").
4. **Describe the Worst Outcome**: Capture the catastrophe you imagine.

Fear Hierarchy Table

Situation I fear will go badly	*Expected anxiety (0%–100%)*	*Expected mistakes*	*Worst possible outcome*
Asking for help in a shop	20%	I won't find the right words	The shop assistant will laugh at me

Reflection after Practice Table

Situation practised	*Anxiety during (0%–100%)*	*Mistakes made*	*What actually happened*

Moving Forward with Compassion

Even if your feared outcome happens (for example, you forget words, feel embarrassed or someone looks puzzled), it is important to learn that you can still cope.

The CRM perspective invites you to:

- Respond with kindness, rather than harsh self-judgement.
- Remember that one imperfect moment does not define you.
- Treat difficulties as opportunities to adapt, learn and strengthen resilience.

The aim is not perfection, but emotional steadiness, to keep moving forward, even when anxiety shows up. Discomfort becomes a catalyst for resilience and growth when met with compassion and adaptive thinking.

For further guidance, see Appendix 7: *Navigating Mind Influencers: Guidelines for Adaptive Thinking* and Appendix 8: *Unlocking Adaptation: A Practical Guide to the Compassionate Resilient Mind.*

Assertiveness and Communication after Brain Injury

Not all communication difficulties after brain injury stem from problems with language, memory or concentration. Some challenges arise from a lack of assertiveness (i.e., the ability to express needs, thoughts and feelings in a confident, respectful way). This difficulty may have existed before the injury and become more pronounced afterwards due to reduced confidence, emotional dysregulation or damage to brain areas involved in impulse control and social awareness. Understanding different communication styles can help you recognise unhelpful patterns and build more assertive, compassionate and flexible ways of interacting with others.

Communication Styles

Passive Communication

People who communicate passively often avoid conflict or discomfort, sometimes at their own expense. This can lead to unmet needs, frustration and being overlooked by others.

Signs of passive communication include:

- Not expressing needs or preferences
- Going along with others to avoid conflict
- Downplaying opinions (e.g., saying, "I'm not sure, but…")
- Speaking quietly, avoiding eye contact, closed body posture
- Frequently apologising or putting oneself down

Aggressive Communication

Aggressive communicators prioritise their own needs, whilst disregarding others' perspectives, often causing tension, fear or resentment.

Signs of Aggressive Communication include:

- Interrupting, loud or hostile tone
- Criticising or blaming others
- Dismissive statements (e.g., saying, "You're wrong")
- Dominating body language (e.g., glaring, towering posture)
- Difficulty listening to or acknowledging other views
- Not considering others' points of view and always assuming that you are right

Passive-Aggressive Communication

This style appears passive, but expresses anger indirectly, often leading to confusion or unresolved tension.

Signs of Passive-Aggressive Communication include:

- Sarcasm or backhanded compliments
- Procrastination or deliberate underperformance
- Withdrawing (e.g., giving someone the "silent treatment")
- Denying feelings (e.g., saying, "I'm fine") despite visible upset

Assertive Communication

Assertiveness is the balanced, respectful expression of your needs, feelings and views, whilst also valuing others' rights and perspectives.

Signs of Assertive Communication include:

- Calm, steady tone and open body posture
- "I" statements (e.g., saying "In my view…")
- Clear, respectful boundary-setting
- Active listening and willingness to compromise
- Expressing disagreement without dismissing others

Assertiveness and the CRM

Assertive communication is at the heart of the CRM approach, which encourages purposeful, flexible and emotionally aware responses. Assertiveness allows you to honour your values, stay connected to others and safeguard your well-being, without falling into patterns of avoidance or aggression.

The key CRM qualities applied to assertiveness:

- **A—Awareness and Acceptance**: Without judgement, tune into your feelings during interactions. Notice if you are silencing yourself out of fear or pushing too hard due to frustration. Accept that these reactions happen and use them as cues for adjustment.
- **C—Cognitive Flexibility**: Assertiveness is not rigid. It adapts to different situations (e.g., sometimes speaking up strongly, other times listening carefully), whilst staying anchored in your values.
- **C—Compassion**: Speak with kindness, both to yourself and others. Value your voice without the need to dominate or to please. Compassion softens interactions and keeps the focus on connection.
- **E—Effort with Balance (Compassionate Persistence)**: Assertive communication requires practice. Balance persistence with self-care: pace yourself, pause when emotions run high and return when ready, rather than giving up or forcing too hard.
- **P—Purposeful Action**: Use intentional strategies, such as "I" statements, a calm tone and open body language. Assertiveness means choosing how to respond, rather than reacting automatically from fear or frustration.
- **T—Tools and Strategies**: Practise role-plays, scripts or structured exercises to prepare for difficult conversations. Using these tools is not weakness, it is a wise, purposeful way of supporting communication.
- **S—Self-Reflection**: After interactions, reflect on what went well and what could improve. Ask: "Did I express myself clearly and kindly? Did I stay true to my values?" Use this reflection to guide growth, not to criticise yourself.

CRM Compassion Goal for Assertiveness

"I can speak up with kindness and clarity. I can listen with respect. I can connect with others in a way that honours both my needs and theirs."

Assertive Strategies for Managing Difficult Interactions

Assertiveness can be particularly challenging in emotionally charged situations. The following strategies, rooted in CRM principles, help maintain emotional control, self-respect and meaningful connection:

RESPONDING TO SOMEONE ELSE'S ANGER

- **Ground Yourself**: Breathe deeply and remember your right to speak calmly and protect your boundaries.
- **Reflective Listening**: "I can see you're upset; can you help me understand?"
- **Validate Feelings:** "I get why that might feel frustrating."
- **Suggest a Pause**: "Let's take a break and talk when we're calmer."
- **Use Calm Body Language**: Open posture, relaxed shoulders, steady eye contact; avoid intimidating or submissive signals.

NAVIGATING DISAGREEMENTS

To help navigate disagreements:

- **Listen First**: Show empathy before expressing your view. "I understand how you feel… My view is different…"
- **Use "I" Statements**: "I feel differently because…"
- **Seek Compromise**: "What if we try it your way today and mine next time?"
- **Respect Differences**: Assertiveness means standing your ground, not winning.

SAYING NO ASSERTIVELY

Especially after brain injury, fatigue and overwhelm make saying no a vital self-care skill. The following can help you to say no assertively:

- **Be Direct, Not Dismissive**: "I'd love to help, but I'm too tired today."
- **If Relevant, Name Fatigue as a Reason**: "If I push through now, I'll feel worse later. I need to rest."
- **Offer Alternatives**: "Not the cinema, but how about coffee?"
- **Use the "Broken Record" Technique**: Calmly repeat your boundary: "I'm still going to say no."
- **Stand Firm without Approval**: It is okay if others do not like your boundary. Your needs matter.

Practising Assertiveness: CRM-Based Strategies

- **Role-play** or script challenging interactions.
- **Reflect**: "Did I express myself clearly and kindly?"
- **Celebrate Small Wins**: Saying no, expressing a preference, asking for help.
- **Self-talk Mantra**: "It's okay to express my needs. My voice matters."

These skills support the CRM values of compassion, resilience and meaningful connection. With practise, you can become more confident, emotionally aware and empowered in your interactions.

See Appendix 19: *Assertiveness Exercise*, for assertiveness exercises and practice tools.

Take-Home Points

- Communication can feel harder after brain injury due to changes in thinking, language, confidence and/or emotional regulation.
- The goal is not perfect communication, but staying connected and responding to difficulties with flexibility and compassion.
- Assertiveness helps you express your needs clearly and respectfully, whilst protecting your energy and wellbeing.
- Confidence grows through gentle practice, reflection and self-kindness, not through pressure or self-criticism.
- Slips and misunderstandings are part of communication for everyone. What matters is how you pause, adapt and try again.
- With the right tools, support and pacing, communication can become more manageable, meaningful and aligned with your values.

14 Mental Capacity and Brain Injury

Selina Holmes

If you have mental capacity, it means you can:

1. Understand information about a decision
2. Weigh up the pros and cons
3. Make and communicate a choice

The law in most countries protects the right to make your own decisions.

It also recognises that sometimes, a person may not be able to decide for themselves. When this happens, there are rules about how to check capacity, how to protect the person's rights and how to make decisions in their best interests. After a brain injury, thinking and communication changes can affect decision-making.

Mental capacity laws aim to:

- Protect personal freedom
- Keep people safe from harm or exploitation

In other words, these laws are there to balance two things: your right to make your own choices, and the need to protect you if a brain injury or similar problem affects your ability to think things through clearly.

Why We Need Laws Supporting Mental Capacity

Losing the ability to make certain decisions can lead to a loss of personal freedom.

The Universal Declaration of Human Rights says all people are "free and equal in dignity and rights." Because taking away someone's decision-making rights is such a serious step, legal systems have built-in safeguards to:

- Maximise the person's control wherever possible
- Prevent abuse or exploitation (e.g., taking money, influencing a will or making medical choices without proper reason)

To prevent abuse, legal safeguards are built in. These are designed to maximise personal control and prevent abuse.

DOI: 10.4324/9781003464655-14

General Principles of Mental Capacity Assessment

Incapacity Must Be Proven

A person can only be found to lack mental capacity if there is clear evidence of a condition or impairment that affects their ability to make a specific decision (e.g., if you have problems with your thinking skills that impair your decision-making ability caused by a traumatic brain injury). If no such condition exists, or if it does not affect the decision being made, you keep the same legal right as anyone else to decide for yourself.

Capacity Is Decision-Specific

Mental capacity is not "all or nothing." Each decision is assessed on its own.

A person may be able to handle some types of decisions, but not others.

Charlie's Story—Two Different Decisions

Charlie has a brain injury that affects his memory, attention and impulse control. This means his impulses and emotions override his reasoning before there is time to think things through. Impulsivity can affect his decision-making in the following ways:

- Making choices on the spur of the moment without considering the bigger picture
- Responding more to immediate feelings (excitement, anger, frustration) than to logic or long-term goals
- Overlooking important details, risks or consequences
- Agreeing to something before thinking about whether it is realistic or safe
- Giving personal information, spending money or doing something without checking if it is a good idea

After his accident, Charlie receives a large insurance payout to fund his care for life. Because of his impulsivity, he is at high risk of being scammed, making poor financial choices and running out of money for his future needs. Charlie is therefore assessed as lacking financial capacity. The court appoints a deputy for finances (a specialist solicitor) to pay bills, approve large purchases and protect Charlie's long-term financial security. Charlie can still receive a weekly allowance in his bank account, pay for groceries, hobbies and social outings, and make other small-scale financial decisions on his own.

A Separate Decision—Making a Will

Later, Charlie decides to make a will. He understands who he wants to include (his family and a charity), understands why he wants to include them and can explain his choices clearly. With support from his deputy to help with memory and planning, Charlie makes informed and balanced decisions about dividing his assets. His solicitor records these wishes in his will.

Key point: Even though Charlie lacks capacity for complex financial management, he has testamentary capacity (the legal ability to make a valid will). With the right support, he can understand the nature and consequences of the decision and make it himself.

Decisions and Decision-Making Ability Can Change

Your decision-making ability is not fixed. Changing your mind, taking extra time or asking for advice is normal; it does not mean you lack mental capacity. Mental capacity can fluctuate during the day or week. It may be better at certain times of the day or worse when you are tired, unwell, on certain medication, or feeling stressed or upset.

You Should Be Given the Best Opportunity to Show Capacity

Wherever possible, the person should be supported to make their own decision.

Nadia's Story

Nadia has aphasia (communication difficulties) after a stroke. She needs to decide whether to move house. To support Nadia in making this decision, the Speech and Language Therapist (SLT) advises the social worker to help her understand the information relevant to her decision by using very short sentences, giving information in bullet points and providing simple written notes to go with the conversation. This extra support means Nadia can take part in her own decision-making.

Key point: Before deciding someone lacks mental capacity, all reasonable steps must be taken to help them decide for themselves.

Unwise Decisions Do Not Mean No Capacity

Even if you make an unwise decision, you still have capacity if you understand the information, can weigh up the pros and cons, recognise the risks and take steps to manage those risks, and can communicate your decision.

Example

Nadia has swallowing difficulties. Her SLT advises her to avoid certain foods that could cause choking. Most of the time she follows this advice, but occasionally she chooses to have a bacon sandwich. She knows the risks and takes precautions by eating when someone is nearby, in case she needs help. She also adds tomato sauce to make swallowing easier. Her daughter is worried, but the SLT explains that this is an unwise choice, not a sign of lacking capacity. Nadia understands the consequences and manages the risks, so she has the capacity to make this choice.

Key point: Mental capacity is about your ability to think through and manage a decision, not whether others agree with it or would make the same choice.

Decisions Made on Your Behalf Must Be in Your Best Interests

If you are assessed as lacking capacity for a specific decision, someone else can decide for you, but only in your best interests. The decision-maker (often a health or social care professional, such as a doctor, Occupational Therapist (OT), SLT or social worker) must consider:

- Your current wishes
- What you likely wanted before your injury, based on your history, culture and values
- The views of your family or people close to you

- In the United Kingdom, if there is no suitable person to speak for you, an Independent Mental Capacity Advocate may be appointed to ensure your interests are kept at the forefront of decision-making

For more serious or complex matters, a best interests meeting may be held, involving a team of professionals to agree on the best outcome for your well-being.

Key point: Any decision must be right for you, even if it does not suit others.

Taking the Least Restrictive Option

When someone makes a decision on your behalf, they should choose the option that limits your rights and freedoms as little as possible. This is called the least restrictive approach.

Chen's Story

Chen is in a rehabilitation unit, six months after a serious accident. She gets confused and overwhelmed, and does not yet understand why her home is unsafe. The question is: should her home be sold? Instead of rushing into a permanent decision, her team chose a flexible, least restrictive option, including extending rehabilitation for another eight weeks, and arranging supported weekend visits home with family and carers. This gives Chen a chance to rebuild skills, develop insight into her needs and limits, try living at home again with support, and be more involved in the final decision. By delaying the sale and choosing a more flexible option, the team protects Chen's best interests, whilst keeping her as involved as possible.

Key point: The least restrictive option keeps as much control with the person as possible, allows for change over time, and supports independence, whilst still keeping them safe.

You Do Not Need to Be Completely Independent to Have Capacity

Mental capacity is not about doing everything alone. You may still have capacity if you understand your situation, use strategies or tools, and accept support when needed in order to make your decisions. Even if you choose not to use help, you may still have capacity, as long as you can weigh up the risks and benefits, and make an informed choice. The key is your ability to understand, reason and decide, even if others disagree.

Insight and Emotional Control as Barriers to Mental Capacity

After a brain injury, a person may lack mental capacity if they do not fully understand the nature, extent or consequences of their difficulties. This is called lack of insight. Without insight into how the injury affects you, it is harder to make well-informed decisions. Developing insight is often the first step towards regaining capacity. Only by recognising how your difficulties affect your daily life, can you properly factor them into your decisions. This can be a frustrating and stressful process. In the short-term, these emotions may make it harder to weigh up information clearly, but over time, improved insight usually brings better control and more balanced choices.

The Role of Emotional and Behavioural Control

After a brain injury, a person might fully understand a decision, and they may also know what actions they should take. However, in real-life situations, they can find it hard to put that understanding into practice. This is because strong impulses or emotions in the moment can override their reasoning. When calm and supported, they might explain the decision clearly, show they understand the risks and benefits, and agree on a sensible plan, but when the situation arises, they may:

- Act impulsively, without thinking through the consequences
- Respond quickly to emotions, such as frustration, excitement or anxiety
- Struggle to follow through on agreed plans due to low motivation, apathy or distraction
- Make a snap choice that goes against what they had reasoned earlier

This gap between knowing and doing is a common effect of brain injury.

It can create barriers to mental capacity, because decision-making is not only about understanding the information, it also depends on being able to apply that understanding in the moment.

Implications of Losing Mental Capacity

If you are assessed as lacking capacity, decisions will be made for you in your best interests. This means you lose some personal control; you may have fewer choices and getting what you want can take longer, as others must decide on your behalf.

When It Affects Finances (United Kingdom Example)

If you lack capacity for financial matters, someone will be appointed to manage your money:

- **Attorney**: A person you choose whilst you still have capacity, through a Lasting Power of Attorney (LPA). This can be a friend, family member or anyone you trust. They do not need legal training.
- **Deputy for Finances**: A specialist solicitor appointed by the court if no attorney was chosen before capacity was lost. They manage your money and report to the Court of Protection.

Important: You can only appoint an attorney whilst you still have mental capacity.

TIP: An LPA for health and welfare decisions is separate from an LPA for property and finances. An LPA for health and welfare allows your attorney to make decisions, such as how you are cared for or what medical treatment you should have, should you lose the capacity to make those decisions for yourself.

Regaining Capacity

In some cases, you may be able to regain capacity, and with it, the right to make your own decisions. For finances, this usually involves a legal process, which varies by country. If you want to try to regain capacity:

- Seek advice from a solicitor experienced in mental capacity law (e.g., your current financial deputy).
- Even if full capacity cannot be regained, you may still be able to take back more personal control with the right skills, strategies and safeguards.

In the following section, we will look at practical steps and worksheets to help you work towards regaining financial capacity or improving your ability to make capacitous decisions.

Taking Steps to Regain Financial Capacity/Improving Your Ability to Make Capacitous Decisions

If you are aiming to regain financial capacity or simply want to improve your ability to make financial decisions, it can be hard to know where to start, or which specific skills need work.

The worksheets in Appendices 36–39 are designed to help you:

- Identify your strengths and weaknesses in financial decision-making
- Pinpoint specific areas for improvement
- Develop a clear, realistic action plan.

For practical strategies (e.g., managing memory or building insight), check the other chapters in this book. And, do not try to go it alone; get support from someone you trust. That might include a family member, support worker or a qualified professional, such as a psychologist or OT.

Take your time. Rushing this process may increase your risk of poor decisions or financial abuse. Focus on building the right skills and putting the right supports in place.

If someone is currently managing your finances (such as an attorney or deputy), involve them in the process, they can help guide and support you on your journey back to independence.

Developing Money Awareness

To build or regain financial capacity, you need a solid foundation of money-related knowledge and everyday skills. These are essential for understanding, managing and making decisions about your finances.

The key areas include:

- **Knowing Your Income and Outgoings**: Be clear on what money comes in (e.g., wages, benefits) and what regularly goes out (e.g., rent, bills, food).
- **Understanding Everyday Costs**: Know the general price of basic items, such as bread, rice and pasta.
- **Recognising Your Personal Spending Needs**: Distinguish between essential spending (e.g., food, utilities) and non-essential spending (e.g., hobbies, luxury items).
- **Planning and Monitoring Your Spending**: Track what you spend, and plan ahead to avoid shortfalls.
- **Using Different Payment Methods**: Be comfortable using cash, bank cards and online banking.
- **Understanding Your Assets**: Know what you own (e.g., money, property) and how much it is worth.
- **Understanding and Managing Debt**: Know what you owe, to whom, and how to handle repayments.
- **Recognising and Avoiding Financial Risk**: Spot the signs of scams, fraud or exploitation.

- **Managing Behaviour in the Moment**: Control impulsive spending or emotional spending triggers (see Impulsive Spending, below).
- **Being Self-aware**: Understand your strengths and weaknesses in managing money (see Self-Awareness section below).
- **Using Strategies and Support**: Know when and how to get help, and use tools to support good decisions (see Action Planning section below).
- **Understanding Consequences**: Realise the impact of poor choices, such as falling into debt or limiting future options.

See Appendix 37: *Understanding Your Own Finances*, for activities to help you map out your income and spending, and begin planning your budget with clarity and control.

Self-Awareness, Insight and Managing Urges to Spend

We all have financial habits, some helpful, some not. After a brain injury, these habits can shift. You may become more vulnerable to spending mistakes or poor decisions, even if you are aware that your situation has changed. Awareness alone is not always enough, your behaviour also needs to adapt.

Use Appendix 38: *Insight and Self-Awareness: Understanding Vulnerability after Brain Injury*, to reflect on the factors that may affect your financial decision-making, such as:

- **Thinking Skills** (e.g., memory, planning, reasoning)
- **Emotions** (e.g., anxiety, stress, low mood)
- **External Influences** (e.g., persuasive advertising, peer pressure)
- **Physical Factors** (e.g., fatigue, pain)

It can be helpful to work through this with a trusted professional, such as a psychologist or OT, who can help you understand how these factors play out in real life.

Try to reflect honestly on real examples and summarise what you learn. This is key to developing lasting self-awareness and regaining control over financial choices.

Impulsive Spending

Impulsive spending happens when we act on an urge without thinking things through. Everyone does it sometimes and retailers even design offers to trigger these behaviours ("Limited time deals", "3 for 2", "Buy now, pay later").

After a brain injury, impulsive spending can become more frequent or harder to control, especially when combined with difficulties in memory, attention or planning.

To stay in control:

- Use Appendix 39: *Smart Spending & Budget Confidence,* to learn how to set a budget and plan purchases ahead of time.
- Use Appendix 39: *Smart Spending & Budget Confidence,* steps 5 and 6, for strategies to manage common triggers, the situations, emotions or thoughts that often lead to impulsive buying.

By reflecting regularly on your actions and identifying your personal patterns, you can build insight, strengthen self-control, and take back power over your financial decisions.

Make a Plan to Address Your Weaknesses

Once you have identified your strengths and challenges, and explored strategies to support your financial decision-making, the next step is to turn insight into action.

If you still have vulnerabilities that have not been fully addressed, use Appendix 40: *Safe Action Planning For Finances,* to create a personal action plan.

This plan will help you:

- Target specific areas that need improvement
- Set realistic goals
- Identify the support or tools you will need
- Track your progress over time

It is best to complete the worksheet in this appendix with someone you trust, such as a family member, support worker or professional, who can offer feedback, encouragement and accountability.

A good plan builds your confidence, reduces risk and supports your journey towards greater financial independence.

Nobody Is Perfect!

Everyone makes financial decisions they later regret; that is part of being human. What matters most is what you learn from these moments, not that you made the mistake in the first place. Try not to beat yourself up. Instead, reflect, adjust and move forward.

Build some flexibility into your budget, so you can enjoy small, spontaneous purchases without derailing your bigger plans. The key is to balance short-term gratification with your long-term goals.

Remember: new habits take time. Embedding financial strategies into your daily life takes patience, practice and consistency.

A Final Thought

Accept support when it is appropriate, focus on building your skills at your own pace and give yourself time to grow. Regaining control over your finances is not about being perfect; it is about becoming capable, confident and in control.

15 Supporting Relationships with Your Children

Cathy Grant and Katie Venables

Having a brain injury is likely to affect your relationships, as both you and your children will need time to adjust to the change that has occurred. Children are more able to understand visible physical changes than the more hidden effects of brain injury. For instance, even young children understand concepts such as headaches and tiredness. In contrast, the cognitive and emotional changes you experience are something that your child will pick up on, but they may need some support from you or another member of the family to understand and adjust to these changes. The good news is that children tend to adjust eventually and there are things that you can do as a family to support that adjustment. Appendix 41: *Key Points for Your Family to Understand about Brain Injury* includes key information on brain injury that would be useful for your child to understand.

Emotional Changes

Young children understand simple emotions, such as happiness, sadness and anger, but they may blame themselves for the emotional changes they see in you, even though they are related to the brain injury. Reassurance using simple language can help a young child understand that you are not sad or angry at them. They need to be reminded that the sadness or anger they witness is the effect of the brain injury. It may be helpful to find a name for the difficulty, such as "poorly brain" or "having a poorly moment" to help your child label and understand what is happening.

Older children have a better understanding of emotions but will still benefit from reassurance. They may get angry in response to your irritability or anger. Older children are likely to benefit from a clear understanding of the effects of brain injury, as well as some strategies to navigate anger (see Chapter 4: F*inding Calm in the Storm: Anger, Irritability, and Compassion,* for guidance on how to navigate anger). Identifying together an adult who they can talk to about their feelings may also help. They may need encouragement to talk with the identified adult about how they feel, and reassurance that they are not being disloyal by talking through the difficulties.

Your children should also be encouraged to talk to you about their feelings. If you struggle with remembering conversations or managing anything beyond small amounts of information, encourage your child to write their feelings in a journal that you can read at your own pace, or to record audio messages that can be replayed.

Sadly it is sometimes the case, that both the child and parent have sustained a brain injury in the same accident. This can make managing emotional change more difficult as your child will also be struggling with regulating their emotions, and may be less able to identify and talk about their feelings.

DOI: 10.4324/9781003464655-15

Table 15.1 outlines some of the common emotional difficulties that present in parenting relationships, and some helpful tips for their management.

Table 15.1 The impact of emotional problems on parenting and tips for managing

Problem	*Impact on relationships*	*Tips for parent/child relationship*
Emotional	Acquired brain injury can result in emotional changes for both the parent and child. Children can find these changes confusing. They may believe that they are responsible and have done something wrong. Anxiety and low mood can result in avoidance of events and activities. When people are anxious, they become short-tempered. Low mood can appear as if you are disinterested and result in less time spent with loved ones. Increased irritability and reduced patience. Easily frustrated by commonly occurring child traits (noisy, messy, restless, argumentative). You may behave in ways that are out of character or say things that upset others.	Develop practical strategies for managing emotions. Involve your children in this and encourage them to use strategies for their own emotions (see Appendix: 42: *Relationships with Children Worksheet (to Complete with Your Family)*). Externalise difficulties together (e.g., the worry monster). Visualising and drawing what this may look like as a joint activity can be helpful (see Appendix 48: *Creating a Worry Monster Worksheet*). Practise child-friendly anxiety management techniques together, e.g., handprint breathing, child mindful breathing (see Appendix 49: *Handprint Breathing*). Discuss any incidents when things are calm. Apologise for irritable behaviour and acknowledge your child's feelings. Agree on strategies on how to move forward and not hold a grudge. Ensure children have a space at home where they can go to feel safe and remove themselves from uncomfortable situations. Jointly devise a (silly) code word that can be used to defuse situations and allow children to express that they are not comfortable/want to leave. Give your child information on emotional problems after a brain injury. Provide reassurance that how you are feeling is not their fault. Normalise and validate your child's emotions and encourage them to share their feelings (see Appendix 46: *Emotions Cards*).

Cognitive Changes

Young children do not have a good understanding of cognition. They are likely to struggle to understand what a poor memory, inattention or difficulties with multitasking mean. They will require reassurance that the resulting situation (e.g., forgotten birthday) was not intentional. Books and films with characters who have cognitive problems may improve your child's understanding. However, as books and films usually do not capture the complexity of cognitive problems, your child is also likely to benefit from very concrete information on your difficulties along with what aspects of cognition are preserved. For example, in Finding Nemo, the film captured Dory's difficulties with laying down new memories, but also portrayed the character as having difficulties with her early childhood memories. Difficulties with memories laid down many years prior to the acquired brain injury are uncommon, so it is important to help your child understand if this is a preserved part of your memory.

Older children are likely to understand that you have difficulties with thinking, learning and concentration. They are likely to benefit from some guidance on what to expect in terms of their interactions with you. For example, they may benefit from help with understanding that, as you are unable to multitask, talking to you, whilst you are already doing a task is not going to be helpful. It is useful to identify a solution together, such as finding a time to talk to you when they can have your full attention. The relationships with your family worksheet (Appendix 42, *Relationships with Children Worksheet (to Complete with Your Family)*) may help you and your child think about difficulties and solutions together.

A child who has also sustained a brain injury, may be having similar difficulties with cognition to your own. Children tend to struggle to recognise their difficulties in the same way as adults, and can fail to appreciate the impact that their cognitive difficulties have on their ability to function.

Table 15.2 outlines some of the cognitive difficulties that can affect parenting relationships, and some tips for management.

Table 15.2 The impact of cognitive problems on parenting and tips for managing

Problem	*Impact on relationships*	*Tips for parent/child relationship*
Cognitive problems	Unable to multitask (e.g., help with homework and make dinner). Make mistakes, not complete tasks resulting in disagreements or guilt. Not able to remember what has happened and to share memories as a family. Feel less confident in taking responsibility for children, such as at parents' evening due to poor memory. Forgetting to pack the things needed for the school day. Forgetting to complete tasks you have agreed to do. Not being able to join in with the "to and fro" of family communication can lead to feeling isolated and less confident. Not able to cope well when your child brings friends home from school. Reluctant to attend social/community activities.	Use a prompt card or sequenced list. Ask your child to help you with tasks they can be part of (e.g., meal prep). Provide praise and reward for "my little helper." Reassure them it is not because things are not important using shared language, familiar characters (e.g., poorly brain, Nemo). Apologise, and discuss incidents after the event. Use visual aids, such as photo books (could produce a scrapbook together, joint activity) to prompt memory and facilitate discussions. Devise memory aids together (e.g., a list of items for school bag/PE). This could also promote positive independence in younger children. Tick off the checklist (e.g., on the wipe-off board, to double-check items). Prepare bullet point notes for important meetings, with things to say/questions to ask. Highlight when a break may be required. Agree on a name, e.g., "quiet time," so there is joint understanding. Agree on an allocated space in the home that is a quiet space. Depending on the age of the child, ask them for support to implement strategies (e.g., only one person speaks at once). Allow additional time for you to process and reduce environmental distractions (e.g., television turned off during times for family talk). Allocate time for family discussions (e.g., meal times together).

Communication Strategies

It can be tricky to think of the words to use with your child, especially if you are feeling upset about things yourself. You may want to work out beforehand what you feel able to discuss and what might need to be left for another time, or for another person to discuss with your child. If things come up that you are not ready to discuss, it is okay to say, "I'm not sure that I can talk about that right now. I'll do some thinking and can we talk about it again tomorrow?" It can help to practise some of the phrases that you want to use to let your child know that you are there for them.

Sometimes, it can feel more comfortable if you are talking side by side, rather than face-to-face. Sometimes, it will be important to show your child that they have your full attention, but other times, talking, whilst having dinner or engaged in a joint activity, such as colouring or having a walk together is better.

It is important to be ready to listen to what your child says to you. Feeling calm and prepared will help you to do this. Do not rush an answer to your child's questions. If you need time to think, be honest and let them know. Here are some phrases that may help you manage your conversation:

"Thank you for telling me how you're feeling."
"I wasn't expecting you to say that, but thank you for sharing. I need a bit of time to think about it."
"What would you like to happen next?"
"How would you feel if…?"
"You can always talk to me. I'm here for you…"

With older children, talking together about the difficulties and coming up with possible strategies that may help, can be powerful. This is a good way to help your child feel heard and to generate a shared understanding of problems and solutions. The worksheet in Appendix 42: *Relationships with Children Worksheet (to Complete with Your Family)* could be used to record the outcome of your discussion. It may be helpful to work through the Values worksheet in Appendix 2: *Your Inner Compass: Exploring Values After Brain Injury*, with older children, so that family values can be identified and used to support the discussion around finding solutions to problems.

Children with brain injury tend to struggle with communication due to their cognitive difficulties and emotional regulation problems. They are likely to benefit from more simple communication methods that allow for lots of repetition over time. Visual information may also help a child with a brain injury keep track of what has been discussed or agreed.

Practise Listening to One Another

Listening is a skill. Children can develop their listening skills through practice. You could agree with older children to practise active listening together. It is important to identify your feelings and to allow your child to feel different, and let them express this. Feelings cannot be right or wrong; they are just feelings.

You can use this exercise to practise together. There are two roles—the talker and the listener.

1. The talker spends 60 seconds speaking about a topic. Make sure to include feelings and thoughts within the topic.
2. After 60 seconds, the listener will repeat back the highlights of what was said, making sure to include the thoughts and feelings.
3. Swap roles and start again.

This exercise can help both you and your child to become better at listening, and picking up on key feelings and thoughts. If it is a struggle to remember what was said, try it again, whilst jotting down key points. You can also try recording it and re-listening.

Online Communication and Safety

It is likely that parents will use online methods (e.g., text, instant messaging, social media) to interact with their child, and this can be a really helpful form of communication, especially for older children. It also opens up your child to online risks, and it is important to regularly talk with your child about how they can keep themselves safe. Show an interest in how their favourite online games or apps work, with an ear for how they allow them to talk with other people. Discuss with your child who they are talking to online and what details they are sharing with others. Agree with your child to have in place settings that limit who can contact them and explain why it is important to do so. For instance, on social media, you can lock the account, so that only people who know your child are able to see their content. You can change privacy settings, so that friend requests are limited or not allowed. Remind your child that it is important not to share personal information with people they do not know (e.g., address, phone number, links to other social media accounts, school/work details). It is important to explain to your child not to accidentally share information that may put them in danger, such as their location, through tagging photos with geo-location, allowing others to track their phone and sharing images with identifiable street names or landmarks. Explain that sharing location details could increase the risk of someone making unwanted contact. Help them to understand the need to be careful when talking to people they do not know online. Remind them that the person may not be who they say they are, or they may intend to cause them trouble using any shared information. Help your child understand that once photos of them are shared, they can be spread very quickly online and be altered.

Let your child know that they should come to you or an identified adult if any communication online makes them feel uncomfortable or worried.

Communication through Play

Young children learn and communicate through play or creative activities, rather than through conversation. Young children tend to enjoy drawing, colouring and simple board games. Activities can be a great way to teach young children about the effects of brain injury and get them to talk about their feelings. Appendix 43*: Best Memory (for Infant and Primary School Age)* includes activities that will help a young child adjust to change, Appendix 44: *Draw a Family (for Infant and Primary School Age)* helps children talk about their family and Appendix 45: *Snakes and Ladders (for Primary School Age)* helps children think about helpful behaviours.

Activities, such as emotion cards (Appendix 46: *Emotions Cards*) and making a worry jar (Appendix 47: *The Worry Jar*) can help older children of seven years and upwards to identify and manage their feelings. It is normal for children to feel worried about the changes that have happened related to a brain injury, and to struggle to manage their worries. The worry monster activity is a playful approach that externalises worry (Appendix 48: *Creating a Worry Monster Worksheet*). This can be very helpful in supporting a child to think about and manage their worries.

Know That You Are Not Alone

Parenting after sustaining an acquired brain injury can take some adjustment for both you and your child. This is normal. Table 15.3 outlines common difficulties reported by parents with an acquired brain injury, and some tips for how to manage the issues that can arise. These difficulties are in addition to the emotional and cognitive changes already covered.

Table 15.3 Other commonly reported problems for parents with acquired brain injury and management tips

Problem	*Impact on relationships*	*Tips for parent/child relationship*
Sleep and fatigue	Feeling too tired to do nice things with your children or feeling tired very quickly when you are out together. Tiredness can result in avoidance of/refusal to engage in activities.	Provide age-appropriate language regarding brain injury and fatigue (e.g., a poorly functioning brain uses more energy, gets tired more quickly). Use a metaphor to aid understanding (e.g., a phone battery that needs to recharge). You could rate your energy (e.g., I've only got 20% battery today) and have a visual image for younger children. Provide examples of what recharges your battery (e.g., a 30-minute nap) and which activities require less battery, so your child can understand why the day is structured as it is. Involve your child in choosing small, manageable, but fun activities. Add a time limit and stick to it (e.g., play computer games for 10 minutes). Engage children in a gentle/relaxing activity that you could do together, e.g., mindful practice suitable for children, such as colouring. Suggest a preferred activity when you need to rest (e.g., you watch an episode of your favourite cartoon, whilst I have a nap).
Guilt/self-criticism and loss of confidence	Guilt and self-criticism are common following a brain injury. Self-criticism and guilt have a negative impact on emotional functioning and can increase symptoms of anxiety and low mood. Self-criticism will leave you with less energy to be involved in relationships/activities and further impact mood and irritability. Avoidance of decision-making and enforcing boundaries is related to low confidence. It can result in being less assertive and less likely to communicate one's own needs.	Focus on the things you can do with your children and the positive aspects of your relationship. Ask your child what joint activities are most important to them and make plans to engage in/prioritise these. Engage with your child to identify favourite things about each other. Devise joint activities based on these qualities. Work together as parents to present a united front, allocate roles and use consistent reinforcement.

(*Continued*)

Table 15.3 (Continued)

Problem	*Impact on relationships*	*Tips for parent/child relationship*
Practical issues	Unable to drive, cannot follow complicated board games to play with child, cannot run and kick a football. Pressure of being at home, rather than at work, and far more time spent together. Change in established relationship dynamics. Change in parenting responsibilities.	Have an open conversation about what will change/has changed and a plan for how to manage things. Identify activities that you can engage in together instead. Involve children in the allocation of new/different roles planning. Explain any changes to children, any change in routine. Could use visual aids/prompts to help implement/embed any changes to routine. Reward and praise children for any support they provide.
Changes in appearance	Facial or motor changes to adjust to and for older children, the need to explain the changes to their friends. Embarrassment. Avoidance of community/social activities. Impact on self-identity. Feel less attractive, self-conscious, resulting in changes in behaviour.	Acknowledge changes, encourage children to ask any questions they have. Normalise that they may feel distant or confused. Reassure them that it does not change the way you feel about them. Draw on remaining characteristics. e.g., "I'm still…" Discuss possible reactions of other people and normalise these. Support them to prepare an age-appropriate response for situations when others may ask questions or make comments. Liaise with schools, so that they can also support, e.g., an education slot in acquired brain injury in lessons and pastoral care. Inform of any bullying incidents. Books, films or support groups that may help with adjustment (e.g., "My Mum Makes the Best Cake" book).
Focus on own recovery	Reduction in time available for children and emotional resources available.	Help your child understand that you need to practise your skills to get better at everyday tasks. Where appropriate, get them involved in your rehabilitation goals, so they can help you monitor your progress.
Changes in child	You may experience less authority from being absent, whilst in hospital or as a reaction to being different from your pre-injury self. This may result in your child questioning or refusing to do what is requested.	This reaction can be extremely distressing; allow time for adjustment. The issue tends to be transient. Worksheet on managing difficulties (Appendix 42: *Relationships with Children Worksheet (to Complete with Your Family)*). Activities (Appendix 45: *Snakes and Ladders (for Primary School Age)*) to discuss behaviour.

Further Resources

Books

For you:

- "Parenting after Brain Injury" by Alex Goody.
- For your children: "My Mum Bakes the Best Cakes" or "My Dad Builds the Best Boats" by Jo Johnson, written for younger children to help them understand brain injury.
- "My parent has a brain injury… A guide for young people" by Jo Johnson, written for older children and adolescents to help them understand brain injury.

Online

The Child Brain Injury Trust has useful online resources to help improve children's understanding of brain injury and cope with the associated changes. Much of the literature focuses on child brain injury, rather than injury in adults. Nonetheless, the information provided is useful for a child whose parent has been injured (https://childbraininjurytrust.org.uk).

16 Returning to Education after a Brain Injury

Cathy Grant

How Can a Brain Injury Impact Returning to Education?

After a brain injury, some of the reported difficulties that can impact education are:

- Slow processing of information can make it difficult to keep up with the pace of lessons or complete work within the given time frame.
- Being easily distracted and struggling to hold information in mind can make it difficult to listen, write and think at the same time (ask an Artificial Intelligence [AI] chatbot for the latest devices and apps that are suited to lectures for recording, transcribing and helping you focus on comprehension, whilst you listen).
- Problems with memory can make learning new information and remembering what has been said or done tricky. It can be difficult to recall information from previous lessons (see Chapter 10: *Catching the Slips: A Compassionate Resilient Guide to Remembering* and Chapter 11: *The Compass of Attention: Guiding Learning with Resilience and Compassion*; ask an AI chatbot for advice for lecture-focused apps and devices to help store, organise and record notes).
- Fatigue, midway through a lesson, can interfere with managing to follow the whole lesson (see Chapter 8: *Pacing with Purpose: A Compassionate Guide to Navigating Fatigue*).
- Increased pain can impact your attention in class or your ability to move between lessons. Ignoring symptoms can worsen things and lead to getting stuck in the "boom-bust" cycle (see Chapter 9: *Finding Strength and Compassion in Living Beyond Pain*).
- Feeling upset or anxious about finding work difficult that you previously found easy. You may worry about what other students think about you or worry that you may not pass your course (see Chapter 5: *Living Beyond Anxiety: A Compassionate, Resilient Approach*).
- Struggle to plan and organise your work, which affects how prepared you are for lessons, or your ability to meet work deadlines (see Chapter 12: *Executive Skills after Brain Injury: A Compassionate Guide to Planning, Problem-Solving, and Self-Control*; ask an AI chatbot for advice on apps and devices for organising and planning work deadlines).
- You may find communicating with others more difficult. You may feel less confident in social situations or struggle with reading social situations (see Chapter 13: *Communicating with Assertiveness and Compassion after Brain Injury*).

For strategies to support you with each of these areas, you can read through the corresponding chapter.

DOI: 10.4324/9781003464655-16

How Will I Know If I Am Ready to Go Back to Education?

Returning to education is likely to help you get back into a routine, which can be helpful. However, the transition back into education should be carefully planned as there is much to consider. In addition to the cognitive, physical and emotional effects of brain injury, it is possible that a lot of time from education has been missed due to hospitalisation. The key is to plan a transition back into education that allows you to gradually build up the amount of time spent there. Before that can take place, the transition process starts with communication with educational professionals and establishing a support plan.

A support plan may involve modifying the learning environment, teaching methods and expectations, as well as support for potential emotional and social challenges you may face. It is important to consider whether restarting an academic year, rather than trying to catch up on missed work, might be most helpful, or whether it is more important to remain with your peer group. It is also important to consider whether you are aiming to study full-time or part-time once the gradual transition back into education is complete.

Although it is likely that many difficulties can be anticipated and support put in place before you return to education, some difficulties may only become apparent once you have returned. Due to difficulties with self-monitoring, some people with brain injury can find it hard to recognise when they are having difficulties. It is therefore important to have a good support network, with clear communication in place, for the remainder of your time in education.

Support from Professionals

If you are returning to school, it is likely that the educational professional responsible for students with additional education needs (called a Special Educational Needs Coordinator or SENCO in England) has already had contact with the hospital or rehabilitation team to develop some understanding of your needs. It is important that you allow school to refer you to any support services deemed necessary to understand your needs or support you better (e.g., educational psychologist, specialist teacher). You will have your own views and goals for education, which will be important for you to share with professionals. It is important to work together to make a plan around what would be suitable for you, and adjustments that may be needed to help you reach your goals.

Mainstream colleges also offer supported learning in much the same way as schools. Colleges in England have an Additional Learning Support Team who can work on a support plan with you. If you need a higher level of support than a mainstream college can offer, specialist colleges are available that offer a high level of support. More information about specialist colleges can be found at www.natspec.org.uk.

Universities also offer support for students with a brain injury, but the burden of responsibility lies with the student to seek the help and support that they require. Support is available by contacting the disability advice team that is part of the university you attend or have applied to attend. You should be allocated a disability advisor who will work with you to identify barriers to learning and recommend reasonable adjustments. In addition to the difficulties experienced on returning to education outlined previously, further challenges relating to managing household activities alongside study are also commonly experienced. As university campuses are often large and can be difficult to navigate, support around these practical aspects may also be necessary.

Whether you are planning a return to school, college or university, good communication with education providers is the key. It is important to monitor and regularly review how you are getting on, so that expectations and support can be adjusted as necessary. The template in Appendix 52: *Education Review Meeting Template* may help you to develop a review and effective communication of your needs in your educational review meetings. Regular meetings are recommended to maximise your educational outcomes.

Before Returning to Education

After a brain injury, everyone's rehabilitation journey will be different. It is important to give yourself time prior to returning to education to think about what needs to be in place to support you to do this.

You could try the following to help you:

- Timetable what your routine would look like when you return to education. What would you need to fit into your day? What things might be more difficult and what might you need support with? The template in Appendix 53: *Timetable Worksheet—Potential Difficulties and What Helps.*
- Slowly build up a routine that would be similar to what you would need to do when you first return to education, e.g., waking up, getting ready to leave the house, packing your bag, having dedicated study time. Monitor how easy it is for you to do this and areas of difficulty. These tasks will help you to understand where extra support might be needed.
- Gradually build up your activity levels and monitor your fatigue/pain levels to understand what is likely to work for you.
- Get feedback from your family and friends about how they think you are managing.
- Sometimes, unhelpful thoughts might stop you from sharing information about your difficulties. Ask yourself, "What would you say to a friend in the exact same situation as you?"

Managing Socially

Previous friends may have moved on if you spent a lot of time absent from education. You may need to rebuild existing friendships or make new friends. Making new friends requires the ability to start and follow conversations, participate in social activities and connect with others who have shared interests. Joining clubs or after-lesson groups are useful ways to build friendships, but these can be difficult if you are struggling with noisy environments or fatigue. It might be useful to aim to build one or two friendships to start with, as engaging in activities where you can interact one-to-one might be easier. If you are struggling to read social situations, it can be helpful to share this with others along with permission to explain things that you have misread. Saying, "I sometimes struggle to spot humour, so if I've misread what was intended to be a joke, please tell me." Planning time together that involves a mix of time for conversation and another activity (e.g., watching a movie) may be helpful if conversations are effortful. Making friends or re-establishing shared interests with existing friends can take time. Schools and colleges may be able to put a "buddy" in place to help you initially.

Conclusion

Returning to education can be a very positive experience, but it is not without its challenges. Communication is the key to ensuring that you have the support needed to manage the transition into learning. It is crucial once you have resumed education to continue to monitor your progress, and adjust the demands and support available as necessary. Good support networks and clear communication throughout your time in education will maximise your ability to complete your studies.

17 Returning to Work after a Brain Injury

Stephanie Keay

How Can a Brain Injury Impact Returning to Work?

After a brain injury, you may experience some of the following difficulties that could impact your return to work:

- **Increased Tiredness and Fatigue**: It can be easy to underestimate the amount of energy required to complete tasks that may have felt automatic before your brain injury (see Chapter 8: *Pacing with Purpose: A Compassionate Guide to Navigating Fatigue*).
- **Increased Pain**: You may no longer be able to carry out tasks in the same way, and certain movements or activities may no longer be possible. Sometimes, people will try and "push through" to carry out tasks the way they previously did, which can lead to more pain and getting stuck in the "boom-bust" cycle (see Chapter 9: *Finding Strength and Compassion in Living Beyond Pain*).
- **Anxiety**: You may experience worries about your work that you did not previously have. You may worry about what people think about you or worry that you may lose your job (see Chapter 5: *Living Beyond Anxiety: A Compassionate, Resilient Approach*).
- **Memory Problems**: Forgetting what people have said or whether you have completed a task, etc. (see Chapter 10: *Catching the Slips: A Compassionate Resilient Guide to Remembering*).
- **Executive Problems**: Difficulties with problem-solving, planning how to do things (see Chapter 12: *Executive Skills after Brain Injury: A Compassionate Guide to Planning, Problem-Solving, and Self-Control*).

For strategies to support you with each of these areas, you can look through the corresponding chapter for a comprehensive guide.

How Will I Know If I Can Go Back to Work?

You may not know if you will find it difficult to return to work until you try it out because work places a higher demand on your thinking skills, emotional resources and fatigue levels. It is therefore important to take some time to think about the difficulties you have experienced since your brain injury and how these might impact the way you work and your role, e.g., being able to problem solve quickly on the spot, having to keep track of several things at once, standing or sitting for extended periods of time.

DOI: 10.4324/9781003464655-17

It is likely you will be able to identify some of these before you return to work and think about ways to manage these. However, other difficulties will become more apparent as you return to work. Things that you were able to do automatically may take more effort and focus, which can understandably result in some anxiety or loss of confidence in particular tasks.

It is also important to note that in some cases, individuals with brain injury can find it hard to recognise when they are having difficulties, because the part of the brain involved in self-monitoring may be damaged.

Before You Return to Work

After a brain injury, everyone's rehabilitation journey will be different. It is important to give yourself time prior to returning to work to think about whether returning to work is feasible and what needs to be in place to support you to do this.

You could try the following to help you see if going back to work is advisable:

- Write a list of what your work routine would look like, what tasks you would need to fit into your day and think about what things might be more difficult now (use Appendix 50: *My Working Week—Potential Challenges and What Helps*).
- Slowly and steadily start to build back a routine that would be similar to what you would need to do if you returned to work, e.g., waking up earlier, tasks that involve different skills, cooking, DIY and shopping. These tasks will help you to start challenging your thinking skills and understand where extra support might be needed.
- Gradually build up your activity levels to see how your fatigue/pain levels are impacted. What can you manage?
- Talk to family and friends, and see how they think you are managing your day-to-day tasks—other people often see things that you do not.
- In some cases, you might find it helpful to refer yourself or be referred to a neuropsychologist who can assess you for difficulties with thinking, mood, anxiety or tiredness to see whether there are ways that these can be helped.

Returning to Work

When planning your return to work, it is vital to have an open and honest conversation with your employer or manager. For them to support you fully and make adjustments, they need to know the difficulties you may experience and the challenges you will face when returning to work.

This can feel tricky to do, and there might be lots of reasons why you might find it difficult to share this information, including you might not want people to know how things have changed; you want to show them you can still do your job; you are worried about what people will think of you; you do not want to have to talk about what happened to you and just want to get back to how things were. These are all understandable responses but can result in you wearing "a mask" at work, pretending everything is okay and that you are not finding things as difficult as you are, but by doing so, you might not get the support you need to be able to do your job well. This could result in an increase in stress, anxiety, fatigue and pain as you push yourself to do your job the way you used to.

Sometimes, unhelpful thoughts might stop you from sharing information with your employer; ask yourself, "What would you say to a friend in the exact same situation as you?"

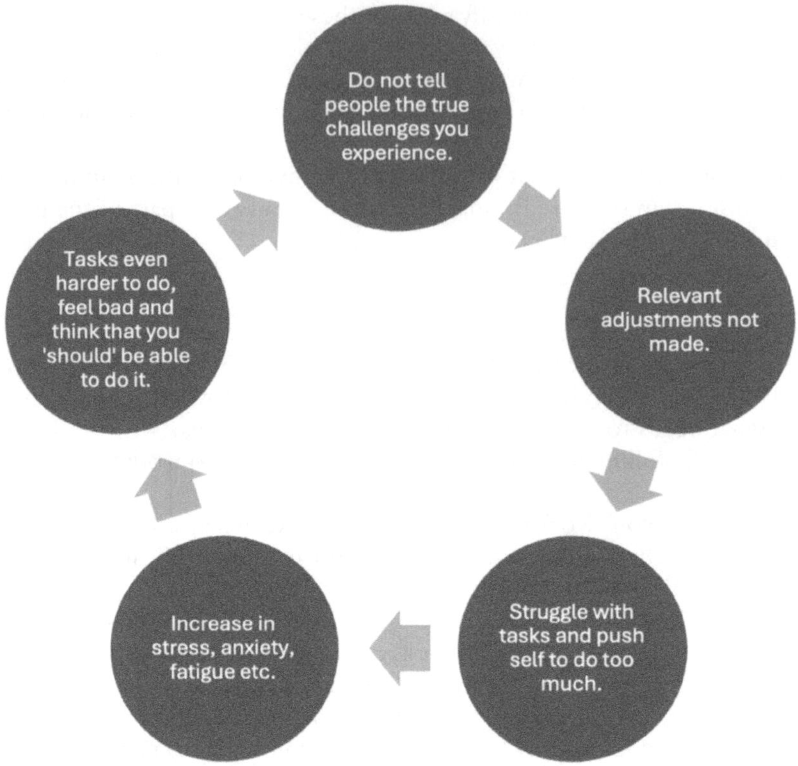

Figure 17.1 "Putting on a Mask" Vicious Cycle Diagram.

Speaking to Your Employer

Prior to returning to work, speak to your employer to let them know about your difficulties and find out ways in which they may be accommodated in the workplace. (Appendix 51: *Employer/Manager Review Meeting Template* can help with this.)

You could try the following to help:

- Arrange a meeting with your employer and try to discuss a phased return to work.
- Write down a clear plan of what the phased return will look like and acknowledge that this is likely to change. Making this clear helps to minimise any additional stress and anxiety for both of you.
- Write down a summary of the tasks you do; rate how you think you will do with these tasks (e.g., can do without difficulty, can do with difficulty or cannot do); and note any strategies or support that may help. Share this with your employer.
- Share what strategies you have put in place to help you with your tasks, e.g., using a diary, alarms and regular breaks.
- Discuss any ideas that you have about ways your employer can support you, and ask whether they have any other suggestions that may help.
- Arrange regular check-ins and have a clear goal for these meetings. Use them as ways to problem solve together; be curious, not critical—what is working and what is not. Is there anything else you or your employer could be doing?

Appendix Number	*Title*	*Author*
1	Building the Basics for Recovery and adaptation	Emma Nicholas
2	Your Inner Compass: Exploring Values after Brain Injury	Emma Nicholas
3	Turning Values into Action: Setting SMART Goals	Emma Nicholas and Vicki Hall
4	Enjoyment and Achievement: Activities to Lift Mood and Motivation	Vicki Hall
5	Shifting Focus: Building Resilience through Gratitude	Emma Nicholas
6	From Resistance to Acceptance: Opening the Door to Adaptation	Vicki Hall
7	Navigating Mind Influencers: Guidelines for Adaptive Thinking	Vicki Hall
8	Unlocking Adaptation: A Practical Guide to the Compassionate Resilient Mind	Vicki Hall
9	Metaphors for a Compassionate Resilient Mind	Vicki Hall
10	Acceptance and Resilience Goals: Choosing Growth over Perfection	Vicki Hall
11	Turning Procrastination into Meaningful Action	Vicki Hall
12	From Perfectionism to Progress: A Compassionate Resilient Mind Exercise	Vicki Hall
13	Rose-Tinted Reflections: Navigating the Good Old Days Bias	Vicki Hall
14	Switching off Automatic Pilot: The Art of Mindfulness	Vicki Hall
15	Mindfulness for Chronic Pain: Meeting Discomfort with Compassion	Vicki Hall
16	Relaxation Skills: Finding Calm and Balance	Vicki Hall
17	Anger Diary	Vicki Hall
18	A Narrative about Riding the Rage Storm: When the Fire Takes Over	Vicki Hall
19	Assertiveness Exercise	Vicki Hall
20	Taming the Dragon: A CRM Relaxation Script for Anger and Embitterment	Vicki Hall
21	Courage in Motion: Practising Safe Exposure	Vicki Hall
22	Therapeutic Letter for Forgiveness and Healing	Vicki Hall
23	Pros and Cons of Remaining Embittered	Vicki Hall
24	Pros and Cons of Forgiveness	Vicki Hall
25	Recognising the Signs of Fatigue	Vicki Hall
26	Fatigue diary: Tracking Patterns to Support Adaptive Pacing	Vicki Hall
27	Evaluating Beliefs about Fatigue and Initiating Compassionate-Resilient Change	Vicki Hall
28	Breaking Out of the "Boom-Bust" Cycle – Pacing Activities	Vicki Hall
29	Rebalancing the Volume: Highlighting What Matters, Softening the Noise of Pain and Fatigue	Vicki Hall
30	Memory Slip Tracker Form	Vicki Hall
31	PQRST Guidelines	Vicki Hall
32	Guidelines for Problem-Solving	Vicki Hall

(Continued)

Appendix Number	*Title*	*Author*
33	Guidelines for Planning Essays after Brain Injury	Vicki Hall
34	Structured Decision-Making Tool: Finding the Best Option for You	Vicki Hall
35	Strengthening Your Mental Brakes with a Compassionate Resilient Mind (CRM)	Vicki Hall
36	Using the Compassionate Resilient Mind (CRM) to Navigate Cognitive Symptoms with ACCEPTS	Vicki Hall
37	Understanding Your Own Finances	Selina Holmes
38	Insight and Self-Awareness: Understanding Vulnerability after Brain Injury	Selina Holmes
39	Smart Spending & Budget Confidence	Selina Holmes
40	Safe Action Planning For Finances	Selina Holmes
41	Key Points for Your Family to Understand about Brain Injury	Cathy Grant and Katie Venables
42	Relationships with Children Worksheet (to Complete with Your Family)	Cathy Grant and Katie Venables
43	Best Memory (for Infant and Primary School Age)	Cathy Grant and Katie Venables
44	Draw a Family (Infant and Primary School Age)	Cathy Grant and Katie Venables
45	Snakes and Ladders (for Primary School Age)	Cathy Grant and Katie Venables
46	Emotions Cards	Cathy Grant and Katie Venables
47	The Worry Jar	Cathy Grant and Katie Venables
48	Creating a Worry Monster Worksheet	Cathy Grant and Katie Venables
49	Handprint Breathing	Cathy Grant and Katie Venables
50	My Working Week—Potential Challenges and What Helps	Stephanie Keay
51	Employer/Manager Review Meeting Template	Stephanie Keay
52	Education Review Meeting Template	Cathy Grant
53	Timetable Worksheet—Potential Difficulties and What Helps.	Cathy Grant

Appendix 1

Building the Basics for Recovery and Adaptation

A brain injury can lead to changes in lifestyle. People may find that they lose their routine, they may not eat as well as they did before, and they may stop exercising and going out. This can lead to low mood and poor physical health.

Routine

A brain injury can significantly disrupt your usual routine. This may happen for many reasons. For example, you may no longer be working, or you find that fatigue or other symptoms mean you need to rest more frequently.

Developing a new routine that fits your current needs can be a way to support your well-being. A consistent routine helps regulate your mood, improve sleep, reduce fatigue, and foster a sense of purpose. These are key elements in maintaining motivation and emotional stability.

Where do I begin?

Wake and Sleep Times: Try to get up and go to bed at regular times each day. This supports your body clock and improves sleep quality.

Regular Meals: Having meals at consistent times helps keep your body nourished and energy levels more stable.

Rest Periods: If fatigue is an issue, schedule regular rest breaks. Planning these can help you pace your energy and avoid burnout.

Meaningful Activities: Include activities that bring you pleasure, a sense of achievement or connection with others. These are vital ingredients for emotional well-being and recovery.

Creating a flexible, supportive routine is not about returning to how things used to be; it is about shaping a rhythm that works for you now.

Eating for Energy and Recovery: After a brain injury, many people notice changes in their eating habits. You might find yourself relying more on convenience or processed foods because of low energy, fatigue or difficulties with memory, planning or coordination. Some people also experience changes in taste or smell, which can affect appetite and enjoyment of food.

Whilst these challenges are completely understandable, nourishing your body with healthy food is an important part of recovery. A balanced diet, rich in protein, whole grains, fruits and vegetables, can support both your physical health and emotional well-being.

Here are some ideas to help you eat in a way that supports your recovery, even if you are feeling low on energy or motivation:

Use Pre-prepared Options: Supermarkets often stock chopped vegetables, ready-made salads or meal kits that reduce prep time.

Cook When You Have Energy: If you feel more alert at a certain time of day, try to prepare meals then, rather than waiting until mealtimes when fatigue may hit.

Batch Cook: Making several portions of a healthy meal and freezing them saves time and effort on days when cooking feels too much.

Get Support If Needed: If you struggle physically with cooking, ask your GP for a referral to an occupational therapist. They can advise on equipment and adaptations that make food preparation easier and safer.

Support Thinking Difficulties: If memory or attention problems make cooking hard, look at the relevant chapters in this book for strategies to help you cook more confidently and safely.

Watch Out for Stimulants: Reduce or monitor your intake of caffeine and sugary drinks, as they may give short bursts of energy; they can also contribute to energy crashes and poor sleep.

Use Trusted Information: There is a lot of dietary advice online. Make sure you use reliable sources, such as the National Health Service (NHS) website or the World Health Organization. If you are outside the United Kingdom, look for advice from your national health provider, or speak with your GP or a dietitian about what is best for you.

Sleep: Sleep can be affected by brain injury. Poor sleep can lower your mood and worsen your experience of difficulties, such as changed thinking skills. It is important to get good sleep in order to function well during the day (see Chapter 7: *Resting with Resilience: A Compassionate Guide to Sleep*).

Exercise: Following a brain injury, low mood, low energy or lack of motivation can affect your ability to participate in exercise. Some people also experience physical changes that make exercise more difficult. Increasing your exercise or activity in any way that you can will support your physical and psychological well-being. Exercise can be any activity that increases your heart rate, so gardening, dancing, walking and even housework can be classed as exercise. After a brain injury, exercise may look different from the things you were able to do before you were injured, but any way that you can move your body will be of benefit to you (e.g., seated yoga or seated workouts).

Daylight: Exposure to daylight is important to support your well-being. Daylight can be helpful for establishing a good sleep routine, especially if you get exposure to daylight early in the day. Below are some ways for you to access daylight to improve your well-being:

- Why not take your breakfast in the garden when the weather permits?
- Go for a short walk in the morning.
- Visit a local park to access daylight in nature, which is also beneficial.

Use the worksheet below to consider if there are areas in your life where you might be able to make some positive changes.

Worksheet 1: Improving the Basics

Example:

Area	*What can I improve*	*Who or what could help*	*Progress*
Diet	Add in some more fruit and vegetables.	Buy frozen vegetables to add to meals.	I'm eating fruit twice a day for snacks.
Sleep	Aim to get 8 hours of sleep at night.	See the chapter on sleep. Reduce napping in the day.	Sleeping 7 hours at night and reduced napping in the day.
Exercise/ movement	Move my body more.	Move my body at regular intervals. Set a reminder to prompt me.	I move every hour for 5 minutes now. I go for a short walk most days.
Daylight	Aim to expose myself to sunlight in the morning.	Stand at the open door, whilst the kettle boils in the morning.	Improved sleep.
Routine	Create a new routine to take account of my new needs, for example, to rest, move, socialise.	See Appendix 4, *Enjoyment and Achievement: Activities to Lift Mood and Motivation*, for how to create a pleasurable activity daily timetable.	Doing things that I enjoy and having a regular routine help my mood and energy.

Worksheet 1: Improving the Basics

Area	*What can I improve*	*What or who can help*	*Progress*
Diet			
Sleep			
Exercise/movement			
Daylight			
Routine			

Appendix 2

Your Inner Compass: Exploring Values after Brain Injury

What Are Values?

Values are the guiding principles that shape how you want to live your life. They reflect what matters to you, the kind of person you want to be, how you want to treat others, and what you want to stand for.

After a brain injury, many aspects of life may change. Values can help you regain a sense of direction by acting as an internal compass, reconnecting you with what is meaningful. This in turn can help you adapt to your new circumstances by shaping a life that reflects who you are now. You may find that your values have changed since your injury, or perhaps they have become even clearer.

Why Are Values Important?

Living in line with your values supports emotional well-being and resilience. It allows you to make choices that feel right, even in the face of setbacks or uncertainty. Values help:

- Anchor your identity after change or loss
- Guide meaningful action, even when things are difficult
- Strengthen motivation when you are feeling stuck
- Foster self-compassion by helping you act in line with what truly matters to you

Values are not the same as goals. They are ongoing directions that give life meaning.

Discovering What Matters to You

There are many ways to explore your personal values. The questions and tools below can help you identify what is most important to you right now.

Reflection Prompts

Your 80th Birthday: Imagine it is your 80th birthday. All the people who are important to you are there. One by one, they stand up to share stories about the life you have lived and the kind of person you have been.

→ What would you want them to say about you? What qualities would you be proud of?

A Role Model: Think of someone you admire (either real or fictional).

→ What traits do they have that inspire you? What values do they live by?

Worksheet A1.1—Discovering and Clarifying Your Values

Step 1: Explore Your Values

Tick the values that feel important or meaningful to you:

List of Values:

Kindness/compassion: to care for, accept and respect myself and others	Resilience: to be able to adjust to change and cope with adversity
Humorous	Adventure: to seek out new experiences
Stand up for myself and others	Community: to be a part of something bigger than myself
Religious or spiritual life	Nature: to be in nature
Health: to take good care of myself	Mindfulness: to practise being in the here and now
Being sporty: to watch or engage in sports	Respect: to respect others and be respected
Creativity: to enjoy being creative	Music: to enjoy listening to or playing music
Challenge: to increase my skills, knowledge or physical abilities	Dependability/reliability (e.g., sticking to my word)
Collaborate: to work together with others on something	Romance: to enjoy a fulfilling love life or partnership with someone
Independence: to do things for myself and make my own choices	Gratitude/grateful: to express thanks for the experiences, relationships and things I have in life
Fun: to laugh and enjoy myself	Friends/connection to others: to have relationships and be a good friend/ mother/father, etc.
Organisation: to be organised and structured	Authenticity/honesty
Responsibility: to be responsible for myself and others	Fitness: to keep physically fit
Self-improvement: to continue to work on myself and develop new skills	Well-being: to feel emotionally well
	Sexuality: to express my sexuality
Security: to feel safe and secure	Risks: to take risks
Generosity: to give my time and resources to others	Genuine: to be my authentic self
Leadership: to lead others	Inspiration: to inspire others, to feel inspired
Write own value here	Write own value here

Step 2: Choose Your Core Values

Now, pick your top 5–6 Core Values—the ones that feel most central to the kind of life you want to live.

1.
2.
3.
4.
5.
6.

Worksheet A1.2—Evaluating Changes in Values Post-Injury

Why Do Values Sometimes Shift?

Following a brain injury, many people experience significant life changes that can affect how closely they live in line with their values. Some values may become stronger or more central. Others may feel harder to live out in the same way as before. This shift is a natural response to change and sometimes it can even reflect growth. When someone moves closer to values, such as compassion, gratitude or resilience after a difficult experience, we call this post-traumatic growth. Taking time to reflect on your values now, compared to before your injury, can help you understand how you have changed, what matters most to you today, and how you can move forward with purpose.

Use this worksheet to explore how your relationship with different values has changed since your brain injury. This process can help you identify growth, how the value is still maintained, areas of loss and areas where you would like to realign.

Worked example:

Value	*How true is this of you now?*	*How true was this of you before your injury?*	*Reason for change/reflection (including how this value is still present)*
Compassion	90%	70%	"Because of what I've been through, I have more compassion for others. I now do voluntary work at an animal sanctuary."
Humour	85%	85%	"I don't laugh as much now, but my sense of humour is still there."
Gratitude	95%	50%	"I'm more aware of what matters. I'm grateful just to be alive."
Fun	80%	90%	"I still enjoy life, but I can't do some of the fun activities I used to (like running)."
Resilience	80%	50%	"Before my injury, I didn't face many challenges. Now, I've had to overcome a lot and I've discovered my strength."

Blank template:

Value	*How true is this of you now?*	*How true was this of you before your injury?*	*Reason for change/reflection (including how this value is still present)*
Compassion			
Humour			
Gratitude			
Fun			
Resilience			

Top tip: Living in line with your values is not about doing it perfectly or getting it right all the time. It is about using your values as a compass, which provides a way to ground and guide yourself, especially when things feel uncertain or challenging. Your values point you in a meaningful direction, but they are not rigid rules. Even small efforts to act in line with your values can help you feel more purposeful and connected.

Worksheet A1.3—Living Your Values Today and Realigning With What Matters

Once you have explored how your values have changed, the next step is to recommit to those that feel most meaningful now. You may wish to integrate them in new ways that reflect your current life.

This process is a key part of developing a Compassionate Resilient Mind (CRM). It helps you move forward with self-awareness, flexibility and purpose.

Use this worksheet to reflect on how you want to bring your key values into your life.

Value	*What does this value mean to me now?*	*How can I incorporate this value into my life today?*
Resilience	Rebuilding my life despite challenges. Overcoming difficulties. Accepting difficult emotions and adapting.	– Practise new skills to navigate my challenges – Work towards self-acceptance – Use tools from this book (e.g., Appendix 7: *Navigating Mind Influencers: Guidelines for Adaptive Thinking*, Appendix 8: *Unlocking Adaptation: A Practical Guide to the Compassionate Resilient Mind* and Appendix 10: *Acceptance and Resilience Goals: Choosing Growth Over Perfection*) – Celebrate small victories
Compassion	Being kind to myself and others. Accepting my symptoms without judgment. Offering myself patience.	– Take breaks when needed – Ask for support – Help others when I can – Practise compassion self-talk (e.g., see Appendix 8: *Unlocking Adaptation: A Practical Guide to the Compassionate Resilient Mind*) – Practise fostering moments of self-compassion (e.g., see Appendix 5: *Shifting Focus: Building Resilience through Gratitude*)

Top tips:

Realigning with your values is not about going back to who you were; it is about becoming who you want to be now.

You may also want to ensure that you incorporate these goals into your life by setting SMART goals (see Appendix 3: *Turning Values into Action: Setting SMART Goals*).

Appendix 3

Turning Values into Action: Setting SMART Goals

This appendix is to help you create clear, values-based goals for a meaningful life.

Set Long-Term, Values-Based Goals

Values act like a compass, guiding us towards what truly matters. Goals are the milestones that we reach along the journey. When our goals are shaped by our values, each step we take moves us closer to living a life that feels purposeful and fulfilling. After a brain injury, your goals may shift, but by returning to your values, you can shape goals that feel personal, motivating and realistic.

Using your values as a guide, think about where you would realistically like to be in five years in the following life areas.

Worksheet A1.1—Long-Term Goals Reflection

For each domain below, write down your hopes or aspirations based on what matters most to you:

Life area	*Where would you like to be in five years?*
Relationships (e.g., Would you like to strengthen a relationship? Meet new people? Be more socially connected?)	
Domestic chores/daily living (e.g., Would you like to be doing more for yourself around the house? Driving again?)	
Support and independence (e.g., Would you like to rely less on support from family or carers? Feel more autonomous?)	
Leisure and hobbies (e.g., Would you like to start new hobbies, return to old ones, or find fulfilling recreation?)	
Occupation (e.g., Voluntary work, paid work, meaningful contribution)	
Education/learning (e.g., Would you like to study something new, take a course or gain a qualification?)	

For more ideas, see Appendix 4: Enjoyment and Achievement: Activities to Lift Mood and Motivation, which includes a pleasurable activities checklist.

Make Your Goals SMART

Once you have identified a long-term goal, it is time to make it SMART (specific, measurable, adaptive, reaslistic and timed):

Specific: Clearly define what you want to achieve.
Measurable: Know how you will track your progress.
Adaptive and **A**chievable: Make sure it supports a meaningful life and aligns with your values.
Realistic: Ensure the goal is achievable within your current capabilities.
Timed: Give yourself a time frame or deadline.
SMART goals help keep you motivated, provide structure and allow you to monitor your growth over time.

Worksheet A1.2—Define Your SMART Goal

SMART element	*Prompt*	*Your response*
Specific	What is your long-term goal? What steps will help you achieve it? What challenges or barriers might you face? What support or resources might help?	
Measurable	How will you know when you have achieved your goal? What will you be doing differently? What can you observe or track?	
Adaptive	How does this goal connect with your values? How will it help you live a more meaningful life?	
Realistic	Is this goal achievable for you right now? What might get in the way? Is it under your control? Can others support you in making it happen?	
Timed	What is your target date for completing this goal? What are the deadlines for each step?	

Top Tip: Set goals that you can control. For example, the goal "I'll contact a friend once a week" is more achievable than "I'll have a day out with a friend every week," which depends on someone else's availability.

Break It Down—Your Action Plan

Long-term goals can feel big, and that is okay. The key is to break them into smaller, manageable steps that you can start working on today. Use the worksheet below to create your step-by-step plan.

Worksheet A1.3—Your Step-by-Step Plan

Goal			
Step	*What will you do?*	*When? (Date)*	*Support/resources needed*
Step 1			
Step 2			
Step 3			
Step 4			

Top Tips:

SHARE YOUR GOALS WITH SOMEONE YOU TRUST

Telling others about your goals can sometimes boost motivation, help you stay accountable and make it easier to ask for support. Support might come in many forms, such as encouragement, practical help, emotional backing or someone checking in on your progress.

CELEBRATE YOUR PROGRESS, ESPECIALLY THE SMALL WINS.

After a brain injury, even tasks that once felt easy may now take courage, effort and resilience. Recognising your achievements, no matter how small, helps protect your mood and supports recovery.

A Compassionate Resilient Mind (CRM) Perspective

Through a CRM lens, setting SMART goals is not about "fixing" yourself; it is about moving towards what matters, even with limitations or setbacks. Try and ensure that you:

- Be kind to yourself as you work through each step.
- Stay flexible- adjust your goals as needed. Focus on meaning, not perfection.

"Success is measured not by where you are, but by what you've overcome to get there."

—*Booker T. Washington*

Appendix 4

Enjoyment and Achievement: Activities to Lift Mood and Motivation

Step 1: Pleasurable Activities Checklist

Part of feeling good is about planning and carrying out activities that we enjoy. Determine the activities that you enjoy doing using the checklist in Worksheet A4.1. Place a tick next to each of the activities you can do that give a feeling of achievement, connection to others or enjoyment.

Worksheet A4.1 Pleasurable Activities Checklist

Community and Trips	*Entertainment*	*Hobbies*
Going on holiday or a day trip Join a community event (e.g., litter picking, volunteering) Going out for dinner Adventure activity (e.g., hiking, hot air ballooning, helicopter ride) Camping Shopping	Going to the cinema Watching TV Watching a movie Going to the theatre Going to a sporting event (e.g., football) Listening to music	Playing an instrument Birdwatching Crafts (e.g., painting) Decorating Photography Woodwork Collecting things
Other: Socialising Speaking to a friend on the phone Meeting someone new Having a discussion with a friend Visiting family or friends Joining a club Giving physical affection Going out to a coffee shop	Other: Games and sports Playing on a games console Playing a board game Playing cards Horse riding Playing sports: golf, football, badminton, swimming Pool or snooker Puzzles, crosswords	Other: Domestic activities Cooking Sewing Bread Making Cake decorating Gardening Fixing things Baking Hosting a dinner party
Other: Education Learning something new Reading Attending a college course YouTube videos on areas of interest (travel, cars, finance, nature)	Other: Health and appearance Buying new clothes Putting on make-up Getting a haircut or beauty treatment (e.g., nails) Eating healthy food Going to the gym or exercising at home	Other: Religious/spiritual activities Going to a place of worship Saying a prayer Reading the religious text Spiritual practices (mindfulness, yoga)
Other:	Other:	Other:

Step 2: Plan to Do at Least One Pleasurable Activity a Day

Write a diary to plan each day or week (see Worksheet A4.2). To help ensure that you carry out pleasurable activities within your day, consider the following points:

- Make sure you schedule at least one of the activities you have identified in Worksheet A4.1 every day at a set time. Set your alarm to prompt you to carry it out.
- Do these activities anyway in spite of how you feel!
- If you have a tendency to put things off, use the guidelines for procrastinating given in Appendix 11: *Turning Procrastination into Meaningful Action* to help you.
- Gradually increase the number of these activities you do over time.

Worksheet A4.2 Pleasurable Activity Daily Timetable

Time	*Monday*	*Tuesday*	*Wednesday*	*Thursday*	*Friday*	*Saturday*	*Sunday*
0600–0800							
0800–1000							
1000–1100							
1100–1200							
1200–1300							
1300–1400							
1400–1500							
1500–1600							
1600–1700							
1700–1800							
1800–1900							
1900–2000							
2000–0000							

Step 3: Pleasurable Activity Log

Use Worksheet A4.3 to record the day and time you engaged in an activity, and how much enjoyment and pleasure it gave you on a scale from 0 to 10 (0 = no pleasure or enjoyment; 10 = maximum pleasure or enjoyment). Also rate how much achievement you felt from doing it (0 = no achievement; 10 = maximum achievement).

Worksheet A4.3 Pleasurable Activity Log

Day, time	*Activity*	*Achievement*	*Enjoyment*
For example: Monday, 29 June, 10.00	Spoke to grandson on the phone	3	8
For example: Tuesday, 30 June, 10.00	Completed 10 minutes of gardening	7	4

Appendix 5

Shifting Focus: Building Resilience through Gratitude

Why Practice Gratitude?

After a brain injury, it is easy to focus on what has changed or what feels difficult. Gratitude practice helps gently shift attention towards the small positive moments that are still present in your day. Gratitude helps us recognise what we have, and helps us recognise what we still have, not just what has been lost.

This practice supports the Compassionate Resilient Mind (CRM) by:

- **Encouraging Cognitive Flexibility**: Allowing your attention to move between difficulty and appreciation.
- **Building Emotional Resilience**: Reinforcing feelings of hope, warmth and connection.
- **Strengthening Self-Compassion**: Reminding you that you are still capable of experiencing joy, meaning and support.

How to Practise Gratitude

Each day, write down three things you feel grateful for or that brought a moment of calm, comfort or connection. Make it part of your routine by linking your practice to something you already do, such as keeping a notebook by your bed or writing in your phone each evening, whilst you unwind.

Examples of gratitude moments include:

- A cup of tea
- A hug or a kind word
- Hearing birdsong
- A funny text from a friend
- Feeling proud of a small step forward
- Warm sunshine on your skin
- Watching something that made you laugh
- Trying something new
- A moment of peace or clarity
- Support from someone who cares

Gratitude Journal—Worksheet A5.1

Instructions: Each day, note three things you feel grateful for or that made you smile.

Date	*Gratitude moments*
7th September	Enjoyed a phone call with my friend—grateful for the connection Ate a lovely lunch—grateful for comfort food Saw a robin in the garden—grateful for nature

Use sentence starters if helpful:

- "Something I appreciated today was…"
- "A moment that felt good today was…"
- "One thing I noticed and valued today was…"

Top tip*:* Even on the hardest days, your mind can learn to notice what lifts you. Practising gratitude is not about ignoring your difficult times; it is about strengthening your ability to see light alongside the dark.

Appendix 6

From Resistance to Acceptance: Opening the Door to Adaptation

Why Is Acceptance Important?

Acceptance means acknowledging the reality of your situation (including losses, symptoms and weaknesses) without judgment or resistance. It does not mean you have to like or approve of these experiences. Instead, it is about observing them, allowing them to be present, and making space for the discomfort and unwanted feelings that they may cause, rather than fighting or pushing them away. In doing so, you create psychological space to adapt, learn and continue building a life of meaning whilst accepting the challenges.

After a brain injury, acceptance can also mean recognising that some things may not improve. This is often a painful realisation, yet it can become a gateway to adaptation, accommodation and growth. By accepting what cannot be changed, you release energy that would otherwise be spent on struggle. That energy can then be directed towards what you can influence, for example, how you respond, how you care for yourself and how you discover new ways of living with purpose and value.

Resistance and Avoidance Are Natural, But Not Always Helpful

It is normal to resist facing limitations, unwanted feelings or difficult sensations, and this resistance can often intensify after a brain injury. You may fear this means weakness, failure or losing who you are. This often activates the "Gatekeeper," a protective mindset that tries to shield you by fighting, denying or avoiding painful experiences.

Sometimes, the "Gatekeeper" uses criticism as part of this "protective mindset". For example, by saying things like "I should be stronger," "I'm useless," "I'll never cope", it tries to push the experience away or gain control over it. These reactions are understandable; they are part of the brain's instinct to protect. Yet, over time, battling your symptoms, shutting down or criticising yourself drains energy, narrows perspective and blocks new ways of coping. The alternative is to meet resistance with compassion. By noticing your patterns with kindness and asking for feedback from people you trust, you open the door to flexibility, adaptation and more purposeful ways of responding.

The following exercise will help you:

- Reflect on how accepting and adaptive your mindset is, both prior to and after your injury
- Recognise patterns of thinking that may support or block adaptation

- Explore the advantages and disadvantages of an accepting and adaptive mindset
- Consider whether you feel ready to let go of resistance, and make space for growth and adaptation

Try to approach this exercise with the qualities of a Compassionate Resilient Mind (CRM): openness, courage and kindness. Rather than criticising yourself for resisting, recognise it as a normal response, and also as an opportunity to grow more flexible, purposeful and compassionate in how you face challenges moving forward.

Step 1: Reflect on Your Pre-Injury Mindset

Think about your typical responses to challenges before your brain injury. For each statement below, tick the box that best reflects how often it applied to you.

Mindset of adaptation/acceptance	*Never*	*Rarely*	*Sometimes*	*Often*	*All the time*
I didn't mind admitting when I couldn't do something well.	☐	☐	☐	☐	☐
I could accept my struggles without blaming others or harshly criticising myself.	☐	☐	☐	☐	☐
I could acknowledge when I made a mistake or forgot something, take responsibility and learn from it.	☐	☐	☐	☐	☐
I could recognise when I had reached my limits.	☐	☐	☐	☐	☐
I accepted my mistakes or imperfections without resentment or self-criticism.	☐	☐	☐	☐	☐
I accepted constructive feedback, even about flaws, without becoming defensive.	☐	☐	☐	☐	☐
I accepted help when I needed it, but remained independent when I could.	☐	☐	☐	☐	☐
I was open to seeing that my point of view might not always be accurate.	☐	☐	☐	☐	☐
I allowed myself to feel sad, anxious or frustrated without judging, avoiding or pushing away those feelings.	☐	☐	☐	☐	☐
I could stay focused on what I wanted, even when difficult feelings showed up.	☐	☐	☐	☐	☐
I viewed challenges as opportunities to learn, even if I fell short.	☐	☐	☐	☐	☐
I was willing to try things I wasn't good at, rather than avoiding them.	☐	☐	☐	☐	☐
I was willing to face uncomfortable situations with balance and compassion, if they connected me to what mattered most.	☐	☐	☐	☐	☐

Optional tip: Sometimes, we are not fully aware of our own mindset, especially when looking back. If you feel comfortable, you might ask a close family member or friend to complete the same table based on how they remember you before your injury. Comparing your responses can offer insight and spark meaningful conversation.

Step 2: Exploring Your Current Mindset

How often do you now demonstrate a mindset of acceptance/adaptation in response to challenges relating to your brain injury?

For each of the statements below, tick the column that best describes your current experience.

Mindset of acceptance/adaptation	*Never*	*Rarely*	*Sometimes*	*Often*	*All the time*
I adjust my daily activities to work around my limitations.	☐	☐	☐	☐	☐
I face situations that reveal my difficulties, instead of avoiding them when it connects me to what matters most.	☐	☐	☐	☐	☐
When my symptoms show up, I notice them without criticising myself or others.	☐	☐	☐	☐	☐
I can attempt tasks at a managable pace, even when they're hard, rather than avoiding them.	☐	☐	☐	☐	☐
I take on helpful strategies (e.g., using a diary) to support myself.	☐	☐	☐	☐	☐
I accept easier ways of doing things when they're needed.	☐	☐	☐	☐	☐
I accept feedback about my limitations or changes without becoming defensive or showing harsh self-criticism.	☐	☐	☐	☐	☐
I accept help when I need it, but stay independent where I can.	☐	☐	☐	☐	☐
I consider other people's perspectives about my symptoms and admit when mine may not be accurate.	☐	☐	☐	☐	☐
I allow myself to feel emotions, like sadness or anxiety in response to my symptoms without judging them.	☐	☐	☐	☐	☐
I see challenges as chances to grow, even if I don't succeed at first.	☐	☐	☐	☐	☐
I am willing to try things, even if I know I won't do them perfectly.	☐	☐	☐	☐	☐
I am willing to tolerate discomfort, with self-compassion and balance, when it helps me move towards what matters most.	☐	☐	☐	☐	☐

Step 3: Reflecting on the Perceived Advantages of Not Accepting/Adapting to Limitations

Sometimes, we resist acceptance because we believe it protects us or shows strength. Reflect on any beliefs you hold that make it hard to accept your limitations.

Examples:

- "If I accept my limitations, it means I've let them win."
- "It's stronger to fight through than to admit weakness."
- "If I accept what's happened, I might fall apart."

Use the space below to write any personal beliefs you have that may prevent acceptance/adaptation:

Step 4: Exploring the Disadvantages of Not Accepting/Adapting to Limitations

Now reflect on how resistance or denial of your difficulties might be holding you back. What does it cost you, not just practically, but emotionally?

You might consider:

- Fighting your symptoms may leave you exhausted, frustrated or ashamed when they emerge.
- Denial may stop you from using helpful tools (like calendars or reminders).
- You might push yourself too hard, only to crash or underperform.
- You may miss out on easier paths, joy and growth by only doing things "the hard way."
- Without acceptance, it is harder to adjust, learn and move forward.
- Non-acceptance can lead to harsh self-criticism and negative self-talk.
- You may miss out on worthwhile things because you avoid discomfort

Refusing to adapt prevents the development of your CRM and keeps you stuck in "Gatekeeper" thinking (i.e., rigid, threat-based patterns that hold you back). Acceptance allows strength, self-compassion and personal evolution. Helpful metaphors to understand and explore these mindsets are within the following appendices:

- Appendix 9a: *Martial Arts Metaphor, Metaphors for a Compassionate Resilient Mind*: Shows how resisting an immovable force can backfire, whilst flowing with it can lead to strength and skill.
- Appendix 9b: *The Unwelcome Guest Metaphor, Metaphors for a Compassionate Resilient Mind*: Describes how constantly fighting symptoms is like battling an unwelcome visitor, exhausting and life-limiting.
- Appendix 8: *Unlocking Adaptation: A Practical Guide to the Compassionate Resilient Mind. Part 2: Narratives.* This appendix provides narratives and exercises to promote acceptance.

Use this space to write any personal costs of non-acceptance you have experienced:

Step 5: Re-Evaluating Resistance—Opening the Door to Flexibility

After reflecting on the possible costs of resistance and the potential benefits of acceptance, take a moment to consider whether your mindset is helping or hindering your ability to adapt.

Remember, the goal is not to argue with or disprove your beliefs about resisting limitations. These beliefs likely developed as protective strategies and may have served you in the past. Instead, the aim is to create psychological flexibility (i.e., the ability to notice these beliefs without being rigidly controlled by them). This flexibility opens the door to adaptation, resilience and compassionate self-support.

By gently softening the grip of resistance, you can begin to explore new ways of responding that honour your reality, without giving up on adaptation or purpose. This is the heart of developing your CRM (i.e., recognising your symptoms, limitations, thoughts, feelings and experiences, and responding to them with awareness, kindness and purposeful action).

Top Tip: Use Narrative Distance to Reflect Objectively

It can be hard to reflect on our own thinking. If you are struggling, it might help to imagine this exercise applied to someone else (e.g., a character or story). What would you say to them?

See *Appendix 8: Unlocking Adaptation: A Practical Guide to the Compassionate Resilient Mind, Part 2—CRM Narrative Exercises*, for guidance.

Appendix 7

Navigating Mind Influencers: Guidelines for Adaptive Thinking

Thoughts and Mind Influencers

Thoughts are normal mental experiences, such as words or images that appear in your mind. They are influenced by, and influence, your sensations (e.g., fatigue, pain), your emotions and your behaviours. One helpful way to understand thoughts is to compare your mind to the internet with your mental experiences being the social media feed. Just like social media, your mind presents you with "posts" (i.e., thoughts); some helpful, some unhelpful. The ones that grab your attention, and influence how you feel or act, are your "mind influencers." You cannot stop them from appearing, but you can choose how to respond to them. The more you engage with a "mind influencer" (liking, following or commenting), the more powerful its influence becomes. But just like social media, you can scroll past or unfollow the ones that do not serve you. By stepping out of "automatic pilot" and cultivating a flexible, reflective mindset, what we call the Compassionate Resilient Mind (CRM), you can reduce the hold these influencers have over you.

Use the following steps to develop more adaptive thinking.

Separating Facts from Opinion

Thoughts can include both facts and opinions. If your mind is presenting an opinion, for example, "I'm useless" or "This will never get better," treat it as a hypothesis, not a truth. Unhelpful "mind influencers" often distort reality by focusing on worst-case scenarios or personal shortcomings. If you automatically accept them as true, they can become more deeply ingrained.

After a brain injury, it can sometimes be difficult to tell the difference between a fact and an opinion. Changes in thinking skills (such as reduced flexibility or difficulty with abstract concepts) may make it harder to question your own thoughts or see them as just one possible version of events. For example, a person might say, "It's a fact that Jane was ignoring me, I know it's true." But that statement includes an interpretation (Jane's intention), which is actually an opinion, not a fact.

Learning to separate facts from opinions helps you step back from "mind influencers" and view them with a more compassionate, flexible mindset. It allows you to challenge unhelpful beliefs, consider alternative perspectives and avoid jumping to conclusions.

Table 7.1 How to Separate Facts from Opinions

Facts	*Opinions*
Facts are observations that can be confirmed with high certainty (95%–100%), like in a court of law.	Opinions are personal beliefs, interpretations or assumptions. They cannot be proven with certainty.
Examples of facts:	**Examples of opinions**:
Descriptions of things you can physically observe (e.g., "She was wearing a red jumper.")	Beliefs about other people's motives (e.g., "He ignored me on purpose.")
Specific actions without assumptions (e.g., "He left the room.")	Predictions (e.g., "She'll probably cancel again.")
Verbatim quotes (e.g., "Frank called me an idiot.")	Judgements or labels (e.g., "He's lazy," or "She doesn't respect me.")
You can directly see, hear or verify facts.	Assumptions about others' thoughts (e.g., "Everyone thinks I'm an idiot.")
	Opinions rely on interpretation and are coloured by emotion, assumptions or personal beliefs.

Practise Exercise: Identifying Opinions

Try to spot the opinions in each of the following scenarios. These are the parts of the statements that cannot be proven with certainty or rely on interpretation:

- "I invited Ed round. He went outside for a cigarette, and I asked him to lock the door behind him. After he left, I found the door unlocked. It must have been Ed, and he must have done it on purpose".
- "I gave Elliot a letter to post. He said he posted it, but my friend never received it. Elliot lied to me".
- "Rachel painted my house, but the paintwork looked uneven. She's a bad painter, so I won't hire her again".
- "I saw a school friend on the street. She looked right at me and walked on. She ignored me because she doesn't like me and thinks I'm an idiot".
- "Edward is tall and has dark hair. He always seems happy, but he's a bit of an idiot".
- "I hired decorators. They're always late. They don't respect me".
- "Jane has brown hair and blue eyes. She's always kind and happy—I like her".

Answers:

1 Ed left the door unlocked on purpose.
2 Elliot lied to me.
3 Rachel is a bad painter.
4 My friend carried on walking because she does not like me. She thinks I am an idiot.
5 Edward is an idiot who seems to be happy.
6 The decorators have no respect for me.
7 Jane is always very kind to people and happy.

Reflection Tip: Can you tell for sure why someone did something, what they are thinking or how they feel, unless they told you? If not, it is an opinion. By learning to spot these "mind influencer" statements, you can reduce their power and avoid reacting as if they are facts.

Liking and Unliking "Mind Influencers"

"Mind influencers" are thoughts, opinions or mental posts that you latch onto when they pop up in your feed of thinking. You latch onto a thought when you "like" or "follow" it. Some are helpful and worth a mental "like" because they guide you towards growth, safety or understanding. Others may mislead you and not be telling you credible messages.

After brain injury, thinking can become narrower and more fixed, especially when emotions are strong. Asking how credible a thought feels helps you step back and reflect on all the available evidence, not just the parts that shout the loudest. This exercise is not intended to make thoughts go away, but to restore perspective and choice when thinking has become narrowed or stuck. It supports flexibility by widening the picture, allowing you to consider context, alternative explanations, and longer-term impact. It is not about arguing with the thought, forcing positive thinking or dismissing real difficulties. Instead, it helps loosen "stuck" thinking patterns, and restores your ability to shift perspective and respond with compassion and purpose.

To decide whether to like a post, it is worth asking:

- "Is it based on solid evidence?"
- "Have I weighed up the facts for and against it?"
- "Could there be other interpretations?"

If you decide they are not credible, you can mentally "unlike" it. Mentally "unlike" does not mean "disliking," it means mentally disengaging from the thought, so it has less power and becomes easier to scroll past.

Not all emotionally charged "mind influencers" are unhelpful. For example:

- A sad "mind influencer" whispering, "You're not good enough," blocks growth.
- An anxious "mind influencer" warning, "You're in danger," could be protective, if accurate.

The key is choosing whether to follow or unfollow:

- Follow: You let its message guide your behaviour.
- Unfollow: You notice the thought, but choose not to act on it.

To consider if you want to follow the "mind influencer," ask yourself:

- Does this "mind influencer" take me towards or away from my values and goals?
- Does it support compassion and resilience?
- Does it help me adapt, or does it fuel slips and avoidance?

Remember: The more you "like" or "follow" a "mind influencer", the more likely that it will reappear in your feed of thoughts. If you notice you are arguing with the thought or getting tangled up in it, label the process ("I'm debating again"), pause, and gently scroll past.

Creating CRM Posts

When an unhelpful "mind influencer" shows up, try posting back with a CRM "mind influencer", which conveys a message of compassion (e.g., name how the thought makes you feel, with kindness instead of criticism) and resilience (e.g., reply in a way that is kind and courageous, helping you face difficulty, whilst keeping focused on your goals). A CRM response balances kindness, acceptance and persistence: it acknowledges mistakes and limitations with compassion, then adapts and keeps moving forward. Compassion reminds you to rest when needed; resilience helps you keep going afterwards.

Ask: "How would a confident, kind, flexible influencer respond to this unhelpful post?"

For more support, see Appendix 8: *Unlocking Adaptation: A Practical Guide to the Compassionate Resilient Mind.*

Top Tip: Unhelpful "mind influencers" often thrive on engagement. Arguing with them, trying to prove them wrong, or repeatedly analysing their posts, can actually give them more attention and power, much like arguing with a provocative account online. You do not need to delete the unhelpful post or convince anyone it is wrong, or that it needs to disappear. When it shows up again, you can simply scroll past it. As your feed becomes populated with more compassionate, resilient posts, it naturally begins to attract other like-minded "mind influencers," reducing the impact and influence of the unhelpful ones.

Worksheet to Create Adaptive, Flexible Thinking

This worksheet helps you notice unhelpful "mind influencer" thoughts without getting pulled into them, and then reflect and respond later from a calmer, wiser place.

Step 1—To Shift from "Automatic Pilot" to Intentional Action

Notice when a strong or repetitive thought appears. Name the experience: "I notice I'm thinking ___________, which makes me feel ___________."

Observe without engaging, like scrolling past a post without clicking.

Use Worksheet 7.1 to write down the "mind influencer's" message and practise responding from your CRM.

Step 2—How Much Are You Liking This Post?

Later, in a calm intentional space, rate believability of the thought from 0% to 100%. The higher the number, the more you have "liked" it, and the more it will appear. Note the believability rating in worksheet 7.1.

Step 3—Why Might You Like It? (Evidence For)

Explore what makes the thought feel convincing. Note reasons in Worksheet 7.1.

Step 4—Why Might You Unlike or Scroll Past? (Evidence Against/Alternatives)

Part A: Note alternative views or interpretations.

Part B: Ask what happens if you act on this post. Does it move you towards your goals and values? Does it support compassion and resilience, or hold you back? If you decide you do not want to "follow" a post that you have already liked, you can always "unlike" it and mentally disengage.

Step 5—Post Back with Your CRM

Imagine your inner wise self posting a reply that is kind, grounded and strong. Write your CRM response in Worksheet 7.1.

Example: Worksheet 7.1—Flexible Thinking Feed Review

Step 1: Write down the "mind influencer's" message	I couldn't follow the conversation with my family. They must think I'm annoying and a burden.
Step 2: Rate its believability (0%–100%)	80%
Step 3: Write down why I might like it (what made this thoughts evidence for)	I had to ask people to repeat themselves. I couldn't keep up, and felt like I slowed everyone down.
Step 4A: Consider alternative views	I'm recovering from a brain injury. No one said anything rude. My family loves me, even if I sometimes need extra support.
Step 4B: Consider the impact if I follow this post	If I get sucked into this post, It'll make me want to avoid conversations, I'll miss out on conversation practice and I'll feel worse.
Step 5: CRM response	I'm doing my best in a tough situation, that's something to be proud of. It's okay to need repetition. Everyone is annoying sometimes, but I can show resilience by keeping on trying.

Step 6: Softening the Grip of Unhelpful Influences and Nurturing Adaptive Ones

Even when you recognise that a "mind influencer's" message is unhelpful, biased or illogical, it can still occupy your attention and affect how you feel. Just like persistent social media influencers, these thoughts may continue to pop up, even after you have "unliked" or "unfollowed" them, particularly if you have had a strong mental connection to them over time.

Whilst you cannot completely eliminate maladaptive "mind influencers," you can change your relationship with them, and reduce their power and influence. If you find that a maladaptive thought is still strongly affecting you, the following strategies can help you scroll past it, minimise its impact, and strengthen more helpful and adaptive "mind influencers":

Redirect Your Attention: When a maladaptive "mind influencer" appears, remind yourself that you control how you interact with it. Shift your focus back to your current activity or to something that truly matters to you (see Appendix 14, *Switching Off Automatic Pilot: The Art of Mindfulness*).

Visualise the Thought Differently: Imagine the message on a screen in a font that is hard to take seriously (like Comic Sans in green). This helps reduce its credibility and emotional pull.

Create a Cartoon Character: Assign a disempowering and silly cartoon persona to the maladaptive "mind influencer." Picture it speaking the messages in a ridiculous or exaggerated way.

Exaggerate the Emotional Tone: Consider what emotional path the thought is leading you down (e.g., doom and gloom, fear or anger). Choose a cartoon character to represent that path (e.g., such as "Eeyore" for gloom or the "Hulk" for anger). Imagine the "mind influencer" speaking in their voice, perhaps sped up to sound silly. When you notice the "mind influencer", you might say: "Hi 'Eeyore', I see you're back to tempt me down the path of doom and gloom again." Then ground yourself by noticing your environment.

Name the Story: Is this thought part of a repeated narrative? Common ones include: "You were better before your injury," "I'm not good enough" or "I never get things right." Label the story: "Ah, the 'good old days' story is back again." Naming it gives you distance.

Nurture Adaptive "Mind Influencers": Choose a helpful thought (e.g., something compassionate or resilient) and imagine it being said by someone you admire. Picture their voice, tone and body language. Step into their mindset: What emotions would you feel? How would you breathe? What is your posture like? Imagine yourself becoming this person and expressing the thought from that place.

See Appendix 8: *Unlocking Adaptation: A Practical Guide to the Compassionate Resilient Mind*, for an alternative way of creating CRM posts, developing alternative perspectives and enhanced strategies to become aware of when you are susceptible to threat-based "mind influencers." These strategies may be more effective if you are struggling to complete the flexible thinking feed review due to problems with cognitive flexibility (shifting your line of thinking).

Appendix 8

Unlocking Adaptation: A Practical Guide to the Compassionate Resilient Mind

Water cuts through hard rocks to shape its path, not by fighting directly against them, but by flowing with patience and persistence.

Compassionate Resilient Mind (CRM) (Water) and Critical, Closed Mind (Hard Rock)

Your brain has an inbuilt alarm system that scans for danger or psychological threats. When it detects a threat, it automatically switches into "survival mode" (protection), triggering fight (anger), flight (anxiety) or freeze (shutdown) responses. This "survival mode" response prioritises protection over growth and adaptation. It narrows its focus looking for danger, and can react quickly without awareness or taking time to stop and think. In this state, your mind tends to focus on threat-based thoughts, shutting out helpful or alternative perspectives. It can also push away difficult experiences (e.g., feelings and sensations), trying to fight them or deny they are happening. This alarm system can misfire, interpreting discomfort, uncertainty or stress as danger.

This alarm system becomes even more active when your brain is under strain. If you are tired, run down, overstimulated or emotionally overloaded, your brain is more likely to sound the alarm, even when the situation is not truly dangerous. That is why self-care, rest, and gentle pacing are so important, not just for your body, but to support your thinking brain and keep the threat system in balance.

After a brain injury, you experience difficult changes, and when this happens, your threat alarm may go off, and you can go into "survival mode". This "survival mode" tries to "protect" you and push away or fight difficult experiences by:

- Denying or minimising symptoms
- Battling through fatigue or pain
- Avoiding challenges
- Blaming others for difficulties
- Looking out for threat (e.g., looking out for and latching onto threat-based thoughts)

This "survival mode" creates a critical, closed mindset, which is rigid, harsh and unaccepting. It may internalise threats, causing frustration, guilt or self-blame, preventing you from learning to adapt. For example, someone struggling with memory slips might call themselves names or feel worthless, rather than responding with compassion.

This kind of mindset can make recovery more difficult and block meaningful adaptation. It may cause you to feel fragile, stuck or hopeless, increasing the risk of low mood and making it harder to engage with strategies that could help. You may want to give this part of your mind a name, such as the "Gatekeeper." It often operates outside of your full awareness, therefore it can be useful to learn to spot the signs of when it shows up (see Table A8.1), and unless you are actually in danger, the "Gatekeeper's" protection may need softening (i.e., the "Gatekeeper" is reacting as if you are unsafe when in fact, you are just uncomfortable or under pressure).

In contrast, a CRM is aware, self-reflecting and takes purposeful action. It helps you respond to life after brain injury with courage, flexibility and self-kindness. This mindset:

- Shows awareness and acceptance of difficult emotions, mistakes and limitations, allowing you to learn and adapt
- Makes space for difficult feelings, telling you it is okay to feel them, without being overwhelmed by them, but at the same time, supports protection by helping you face fears and difficult feelings gradually, rather than avoiding them entirely
- Combines kindness with accountability: forgiving mistakes, but still learning from them
- Encourages rest when needed, but supports persistence when it is possible
- Supports steady problem-solving instead of withdrawing or blaming
- Creates an inner environment that is open to learning, reflection and new perspectives

This CRM allows you to accept and work with your difficulties, rather than fighting against them, supporting a healthier, more adaptive recovery path that builds strength from within. You may wish to name this mindset (e.g., "Eve Olve") and recognise the signs when it is present (see Table A8.1).

Table A8.1 Signs of each mindset

Signs that the "Gatekeeper" part of your mind is present	*Signs that "Eve Olve" is present*
Says "I can't, I won't, I'm rubbish."	Says "I can't yet but I will try"
Says "I give up" or shows it by becoming distracted.	Takes on feedback and remains engaged.
Body posture becomes floppy or slouched.	Upright and relaxed posture shows confidence.
Body becomes overly tense (anger/anxiety).	Appears calm and ready to learn.
Refuses or ignores feedback.	Says "It's okay to make mistakes; I can learn from them."
Blames others for mistakes.	Takes responsibility and tries a new approach.
Avoids challenges and procrastinates.	Continues after mistakes and frustration.
Reacts quickly without thinking.	Stops and thinks before responding.

The signs of the "Gatekeeper" might not always be obvious; "survival mode" often operates on "automatic pilot" and outside of our conscious awareness. Asking trusted people around you to reflect on your reactions and body language can help you spot when your mindset has shifted.

See also Appendix 9: *Metaphors for a Compassionate Resilient Mind*, for alternative ways to think about these mindsets.

Important: Naming parts of your mind (like the "Gatekeeper" or "Eve Olve") is just a tool, not a rule. It is meant to help you create distance from your thoughts and feelings, so you can observe them without getting pulled in or overwhelmed. They are just modes or experiences for you to observe.

If naming parts of your mind makes you feel confused, anxious or upset, you do not need to use that approach. You might instead say:

- "Part of me is being very self-critical right now."
- "That sounds like my threat system reacting."
- "That's an old habit trying to keep me safe."

The key idea is this: you can notice your thoughts without becoming them. That is the first step towards responding more wisely and compassionately.

Responding to the "Gatekeeper" Part of Your Mind with "Eve Olve"

The first step is noticing when the "Gatekeeper" appears. By recognising its pattern, you create the space to choose your response with awareness and compassion, rather than being pulled along automatically by it. When you notice the "Gatekeeper" is active, you can invite in your CRM to respond. A therapist or rehabilitation professional may also support you in spotting these signs and help you practise more adaptive responses. They may also help you find more helpful "Eve Olve" ways to respond.

"Eve Olve" recognises that the "Gatekeeper's" intentions are not bad; its role is to protect, and its concerns about your safety are valid, but its methods can sometimes be too rigid or harsh. "Eve Olve" does not fight against the "Gatekeeper," but works alongside it, listening to his worries, respecting his need to shield you, and then gently showing him kinder, more flexible ways of protecting you. Over time, "Eve Olve" helps the "Gatekeeper" to soften, to trust that compassion can be protective too, and to gradually reduce the level of resistance. In this way, the "Gatekeeper" does not disappear, but becomes a wiser partner in your adaptation to your brain injury and your personal evolution.

Caution for therapists: If a person is frequently operating in "Gatekeeper" mode, it may feel invalidating or overwhelming to repeatedly bring attention to it. Pointing out these signs should therefore be used under the guidance of a clinical psychologist or neuropsychologist, who can help tailor the approach to the client's readiness and emotional resilience, alongside the right timing. It can sometimes be more helpful reflecting on "Gatekeeper" signs after his resistance has been loosened and he is no longer present.

Below are some examples of common critical, closed-minded statements ("Gatekeeper" comments) and how "Eve Olve" might respond:

Table A8.2 Examples of "Eve Olve" responses to "Gatekeeper" thoughts

Thoughts caught by the "Gatekeeper"	*"Eve Olve" response*
"I lost my balance again. I'm useless. I should just give up."	"[Name], it's okay that you lost your balance. You should be proud of showing resilience by overcoming the obstacle and making it there anyway. Keep adapting and trying."
"I got anxious again. That's a sign of weakness. I'm pathetic."	"[Name], it's human to feel anxious. Feeling anxious gives you an opportunity to show courage."

(*Continued*)

SUPPORT MATERIAL

Table A8.2 (Continued)

Thoughts caught by the "Gatekeeper"	*"Eve Olve" response*
"I couldn't find the right words. I look stupid. It must be Roger's fault for distracting me."	"[Name], it's okay if you couldn't quite find the right words. If you accept what happened, you can keep adapting. Try to explain it in another way."
"I forgot my daughter's PE kit. It's the fault of the person who hit me. I hate them."	"[Name], even if it was someone else's fault, don't let them win. Show how you can grow and adapt, that's how you beat the experience."
"I'm a failure because I'm not progressing like I want to."	"[Name], it's admirable how much progress you've made whilst dealing with your difficulties. Remember: "Success is to be measured not so much by the position one has reached… as by the obstacles overcome" Booker T. Washington."
"I'm tired and making mistakes, but I can't stop, that would show weakness."	"[Name], it's okay to rest. Rest isn't quitting, it helps you refuel, so you can keep going stronger."
"I snapped again. I'm just an angry, horrible person now."	"[Name], I can hear how upset you feel. Snapping doesn't make you a horrible person; it means you were overwhelmed. This is the 'Gatekeeper' trying to protect you, not who you truly are. Try offering yourself the same compassion you'd give someone else. You're learning your triggers and growing; that takes real courage and strength."

Increasing the Presence of Your CRM

You can strengthen your CRM mindset by creating personalised, encouraging statements that "Eve Olve" might say to you in challenging moments. Here are some examples to get you started:

Compassion-Focused

"Today, I'll meet challenges with kindness."
"When I notice a struggle, I'll respond with kindness, not criticism."

Resilience-Oriented

"I've faced and worked around difficulties before. I can draw on that resilience again."
"Each step I take today, however small, is part of my growth."

Purpose and Values

"I choose to act in ways that reflect my values, even in small things."
"I can pause, reflect, and choose responses that align with what matters most to me."

Self-Awareness and Perspective

"Whatever feelings come today, I can notice them without judgement."
"I have the capacity to step back, see the bigger picture, and choose wisely."

Practising this daily helps reinforce the voice of "Eve Olve" and supports you in navigating your recovery with greater self-compassion, resilience and hope.

Part 2: Narratives

The following narratives may help to illustrate how your mental "Gatekeeper" ("survival mode" that tries to protect), although well-meaning, prevents you from moving forward, and how "Eve Olve" (your CRM) can help. You could also write your own stories about how "Eve Olve" helps the "Gatekeeper," so that it is more suited to your narrative, and can strengthen narratives for your mind.

A Narrative about Accepting Emotions and Sensations

The "Gatekeeper" was a rigid creature who was set in his ways. He had a padlock on his mind and heart, and an armoured helmet, which kept his thoughts spinning inside. Nothing could get in or out. He said, "I must keep away from anything that makes me feel uncomfortable, sad or anxious, and I can't get my feelings out. This is what keeps me strong. If I don't do this, I might fall apart."

"Eve Olve" was a shape-shifter. When difficult feelings or sensations came in, she did not push them away; she just stretched to make space for them.

The "Gatekeeper" and "Eve Olve" lived inside Charlie's mind. One day, Charlie had a very big fall and sustained a brain injury. After this, his world did not make much sense and everything seemed more difficult. Words got stuck and emotions leaked out. The "Gatekeeper" told him, "This should not be happening. You need to keep those feelings locked away and make sure you keep away from anything that's scary or difficult to protect yourself." The "Gatekeeper" built a fence with a locked gate around Charlie to keep him safe, and put a sign up saying "keep feelings and difficult experiences out." This meant that Charlie could not go out and experience life; he remained trapped inside a prison created by the "Gatekeeper," but his feelings did not go away. They banged hard against the gate, and he felt their tension as they pushed to get out. Charlie felt exhausted from having to be on guard all the time to keep the feelings out.

One morning, "Eve Olve" walked past the gate and gently approached the "Gatekeeper." She said, "Why don't we try opening the gate just a little?", but the "Gatekeeper" warned Charlie, "Don't open it. You'll fall apart if you do. I'm only trying to protect you."

"Eve Olve" nodded with understanding.

"I know you're trying to keep Charlie safe. You've worked so hard, holding everything in for so long, but feelings aren't dangerous; they help us feel alive and signal when something meaningful has happened. If we give them space to move, they rise, they peak, and then they pass, just like waves."

The "Gatekeeper" paused. No one had ever thanked him before. "Eve Olve" continued, "Shall we try it together? You don't have to let go of control all at once. I'll stay with you. We can open the gate a little at a time and if it feels too much, we can pause and breathe."

The "Gatekeeper" felt reassured that he was not alone in trying to protect Charlie, so he stepped aside to give Charlie the space to slowly and gently open the gate. When the gate opened a little, Charlie did not crumble, so he gently opened it a little wider. The feelings that had once felt overwhelming began to flow. Some were strong, but with "Eve Olve's" calming presence and the "Gatekeeper" learning to trust the process, they passed like waves. Slowly, the tension faded.

Eventually, Charlie stepped through the gate. The "Gatekeeper," still present, no longer felt the need to hold it shut so tightly. The "Gatekeeper" knew he might still feel the urge to close the gate again, especially when fear or pain returned, but now he trusted that "Eve Olve" would be there to help him pause, breathe and respond differently. The "Gatekeeper" still remained with Charlie, but their relationship had changed. With "Eve Olve" guiding them both, they had found a gentler, more flexible way forward, one that honoured safety, whilst making space for life to be lived.

Reflect and explore:

- Do you have a gate that is keeping difficult feelings or sensations out?
- What is it keeping out?
- What are the disadvantages of keeping the gate closed?
- Are you missing out on anything by keeping it closed?
- How could you open it slowly and gradually?
- How could an "Eve Olve" help you?
- What would he/she say/do?

A Narrative about Accepting Imperfections and Adapting to Limitations

Your mind is like your house that you have lived in all your life. It feels like home, and it is comfortable because it is so familiar to you. You know how to turn the lights on. You know where everything is and how to move around inside. The imperfections can especially bring comfort. A small crack by the light switch or the uneven floorboard near the door are all part of the emotional landscape of "home" because they feel familiar and lived in; they give you a sense of belonging and give character, feeling like they are truly yours.

Suddenly, a storm arrives, like a brain injury, and everything changes. After the storm, Charlie woke in the same house, but it was not the same. The wiring was unfamiliar; the light switches no longer worked the way he expected. He did not know where anything was. He could not find his words, and he kept forgetting things. The home he knew had become unfamiliar and no longer felt like home. Charlie felt uncomfortable and confused.

Inside this altered landscape, two forces lived within Charlie's mind. One was "Eve Olve," a fluid, adaptable shape-shifter. "Eve Olve" thrived on progress, not perfection. As a shape-shifter, "Eve Olve's" power came from her ability to change; as she leant into new experiences (even messy, painful ones), she grew a new layer of strength.

Opposite this was the "Gatekeeper" who was a rigid, black-and-white creature who resisted change, feared vulnerability and demanded the old order be maintained at all costs. The "Gatekeeper" insisted on perfection, rejected feedback and tried to protect Charlie by encouraging him to deny the changes, pretend nothing was different, and cling to old habits no matter how futile.

When Charlie attempted to cook in his unfamiliar house, he became confused; he forgot steps and missed timings. The "Gatekeeper" tensed and whispered sharply, "Stay away from this. You're not good enough anymore. Pretend you're the same. Don't let anyone see you struggle." Anger and frustration welled up inside Charlie, and he felt the urge to give up.

Then "Eve Olve" stepped forward, not to silence the "Gatekeeper," but to join him. She gently said,

"I know this feels overwhelming. You're trying to protect Charlie from failing and feeling exposed, and that's understandable. But we can support him together. The new wiring is confusing, but his home isn't broken; it's just different. Let's take it one step at a time."

She turned to Charlie with warmth. "Let's use strategies. Let's follow step-by-step recipes, check off each step, set reminders. You're not alone in this."

With the "Gatekeeper's" careful watch still present, but less tense, and "Eve Olve's" guidance, Charlie took cautious steps forward. Slowly, confidence began to return. The "Gatekeeper" no longer stood in the way, but stood alongside, watching with care, ready to speak up if needed, but also learning to trust "Eve Olve's" words and take a step back.

With each mistake accepted and each limitation acknowledged, Charlie discovered more about his new wiring. He learned sometimes, to compensate for his limitations it and sometimes, just to live with them peacefully whilst navigating his way towards what matters most.

Gradually, the unfamiliar began to feel familiar. The cracks, the uneven floors, the quirks all became part of a renewed home. Not the one he had before, but one he could truly call his own. With both protection and compassion working together, acceptance transformed the house into a place of belonging. And slowly, it began to feel like home again.

Reflect and explore:

- Are there any ways in which your "house" is different now?
- Are there ways in which it is the same?
- Do you have a part of your mind that acts like a "Gatekeeper" and does not like change or accepting mistakes?
- Is it trying to protect you from anything (e.g., fear of failure/shame)?
- Does it cause any problems?
- What would be the disadvantages of letting the "Gatekeeper" part of your mind run loose without having an "Eve Olve" there to help it?
- Are there ways in which "Eve Olve" could slowly, but gradually, help you face difficult things?
- What would "Eve Olve" say to help you?

Appendix 9

Metaphors for a Compassionate Resilient Mind

The "martial arts" metaphor helps you to understand that by putting up resistance against intrusive experiences, you increase their tension against you; they become stronger, and they are more likely to have a stronger grip on you. Once you learn to embrace them by relaxing into them, their tension reduces, they become more pliable, and you can find ways to work with them and/or around them, which enables you to adapt and learn from them.

Whilst it may sometimes be necessary to focus on your unwanted, intrusive experiences to navigate them, and grow and learn from them, this is not always helpful, and sometimes, it may be important to change your focus to your wider values, which help you to enjoy living life. For example, sometimes, people develop an obsessive focus on their symptoms (e.g., anxious thoughts, pain and fatigue), which prevents them from getting on with their life. The "unwelcome guest" metaphor is a useful metaphor taken from Acceptance and Commitment Therapy (ACT), which helps you to understand that if you spend all your time fighting intrusive experiences (e.g., thoughts, fatigue, anxiety and pain), you can miss out on life and magnify the intrusive experiences; whereas, if you accept them, you can learn to live beyond them and get on with your life (Luoma, Hayes, & Walser, 2007, pp. 39–40).

Appendix 9a

Martial Arts Metaphor

In martial arts, pushing against resistance (or your opponent) can make things worse. If you push hard against your opponent and become tense, several things happen:

- You feel more resistance pushing back against you.
- You become less sensitive to your opponent's movements, and you lose awareness of where they might go next.
- Your body stiffens and your movements slow.
- You expend more energy in the wrong direction, and can feel more exhausted.

Instead of pushing, skilled martial artists learn to embrace the resistance and relax into it. Resistance is not the enemy, but the partner in movement. By softening movements and responding with awareness in the moment, martial artists can:

- Move around resistance, rather than getting stuck in it.
- Redirect energy, rather than being overwhelmed by it.
- Use the opponent's force to gather momentum, turning it into something constructive.

Whilst in martial arts, the strategy of yielding and flowing is used to eventually overpower the opponent, the Compassionate Resilient Mind (CRM) aim is different, and we are not seeking to defeat symptoms or force them into submission. Instead, we take inspiration from the method: meeting what arises with softness, awareness and adaptability. The goal is not victory, but wise partnership with our experience; learning to adapt and evolve from it, shaping a new path to a meaningful life:

Water cuts through hard rocks to shape its path, not by fighting directly against them, but by flowing with patience and persistence.

How This Relates to a Compassionate Resilient Mind (CRM) Response to a Brain Injury

After a brain injury, it is natural to feel like you are constantly battling your symptoms, trying to force memory lapses to stop, pushing through fatigue or getting angry with your brain for "not working like it used to."

SUPPORT MATERIAL

But the CRM takes a different path. It invites you to:

- Notice what is happening without judgment
- Stay grounded in the present moment
- Adapt with flexibility, compassion and strategy

Just as a martial artist is trained to meet force, not with brute strength, but with skilled, strategic movement, the CRM helps you meet life's disruptions with thoughtful, flexible action. Rather than pushing away your experiences, you learn to work with them constructively; adapting, flowing and responding with resilience. This is not about resisting symptoms, but understanding them as challenges that signal where adaptation and learning may be possible.

Reflective Worksheet: Pushing or Adapting?

Use this worksheet to explore areas where you may be reacting rigidly (pushing), and how you can begin to respond more adaptively.

Table A9.1 Applying the martial arts method

Challenge/symptom	*What I usually do (PUSH reaction)*	*What happens when I push*	*What I could do differently (ADAPT response)*
E.g., I keep forgetting appointments	Get angry with myself, say "I'm useless"	Feel demoralised, avoid making plans	Accept that this happens, use calendar + reminders, praise myself for problem-solving

Appendix 9b

The Unwelcome Guest

The Embarrassing Neighbour (aka Mo)

Charlie decides to host a party for his friends and neighbours. He has just moved into the area and has got to know people already. The party is going well, but then there is a knock at the door. His heart sinks when his neighbour, Mo, turns up. Mo is an annoying neighbour who smells of fish and wears an 80s wig. She is arrogant and embarrasses him in front of his guests. She is the "unwelcome guest".

Charlie is mortified. He tries different strategies to deal with her:

Strategy 1: Slam the Door

Charlie tells Mo to leave. But since the door must remain open for other guests, she just comes back in and is smelly, loud and annoying.

Consequence: Mo keeps coming back, and Charlie gets more stressed each time.

Strategy 2: Stand Guard

Charlie tries to prevent Mo from coming in by standing by the door, determined to block her re-entry.

Consequence: Whilst everyone else enjoys the party, Charlie misses out entirely.

Strategy 3: Keep Her Contained

Fed up with missing the fun, Charlie lets Mo in, but spends all his energy trying to stop her from being annoying.

Consequence: She gets louder and demands more attention. Charlie is still not enjoying the party.

Strategy 4: Acceptance (Enter "Eve Olve")

Eventually, Charlie (guided by his inner "Eve Olve"; his CRM) decides to take a different approach. He accepts that Mo will always be there, but instead of trying to get rid of her or giving her the spotlight, he lets her do her thing, whilst he shifts his focus back to enjoying his guests. In other words, he does not fight or control her. He adapts to her being there.

Consequence: Mo is still there, but she is no longer dominating Charlie's attention. When the spotlight is no longer on her, she starts to calm down. Charlie learns he can have fun, even with her in the background.

The CRM Perspective

Mo represents the unwanted experiences that often follow a brain injury (e.g., memory slips, fatigue, anxiety or emotional outbursts). She is the "Gatekeeper" part of your mind that wants to bar the door, fight these symptoms or make them disappear. But the more you resist, the louder and more disruptive they become.

"Eve Olve" (your CRM; the flexible and adaptive part of your mind) understands that life after brain injury is unpredictable. She does not waste energy trying to get rid of symptoms. Instead, she lets them be there without letting them take centre stage, and gets on with what is meaningful to her.

Reflection Questions:

- What are the "Mo moments" in your life? (e.g., symptoms, emotions, worries that keep showing up uninvited).
- How do you usually respond when these show up?
- Is your "Gatekeeper" in charge (e.g., trying to slam the door or guard the room?)
- How might "Eve Olve" handle these situations differently?
- Are you willing to let "Mo" be there in the background, whilst you return to the party?

Reference

Luoma, J. B., Hayes, S. C., & Walser, R. D. (2017). *Learning ACT: An acceptance and commitment therapy skills training manual for therapists.* New Harbinger Publications.

Appendix 10

Acceptance and Resilience Goals: Choosing Growth over Perfection

People sometimes avoid setting goals because they have a fear of not getting things right, or fear that their weaknesses or symptoms will be exposed if they try (see Appendix 12: *From Perfectionism to Progress: A Compassionate Resilient Mind Exercise*; see also Chapter 5: *Living Beyond Anxiety: A Compassionate, Resilient Approach*). Difficulties accepting personal limitations can also lead to resistance in using helpful strategies, for example, refusing to use a diary to compensate for memory problems.

It takes courage and kindness to accept symptoms, mistakes and weaknesses. It is only by accepting them that you can begin to adapt, learn and grow. If we were perfect, we would never have opportunities for growth. Avoiding goals because of fear, means avoiding what is meaningful to us. By contrast, accepting challenges, rather than resisting them enables adaptation (see *Martial Arts* metaphors in Appendix 9: *Metaphors for a Compassionate Resilient Mind*).

Setting Resilience and Acceptance Goals

Instead of only focusing on outcome-based goals (e.g., "I'll walk 100 metres without losing my balance"), it can be more helpful to set Compassionate Resilient Mind (CRM) goals, i.e., goals that focus on the process of showing resilience, persistence and compassion when things are hard (e.g., "I'll attempt to walk 100 metres and keep going even when it's difficult. I'll then be kind to myself and take a rest").

You can also set acceptance goals, which help you to acknowledge, adapt to and respond helpfully to your symptoms or limitations. These may include:

1. Learning to cope with mistakes (e.g., making mistakes on purpose to build tolerance)
2. Recognising limitations or errors as they occur
3. Using strategies to compensate for difficulties
4. Responding to challenges in a compassionate, resilient way

Making Your Goals SMART

Formulate your goals using the SMART framework:

- **S**pecific: Clearly defined
- **M**easurable: You can tell when it is achieved
- **A**daptive: Moves you towards your values

SUPPORT MATERIAL

- **R**ealistic: Achievable given your current circumstances
- **T**imed: Includes a clear time frame

Table A10.1 Examples of resilience and acceptance SMART goals

Resilience/acceptance goal	**SMART goal formulation**
"Talk to myself with a compassionate resilient mind (CRM) when I make a mistake."	"Next time I make a mistake, I'll replace a self-critical comment with a compassionate response (see Appendix 8, *Unlocking Adaptation: A Practical Guide to the Compassionate Resilient Mind*)."
"Accept doing things in a simpler way when needed."	"Tomorrow, I'll make a sandwich, whilst sitting on my perching stool to conserve energy."
"Recognise when I haven't done things perfectly."	"Next week, my therapist's rating of how many prompts I need during a task will match my own self-rating."
"Tolerate mistakes in a safe environment."	"Tomorrow, I'll deliberately mispronounce two words during a conversation with my partner to practise accepting small mistakes."
"Keep going when things are difficult."	"I'll stick to my physiotherapy exercises for 5 minutes, focusing on persistence, not perfection."
"Show resilience in action."	"I'll record my physio session and count how many times I'll respond to challenges, setbacks or the 'Gatekeeper' with my CRM (Goal: at least three 'Eve Olve' responses.)"

Worksheet A10.1—New Goals for Acceptance Template

Use this worksheet to create your own personalised resilience and acceptance goals. Reviewing your progress regularly can help you celebrate growth, refine your strategies, and build confidence in your ability to adapt and thrive.

Resilience/acceptance goal	*SMART goal formulation*

Appendix 11

Turning Procrastination into Meaningful Action

Why Do We Procrastinate?

Procrastination is a common human experience, especially when a task feels boring, difficult, overwhelming or unpleasant. Sometimes, procrastination can also happen simply because your attention gets sucked into something more enjoyable or stimulating, such as checking your phone, watching TV or doing an easier task instead.

When you procrastinate, it can be your mind's way of protecting you from discomfort, whether that is fear, a boring task, self-doubt, overwhelm or the worry that you might fail. These feelings trigger the brain's "survival mode", a protective state symbolised by the "Gatekeeper" (see Appendix 8: *Unlocking Adaptation: A Practical Guide to the Compassionate Resilient Mind*). The "Gatekeeper" prioritises short-term relief by steering you away from the task, even if that means avoiding things that truly matter to you. This means that you get drawn into pleasurable distractions by the impulsive part of your brain that simply seeks immediate gratification without thinking through long-term consequences. After a brain injury, the part of your brain that helps you "stop and think" may not work as well. This can make it harder to step back and consider whether acting on an impulse will lead to a helpful outcome. As a result, you may find yourself putting things off or procrastinating more often.

After a brain injury, it can become even harder to get started. Fatigue, reduced motivation and fear of failure can all contribute to putting things off, and you may have difficulties in stopping yourself acting on your impulses to seek immediate gratification. You may find yourself saying, "I'll do it later," but often, later never comes.

The Cycle of Avoidance

Avoidance may offer short-term relief, but it tends to create long-term consequences. You may find tasks pile up and pressure builds. You may feel frustrated, guilty, or low in mood, which can make it even harder to begin. This cycle can leave you feeling "stuck" in a cycle of avoidance. With the help of compassion, resilience and structure, you can shift out of this "stuckness" and begin moving forward. This worksheet is designed to help you turn avoidance into purposeful action.

Step 1: Reframe the Task as a SMART Goal

The first step in overcoming procrastination is to make the task clear and manageable.

Use the SMART goal format:

- **S**pecific: "What will I do?"
- **M**easurable: "How will I know when I've finished?"
- **A**daptive: "Does it help me move towards a meaningful or valued life?"
- **R**ealistic: "Can I do it within my current abilities?"
- **T**imed: "When will I start, and for how long?"

Example SMART Goal

"I'll do the housework at 9:00 a.m. on Tuesday mornings for 30 minutes or until I've vacuumed the whole house."

Step 2: Notice the Reasons You Put It Off

We all have thoughts or "excuses" that show up when we want to avoid a task. Instead of judging yourself for them, write them down and explore their impact.

Table A11.2 Reasons and disadvantages

Reason for putting it off	*Disadvantage of avoiding it*
"I'm tired; I'll do it tomorrow."	"I'm always tired, if I wait until I feel full of energy, it may never get done."
"I don't like doing it."	"I usually feel better once it's done. Leaving it makes me feel more stressed."
"I'm too busy; I'll do it another day."	"I keep saying that, and it keeps getting pushed back."
"Someone called, so I stopped."	"I could've scheduled the call later. If I stop every time something else comes up, the task never gets done."

Step 3: Explore the Pros and Cons

Next, reflect on the short- and long-term consequences of both doing the task as planned and putting it off.

Worksheet A3.1—Pros and Cons

	Short term		*Long term*	
	Advantage	*Disadvantage*	*Advantage*	*Disadvantage*
Putting off the task	Comfort now Do something more enjoyable	Guilt Pressure builds Loss of momentum	None, it usually stays undone	Increased stress Loss of self-confidence
Doing It as planned	Sense of progress The task gets completed and I stop worrying out it	Mild discomfort Tiredness	Feel accomplished Build motivation and routine	May still feel hard, but I grow stronger and more capable

SUPPORT MATERIAL

Step 4: Create Motivating Reminders

Now think about the excuses you usually make to yourself when you put a task off. Think about how you would respond to them with your Compassionate Resilient Mind (CRM), which instills purposeful action and compassion. You can use these as self-reminders when you feel like putting the task off. The CRM acknowledges feelings, validates struggle and gently redirects towards purposeful action.

Excuse-maker says…	*CRM-inspired purposeful action replies…*
"I'm tired, I'll do it tomorrow."	"It's understandable I feel tired. I can still take one small step now; my future self will thank me for lightening tomorrow's load."
"I don't feel like it now, I'll do it tomorrow."	"It's okay not to feel like it. Feelings don't have to decide for me; one small step now will bring me relief and pride later."
"I'm too busy, I'll do it another day."	"I see that I'm busy. Doing a little today prevents the stress from piling up tomorrow and helps me feel more in control."
"I don't want to do it, it's boring. If I leave it, someone else will do it."	"I can acknowledge it's boring, but my values matter. Doing it myself now honours my responsibility and frees me to enjoy other things later."
"It'll be uncomfortable."	"Yes, it may feel uncomfortable. I can breathe through it, knowing the discomfort will pass and the sense of achievement will last."
"It won't matter if I delay."	"It may feel like it doesn't matter, but each delay adds up. Taking action now helps my future self."

Step 5: Gently Use Rewards

It is okay to motivate yourself with small, meaningful rewards. In fact, it can make the process more enjoyable and sustainable. You can even turn your procrastination activity into your reward.

Procrastination diversion activity	*Use it as a reward for*
Phoning my friend	After 30 minutes of focused work
Making a cup of coffee	After completing one part of the task
Watching TV	Once the task is done for the day
Playing on my phone	After taking one small action step

Step 6: Surf the Urge

When you feel the urge to procrastinate, you can practise urge surfing (see Appendix 35: *Strengthening Your Mental Brakes with a Compassionate Resilient Mind (CRM)*. It involves noticing the urge, pausing and letting it pass without reacting. This helps you move from your impulsive "Primitive Brain" and the "Gatekeeper" urges to reduce discomfort at all costs, to your wise and intentional CRM.

You might say:

- "I notice the urge to avoid this task."
- "Hello 'Gatekeeper', I know you're trying to protect me from discomfort by getting me to avoid what is difficult or boring, but I don't have to listen to you."

- "Let's ride this wave and choose what really matters."

Over time, this strengthens your "mental brakes" and builds emotional resilience.

Step 7: CRM Action Planning Sheet

This worksheet integrates CRM strategies and strategies for how to navigate impulses from Appendix 35: *Strengthening Your Mental Brakes with a Compassionate Resilient Mind (CRM)*, helping you take intentional action, even when strong urges or avoidance show up.

Worksheet A7.2—CRM-Based Action Plan

What task are you avoiding?
Why does this matter to you? (what personal value is it linked to?)
What are you tempted to do instead? (what are your impulses telling you to do?)
What would the "Gatekeeper" (the part of the brain that is trying to protect you from discomfort) say to get you to avoid discomfort? (see Appendix 8: *Unlocking Adaptation: A Practical Guide to the Compassionate Resilient Mind.*)
What would your CRM ("Eve Olve") say in response?
What is the smallest action you can take today?
What strategies can help you apply your "mental brakes"?
What reward or encouragement will help reinforce this?

Appendix 12

From Perfectionism to Progress: A Compassionate Resilient Mind Exercise

Perfectionism is the belief that you must meet high (often unrealistic or unrelenting) standards in order to feel okay about yourself or to avoid failure, criticism or disapproval. It can feel like a necessary driver of success, as if letting go of it might mean lowering your standards, losing motivation or losing control.

Hidden Costs of Perfectionism

Perfectionism is often fuelled by a fear-based mindset, a belief that mistakes are unacceptable and flaws must be avoided or hidden. In this mindset, self-worth depends on getting everything "just right"; mistakes (which are inherently human) feel intolerable; feedback can feel threatening; learning feels unsafe; and we can become hypercritical of both ourselves and others. This, in turn, creates difficulty adapting to change or limitations.

This way of thinking is also a form of the "Gatekeeper" mindset. The "Gatekeeper" is trying to protect you, guarding against the pain of failure, rejection or shame. One of the ways it does this is by criticising harshly, sending messages like "You're not good enough," "You should have done better" or "You'll never succeed unless it's perfect." The "Gatekeeper" believes this tough inner voice will keep you safe and motivated, but instead it fuels self-doubt and pressure. By clinging to rigid standards, it aims to keep you in control. However, in doing so, it closes the door to adaptation, flexibility and resilience, and can lead to worse outcomes by causing you to:

- Give up because you are not doing something perfectly
- Feel paralysed by fear of making mistakes
- Be overly self-critical when goals are not met
- Avoid new opportunities that feel too difficult in case you fail
- Focus too much on the detail and miss the bigger picture
- Experience performance anxiety that worsens outcomes
- Put things off (procrastinate) and avoid completing them because of fear of not doing them well enough
- Refuse to take breaks when you need them, leading to exhaustion
- Set goals that are too easy because you are worried about making mistakes
- Struggle to accept mistakes, and therefore miss out on learning from them
- Dismiss perspectives that differ from your own, creating relationship difficulties, blocking learning and reducing cognitive flexibility

From Fear to Flexibility: Activating Your Compassionate Resilient Mind

A Compassionate Resilient Mind (CRM) does not ask you to stop caring or striving. It does not reject high standards; instead it reframes them with purpose, perspective and psychological flexibility.

When you activate your CRM (see "Eve Olve," Appendix 8, *Unlocking Adaptation: A Practical Guide to the Compassionate Resilient Mind*), you are not driven by fear, but by wisdom and care. You can act intentionally, not in denial of your imperfections, but in full awareness of them, choosing what is helpful, meaningful and realistic in each moment, rather than chasing what is flawless.

The CRM mindset is:

- Open to learning from mistakes
- Flexible in how it defines success
- Adaptable in the face of change, limitations and uncertainty
- Compassionate towards imperfection, both your own and others'

Your CRM (or "Eve Olve") might respond to the "Gatekeeper's" harsh criticism like this:

"Thank you for trying to keep me safe by pushing me to do better. I know you don't want me to fail, but I don't have to be flawless to be worthy or to make progress. Mistakes help me learn, and calm, flexible effort will take me further than fear ever can."

Letting go of perfectionism does not mean lowering your standards, it means liberating your potential.

Reflection Exercise: How Does Perfectionism Affect You?

What does perfectionism push you to do (or avoid)?

When has perfectionism helped you?

When has it held you back or caused problems?

Reflection: What Mindset Do You Want to Choose?

What does your "Gatekeeper" ("survival mode" part of your brain) say when you fear making a mistake, or when you have made a mistake or fallen short of achieving your goal?

What would "Eve Olve" (your CRM) say instead? (i.e., what is a response that shows compassion and keeps you aligned with what matters to you).

What does "good enough" look like for you today?

____

How can you act with purpose, rather than perfection?

____

Purposeful CRM Actions

Choose one task where perfectionism is getting in the way.

1. The task is:

   ____

2. My perfectionistic fear is:

   ____

3. One compassionate action I can take:

   ____

4. How I will remind myself that I am enough:

   ____

CRM supportive statements for when you fall short of your goals or make mistakes:

- "I am worthy and enough, even when I make mistakes."
- "Mistakes are learning opportunities; they don't define my worth."
- "Not achieving perfection doesn't mean I've failed; it means I'm human."
- "My value as a person comes from who I am, not from flawless outcomes."
- "Not achieving my desired outcome provides opportunity to reflect, adjust and move forward, one step at a time. This is how I adapt and evolve."
- "I can celebrate my effort, not just the result."
- "By responding with compassion and flexibility, I make space for progress, learning and growth, without needing to be perfect."

Appendix 13

Rose-Tinted Reflections: Navigating the Good Old Days Bias

"Good Old Days" Bias

After a brain injury, it is common to compare how you are now with how you believe that you were before, but these comparisons are often distorted. This is because people often remember their pre-injury selves through a selective or idealised lens (e.g., thinking things like, "I never made mistakes" or "My memory was perfect"), whilst viewing their current selves through a much more critical filter (e.g., "I always get things wrong now"). This pattern, known as the "good old days" bias, can lead you to:

- Overestimate how much you have changed
- Underestimate your past difficulties or flaws
- Ignore your current strengths and adaptability
- Feel stuck in a "then versus now" narrative (e.g., "I was so much better before")
- Miss other contributing factors (e.g., stress, fatigue, ageing, life complexity) that might also explain your current difficulties

This distorted comparison can also deepen grief. If you saw your pre-injury self through rose-tinted glasses, the sense of having lost that version of yourself becomes even more painful. You may mourn an identity that was never entirely accurate to begin with, which can:

- Prolong emotional suffering
- Make it harder to engage with rehabilitation or growth
- Lead to feelings of disconnection, shame or failure

How It Blocks Adaptation

This distorted self-image, which can make you appear as though you have lost your old self, can activate your brain's threat system, known as "survival mode" ("Gatekeeper") (see Appendix 8: *Unlocking Adaptation: A Practical Guide to the Compassionate Resilient Mind*). In "survival mode", your nervous system prioritises protection over learning. Your brain is on alert, scanning for danger, including psychological threats, such as failure, loss or shame. It constrains flexible thinking, narrows attention, and often relies on rigid patterns or avoidance as a form of self-protection. This automatic "survival mode" can block the very processes needed for recovery and adaptation.

Here is how it can play out:

- Your perception of yourself will remain rigid, and your mind will not be open to information that conflicts with your existing perception.
- You may dismiss small achievements because they do not measure up to your imagined "old self"
- You may avoid trying new things out of fear that they will confirm your "decline".
- The "good old days" bias will distort the picture of who you are. As a result, you may stay emotionally stuck, unable to acknowledge or respond to the reality of your current needs, as adaptation begins with accurate self-awareness.

A Compassionate Resilient Mind Perspective (CRM)

This exercise helps you to reassess past and present thinking through a balanced lens. It encourages you to approach your experience with a balanced, flexible mindset, led by your CRM, rather than by self-criticism or emotional distortion. It is not about denying the challenges of brain injury, but about recognising nuance, context and other contributing factors that may help you respond more usefully to your current difficulties.

Use Worksheet A13.1 to reflect on the following:

1. List cognitive and emotional difficulties you notice now (e.g., memory problems, slowed thinking, increased irritability, anxiety).
2. Consider how often or intensely you experienced similar problems before your injury.
3. Explore other possible reasons for changes, things that may be contributing now, even if they are not directly caused by your brain injury (e.g., fatigue, stress, increased life demands, mood).

Other important notes:

Identifying other factors does not mean your symptoms are "not real" or "not brain-injury related." Many post-injury challenges arise from a combination of neurological, psychological and situational influences. A more complete picture helps guide more effective coping and self-support.

This exercise is also not about proving your thoughts "wrong" or silencing them. Your beliefs, especially ones shaped by loss, grief or identity disruption, are often rooted in valid experiences and protective intentions. In CRM work, we are not trying to silence those beliefs; we are simply trying to help you meet them with more curiosity, flexibility and compassion. The following exercise is designed to help you view the changes through the more flexible lens of the CRM.

Table A13.1 Example: widening your lens of flexibility to evaluate pre- and post-injury difficulties

Current problem	*How was this before your injury?*	*Other possible contributing factors (besides brain injury)*
"I feel like my thinking is slow all the time, but it doesn't stop me doing things."	"I noticed slower thinking occasionally, especially when tired."	"I've been working overtime since returning to work, and I'm constantly exhausted."
"I forget to lock the door around twice a month."	"I occasionally forgot when I was very stressed, maybe once or twice a year."	"I'm under significant stress at the moment, especially around finances."
"I get angry and shout at my husband nearly every day."	"I used to argue maybe once a week, but not as often."	"We've had a lot of financial pressure recently, and we're arguing more overall."
"I forget around 50% of my appointments."	"I hardly ever missed appointments before."	"I now have many more appointments to manage than I used to."

Reconnecting with Your CRM

Take a moment to pause, breathe and consider the following questions, not from the voice of the "Gatekeeper" ("survival mode"; see Appendix 8: *Unlocking Adaptation: A Practical Guide to the Compassionate Resilient Mind*), but from your CRM:

- Has your view of your pre-injury self shifted in any way?
- What are you beginning to notice that you may have overlooked before?
- How might a more balanced perspective help you support yourself more effectively?
- What would it be like to respond to yourself with compassion, rather than comparison?

You might try some of the CRM-based affirmations to help anchor a CRM mindset, for example:

> "I can notice difficulties and differences without judging myself for them."

Responding to the "Good Old Days" Bias

Think of a way in which you would like to respond to the "good old days" bias dialogue with your CRM ("Eve Olve") next time it turns up. Examples are below:

- "Hello, 'good old days' bias story. I see you're back again. I know you're showing up because something feels difficult right now. You're trying to protect me from that pain by reminding me of how things used to be, but this doesn't help. I also know that your version of the past isn't the whole truth; it's rose-tinted, and whilst I understand why you long for how things were, clinging to that version keeps me stuck, disconnected and self-critical. So, thank you for reminding me of what mattered to me then, but today, I will choose to meet today's reality with compassion and resilience by supporting myself in the present, rather than comparing myself to the past. I'm allowed to grieve, but I'm also allowed to adapt and move forward."

- "Hello 'good old days' bias story. Thank you for the reminder, but today I'm choosing compassion and adaptation over comparison."
- "Hello 'good old days' bias story. Old me isn't gone, s/he's just evolving. Today I choose not to listen to you."
- Write your response here or you can choose one of the responses above:

See Appendix 14: for *Switching off Automatic Pilot: The Art of Mindfulness*, mindfulness strategies to redirect your attention, if you find yourself stuck ruminating in comparisons of how you used to be.

SUPPORT MATERIAL

Appendix 14

Switching Off Automatic Pilot: The Art of Mindfulness

What Is Mindfulness?

When we feel anxious, low or overwhelmed, our attention often gets hijacked by:

- Worry about the future
- Rumination about the past
- Harsh self-judgment or imagined threat

This narrows our perspective, fuels emotional reactivity, and can leave us feeling stuck. Our minds can be more easily hijacked by unwanted thoughts and feelings after a brain injury, as the purposeful "stop and think" part of the brain may not work as effectively, making it harder to pause and step back from these reactions. This can lead to being on "automatic pilot," where your reactions are driven more by habits, impulses or strong emotions than by conscious choice and reflective awareness. Mindfulness is the practice of gently guiding your attention to in the present moment, without judgment. It helps you to stop, think and become aware by interrupting "automatic pilot" and training your mind to shift focus towards what is happening right now, both within you and around you. This creates a space between what is going on in your internal world and how you respond. In that space, your rational, purposeful, Compassionate Resilient Mind (CRM) can lead the way, rather than letting the "automatic pilot" (reactive) parts of your mind (like the "survival mode" the "Gatekeeper") take over. You become the agent of your attention, shaping your response in a way that reflects what will support you right now, not just what emotion, sensation or thought is shouting the loudest. This is the start of reflective awareness, purposeful action and you taking control.

Everyday Mindfulness Practice

Mindfulness is about how you relate to experience. You can begin practising it through small, sensory-rich activities in daily life.

Bodily Awareness Practice

Imagine you have just woken up in a new body, every sensation is fresh. Try noticing:

- The feeling of your breath entering and leaving your body
- The movement of your arms or legs

- The contact between your body and the ground
- Describe what comes through your senses in detail

(See Appendix 16: *Relaxation Skills: Finding Calm and Balance* for more sensory grounding.)

Mindful Activity Practice

Use everyday moments as mindfulness opportunities:

- Mindful walking (e.g., walking the dog):
    - Tune into your footsteps
    - Notice the breeze, sounds, smells
    - Feel the leash in your hand, the rhythm of movement
    - Describe what you can see
- Mindful chores (e.g., washing dishes):
    - Focus on the water temperature
    - Watch the bubbles form and pop
    - Feel the texture of objects, hear the clink of crockery

Welcoming Uncomfortable Experiences

When discomfort shows up (e.g., in the form of fatigue, anger, pain, sadness, intrusive thoughts), mindfulness teaches you to accept these experiences and make space for them, rather than block them. The following mindfulness strategies help you to do this:

Name the Experience: "Hello anger, we must stop meeting up like this."

Soften Around It: Imagine relaxing into the feeling, rather than tensing against it.

Surf the Wave: Let it rise and fall as you breathe in and out.

Refocus Attention: Gently return to sensation or sound.

Use the "martial arts" Metaphor (Appendix 9a: *Metaphors for a Compassionate Resilient Mind*), to visualise yielding to, and not resisting, what cannot be pushed through.

Working with a Wandering Mind

It is normal for your mind to wander. Mindfulness is not about stopping this, it is about noticing when it happens and gently guiding your attention back.

Try:

- Imagining your thoughts drifting past in balloons
- Watching your thoughts scroll across a screen, just observing, not reacting

CRM Reflection: Your thoughts may arise automatically, but you are not bound to follow them. With awareness, you can notice them, pause and choose how to respond. Mindfulness builds the foundation of your CRM, by helping you pause, choose and respond, and build purposeful action. Not through control or suppression, but through gentle, open attention.

Appendix 15

Mindfulness for Chronic Pain: Meeting Discomfort with Compassion

Mindfulness helps you to emotionally detach from the pain and relax into it. This helps us to stop fighting or putting up resistance against the sensations, which softens their tension, making them more pliable. This allows us to adapt to them in a compassionate and resilient manner (see "martial arts" metaphor, Appendix 9a: *Metaphors for a Compassionate Resilient Mind*).

Exercise 1: Befriending Pain—A Compassionate Dialogue

This mindfulness exercise helps externalise pain, creating psychological space between your awareness and the sensation. It helps externalise pain so you can relate to it with kindness, rather than judgment or fear.

Step 1: Externalise the Pain

- If you could place the pain outside your body, what would it look like?
- Consider its shape, size, texture and colour
- Does it stay the same, or does it change over time?

Step 2: Name the Pain

- What name would you give this pain? (e.g., "Morph," "Spike," "Bluey")
- Giving it a name can help you build a relationship with it

Step 3: Understand Your Pain-Character

- If "Morph" were a being, what would it be like?
- How do you know it is in pain?
- What facial expression or body posture does it have?
- What is its colour, voice, tone and movement like?
- Is it floppy or tense?
- What are its eyes like?
- What thoughts or emotions might be going through its mind?

Step 4: Soothe and Transform the Pain

Imagine gently stroking "Morph," comforting it as you would a distressed friend or animal.

As you soothe "Morph," observe whether it changes in shape, colour or emotional state.
Watch as "Morph" begins to soften as it responds to your kindness.

Step 5: Reintegration with Compassion

Now imagine placing "Morph" gently back inside your body.
Can you continue treating it with compassion and warmth?
Can you continue to be gentle and kind with this part inside you?

Exercise 2: Mindful Observation of Pain

This guided practice helps you tune into pain with curiosity, rather than reactivity, inviting a gentle shift in your experience. Mindfulness does not erase pain, but it changes how we relate to it. By softening resistance, we can meet our experience with greater flexibility and compassion.

Step-by-step Script

1. Begin by Settling:

   Find a comfortable position.
   Close your eyes.
   Begin to breathe slowly and evenly. Let each breath guide you inward.

2. Observe the Breath:

   Focus on the rhythm of your breathing.
   Inhale slowly in … and exhale gently out…
   Let your breath be like a gentle wave, slowly coming and slowly going.

3. Invite Awareness of Pain:

   As you slowly inhale, allow your awareness to move towards the area of pain.
   Notice how it feels: is it tight, sharp, dull, throbbing, heavy or tingling?
   Where does it begin and end? Are its edges smooth or jagged?
   What shape or texture does it have?

4. Be Curious, Not Critical:

   Imagine the pain as a warm flow of energy.
   Watch it slowly coming in and out as you breathe slowly in and out.
   Watch how it moves or shifts, rather than trying to change it.
   Welcome any thoughts, emotions or memories that arise. Simply acknowledge them and let them pass.

5. Breathe Into the Pain:

   With each inhale, gently breathe into the area of discomfort.
   With each exhale, allow your body to soften, becoming heavier, floppier and more relaxed.

6. If Overwhelmed, Shift Focus:

   If the sensations feel too strong, move your attention to your chest or your breathing.
   Feel the rise and fall, the warmth and calm of your breath.
   As you breathe slowly in and out, feel your body becoming warm, floppy and deeply relaxed.

7. Expand Your Awareness:

   Now, bring attention to your whole body.
   As you breathe slowly, notice any tension.
   Breathe out and allow yourself to sink deeper into relaxation. As you do this, you feel your body getting warmer and floppier and more relaxed.
   Continue this gentle rhythm, slowly breathing in and out.

8. Return Gently:

   When you feel ready, count slowly backwards from 10 to 1.
   Gradually open your eyes and return to the present moment, carrying this sense of calm with you.

Appendix 16

Relaxation Skills: Finding Calm and Balance

What Is "Relaxation"?

"Relaxation" is a way of releasing pent-up tension. By relaxing, we can help lower our levels of stress, arousal and tiredness. It can help to reduce our adrenaline levels and calm our body down when we experience the following:

- fast breathing
- increased heartbeat
- tense muscles
- sweating

Relaxation Techniques

There are several techniques that you can use to help you relax, including the following.

Quick Fix

If you find that you become stressed or tense whilst you are doing something, here is a quick way of helping you calm down:

1. Stop what you are doing.
2. Pay attention to where you feel tense in your body and try to relax those areas.
3. Breathe in through your nose and breathe out slowly and deeply through your mouth.
4. Do this a few times and then resume what you were doing.

Colour Breathing

This is a well-known technique that helps calm you down very quickly.

1. Imagine the colour blue and, as you breathe in, imagine you are breathing in blue calmness.
2. As you breathe out, imagine you are breathing out all of the red tension and replacing it with blue calm. Again, make sure you slowly breathe in through your nose and out through your mouth.

Progressive Muscle Relaxation

1. Sit or lie down comfortably and close your eyes.
2. Let the tension in your body go as you take some slow, deep breaths (slowly breathe in through your nose and out through your mouth).
3. Take note of how your head feels, especially your forehead and whether there is any tension there, and then release it.
4. Let your whole face relax.
5. Move to your neck and shoulders; let the chair or floor take the weight of your head and let your shoulders and neck relax.
6. Be aware of how your body feels as you let go of the tension.
7. Let your arms and hands sink into the chair or floor.
8. Let go of the tension in your back, and sink down into the chair or floor. Let your hips roll out.
9. Let each breath gradually become deeper and slower; take note of how your stomach is moving.
10. Slowly and gradually work through each part of your body, being aware of whether it feels tense, and slowly letting any tension drift out as you allow that part to feel heavier, floppier and more relaxed.
11. Once you have completely relaxed your body, lie still and breathe slowly and deeply.
12. When you are ready, slowly count back from 10 and open your eyes. Slowly start to move your hands and feel and stretch your body out. Take a look around the room, and then, when you are ready, slowly get up.

Appendix 17

Anger Diary

Use the anger diary below to record times when you get angry. Include the following information:

Direct Triggers: What caused you to get angry at that moment in time.

Indirect Triggers: Any things that may have reduced your frustration tolerance, making it more likely that you were going to blow up at that time.

Anger Intensity: How intense your anger was on a scale of 0–10.

Worksheet A7.1 Anger Diary

Date	*Direct trigger*	*Indirect trigger*	*Anger intensity*
	What happened to make you angry at that point in time? Who was there? What was said?	What was going on at that time or during the day that would have reduced your frustration tolerance (e.g., lots of noise, tiredness)?	Circle how angry you were on a scale from 1 to 10 (1 = not at all angry; 10 = the most angry you could possibly be).
			1 2 3 4 5 6 7 8 9 10
			1 2 3 4 5 6 7 8 9 10
			1 2 3 4 5 6 7 8 9 10
			1 2 3 4 5 6 7 8 9 10
			1 2 3 4 5 6 7 8 9 10

Appendix 18

A Narrative about Riding the Rage Storm: When the Fire Takes Over

The following story uses metaphors to describe what happens in the brain during anger surges after brain injury. Some people find stories help them notice patterns more easily than technical explanations. Take what fits, and leave what does not. You can change the story according to your preferences.

Narrative:

Charlie had a storm inside him. Since his brain injury, anger arose like a flash flood. It appeared suddenly and felt overwhelming. He shouted, swore and sometimes he broke things. After the storm passed, he felt worried and confused.

Inside his mind, the "Gatekeeper" was on high alert, panicking and shouting: "They can't treat you like this! You have to stop them! Protect yourself! Shout at them, call them names!" The "Gatekeeper" believed anger was the shield that would keep Charlie safe. However, in its desperation to guard him, it only fuelled the storm, until everything boiled over.

Then "Eve Olve" appeared, not to stop the storm, but to ride it with him. She said, "This storm is part of you, but it's not all of you. Let's learn how to sail through it."

"Eve Olve" shapeshifted into a skilled sailor. She taught Charlie that storms do not stop because you yell at them; they stop when you understand the signs, prepare the sails, and learn how to move with the waves. She showed him:

- The early wind signals in his body: heart racing, breath faster, jaw clenching. This is the build-up the moment before the outburst when the wave could still be directed.
- The first sign the weather was turning: not being able to do something or when he was asked to do something. Now he recognised this, it would help him catch the wave early.

She helped him create an internal anchor of the ship, a simple phrase he could use to pause, to give him time to set the sails up: "'Eve Olve,' help me to ride this storm." She taught him how to drop the anchor: "Step away, breathe out slowly and relax your fists."

At first, the storms still came, but "Eve Olve" stayed with him and helped him ride them out. She did not shame him, but soothed him. With her help, Charlie began to recognise the pattern and prepare. Sometimes, he could catch the storm early. Other times, he needed to recover after to apologise, to repair. And slowly, he learned how to ride the rage and he restored his self-respect.

The "Gatekeeper" began to soften, too. He stopped panicking and started cooperating. He started to say, "Let's listen to 'Eve Olve,' let's spot the signs earlier and practice dropping our anchors."

Over time, Charlie still had storms, but they no longer controlled him. He was learning to become the captain of his own ship again.

Reflect and Explore

- What is your "storm" like? What happens in your body and thoughts before an outburst?
- Can you identify the first signs before the rage builds?
- Do you have a part of your mind that acts like the "Gatekeeper" and panics or makes the storm worse?
- What kind of "anchor" could help you pause or steady yourself when you feel it coming?
- What might "Eve Olve" say to you before, during or after a storm?
- How might she help you rebuild trust in yourself or rebuild your relationships, after the storm has passed?

Ride the Rage Storm Worksheet:

Section	Guided prompts	Your reflections
Name your storm	What do you call your anger outbursts? (e.g., "Hurricane Hugo," "The Red Mist")	
Storm signals: what are the early signs?	Body signals: (e.g., clenched fists, heart beats fast), thought signs: (e.g., "It's not fair," "I can't do this"), situational triggers: (e.g., noise, being interrupted, being told "no," being told to do something)	
Build your anchor: what helps you pause?	What could help ground or pause you? (e.g., deep breaths, relax your fists) "Eve Olve" phrases to help: "I know this feels overwhelming. Let's pause to give us space to put the sails up." "What's important is not to win against the other person, but to feel in control of yourself." "Walking away isn't weakness, it's your strength." "We can say what matters later, when the storm passes."	

Appendix 19

Assertiveness Exercise

Exploring Different Communication Styles

After a brain injury, difficulties with emotional regulation or confidence may make it harder to express yourself clearly, say no, or deal with conflict. This exercise invites you to explore different styles of communication (aggressive, passive-aggressive, passive and assertive) and reflect on how each affects relationships, emotional well-being, and mutual respect.

Use the example scripts and prompt questions below to practise identifying communication styles and thinking about how situations could be handled more assertively. Assertiveness means being able to express your needs and opinions clearly, calmly and respectfully, without violating the rights of others or ignoring your own.

Scenario 1—Aggressive Communication

Script

Bob is watching television when Sam walks in and says, "I don't want to watch this rubbish, I'm turning it over."

Bob replies, "But I was enjoying this."

Sam says, "I don't care, I'm changing the channel."

Prompt Questions:

- What communication style is Sam using: aggressive, passive, passive-aggressive or assertive?
- How do you think Bob might feel in this situation?
- What problems could arise from Sam acting this way?
- How could Bob have responded differently to assert his needs, whilst seeking compromise?

Scenario 2—Passive-Aggressive Communication

Script

Dave feels reluctant to spend the whole day in town with his younger brother, Rob. Whilst he wants to maintain a good relationship, he often gets frustrated after long stretches together.

When Rob asks to go out for the day, Dave agrees, but purposefully keeps coughing throughout the trip, knowing it annoys Rob, and says "sorry" each time.

Prompt Questions

- What communication style is Dave using: aggressive, passive, passive-aggressive or assertive?
- How do you think Rob might feel in this situation?
- What issues might this behaviour cause in their relationship?
- How could Dave have expressed his feelings more directly and respectfully?
- Prompt: Consider how he could set limits without hurting Rob's feelings.

Scenario 3—Passive Communication

Script

Jim's favourite food is curry, and he likes eating it every day. Sue does not enjoy curry, but has not said anything. Instead, she quietly eats it every night without complaint.

Prompt Questions

- What communication style is Sue using: aggressive, passive, passive-aggressive or assertive?
- How do you think Sue might feel over time?
- What problems might arise if Sue continues not to speak up?
- How could Sue express her needs more openly, whilst preserving harmony in the relationship?

Scenario 4—Assertive Communication

Script

Craig and Steve are out shopping. Steve asks to borrow some money, saying he forgot his wallet. They are planning to go to the cinema later. Craig replies, "Sorry mate, you still owe me £10 from last week. I can't lend you more until that's paid back."

Prompt Questions

- What communication style is Craig using: aggressive, passive, passive-aggressive or assertive?
- How does Craig show respect for both his own boundaries and his friendship?

Appendix 20

Taming the Dragon: A CRM Relaxation Script for Anger and Embitterment

Taming Your Inner Dragon

Anger and embitterment after brain injury are not signs of weakness or failure. They are often the result of a brain that has learned to stay on high alert after loss, injustice, or repeated frustration. When this happens, anger can feel intense, automatic, and difficult to control.

This exercise uses guided imagery and breathing to help you work with anger, rather than against it. The imagery of a "dragon" is a metaphor for the brain's protection system (the "Gatekeeper"): powerful, fast-acting, and originally designed to keep you safe. When this system is overwhelmed or stuck, it can express itself as rage, bitterness, or a constant sense of being under attack.

Some people find imagery helpful because it allows them to notice emotional patterns without becoming flooded or self-critical. If the imagery does not suit you, you are free to adapt it, simplify it, or set it aside.

Creating a Calming Space to Welcome the Dragon

Begin by gently closing your eyes. Take a slow breath in through your nose… and slowly out through your mouth. Again… slowly in through your nose… and out through your mouth.

As you continue breathing at this gentle, steady pace, notice your body beginning to soften. Let your shoulders drop. Let your arms feel heavy. Let your body become loose and floppy, and relaxed.

Observing Your Dragon

Imagine that you are standing just outside a cave, which is the home of your inner "dragon".

Give your "dragon" a name. This helps you relate to it as something you can approach and understand. Examples may include "Herbert," "Typhon," "Draco" or anything that feels right to you.

As you peer into the cave, you see your "dragon" resting. You notice fire coming out from its nostrils as it breathes in… and out. This fire is a symbol of its fury, its anger, bitterness or frustration. But as you look more closely, you begin to see that beneath the fire, there is something softer, something more vulnerable.

Beneath the anger, there may be feelings, like hurt, fear, sadness or shame. Just observe these quietly. Notice if they have a shape, a colour or a movement to them.

Keep breathing with the "dragon". Slow, calm breaths in… and out… watching your "dragon" breathe in…. and out as well.

Connecting with the Dragon Using Compassion and Resilience

Now, speak gently to your "dragon".

You might say, "Draco, I see you're feeling this way. I'm here to understand, not to judge. What are you really feeling underneath the fire? What do you need to feel safe, soothed and seen?"

Listen for what the "dragon" might say. Let your response come from your compassionate resilient mind, the part of you that can offer warmth without being overwhelmed.

Now, invite the "dragon" to come out of the cave. When he does, gently place a hand on his scales. Stroke him with kindness, like you would comfort a frightened creature. As you do, notice whether the colours of his feelings shift. Do they become lighter, softer or more peaceful?

As you stroke the "dragon," he begins to breathe differently. The fire fades. With each breath out, he releases calm, silvery smoke, instead of flames. This is a smoke that is energising and soothing.

Now ask your "dragon":

- "How can you live more in line with what truly matters to you?"
- What is your fire getting in the way of?
- "What would it look like to respond with calm strength and kindness, instead of fire?"

Watch how your "dragon" changes as he connects to his values. Does his posture change? Does his face soften? How do his thoughts feel now?

Keep breathing together - in… and out…

Feel the "dragon" becoming more grounded, more peaceful, more purposeful.

Completing the Journey

As your "dragon" settles into this new way of being. You can see that he is starting to glow with calm, peaceful energy. His breathing is slow and relaxed.

Now, imagine him walking slowly, contentedly, back into the comfort of his cave; not to hide, but to rest. You watch him curl up, relaxed and safe.

As you breathe in and out, sense the peaceful energy he leaves behind. You can return to this place whenever anger flares or your fire feels out of control.

Take one more deep, calm breath in…

And a long, slow breath out.

When you are ready, gently open your eyes. Look around the room and name what you can see.

Appendix 21

Courage in Motion: Practising Safe Exposure

"Systematic desensitisation" is a technique involving you gradually and repeatedly exposing yourself to what you fear or find uncomfortable in a safe and controlled way. During this exposure process, you learn to ride out feelings of anxiety and/or discomfort until they pass.

Through repeatedly facing your fear and/or discomfort in this way, you may begin to realise that the worst will not happen, and you will start to feel more confident and in control.

There are three parts to "systematic desensitisation":

1. Identifying a fear or discomfort that you want to navigate.
2. Putting together an "anxiety or discomfort hierarchy" to gradually expose yourself to this fear or discomfort. Exposure can either be in the actual situation or in imagined situations.
3. Using relaxation techniques when you expose yourself to the things in your hierarchy (see Appendix 16: *Relaxation Skills: Finding Calm and Balance*, for relaxation techniques).

Anxiety/Discomfort Hierarchy

An anxiety or discomfort hierarchy provides a framework for gradually exposing yourself to scary situations in a graded way. You can either directly expose yourself to the situation or expose yourself to the situation in your imagination.

Use Worksheet A9.1 to create a hierarchy of scary situations.

1. Think of approximately ten scenarios that each have a different intensity of what you are particularly afraid of (e.g., fear of social situations) or find uncomfortable (noisy environments). Write them down and make sure they are well described. For example, if you feel discomfort in noisy or busy environments, a really uncomfortable situation might be having to travel on a very overcrowded train, and a less uncomfortable one might be being in a supermarket at off-peak shopping times, or imagining that you are on a bus with only a few people.

2. Give each scenario a score out of 100 according to how scared or uncomfortable it makes you feel (0 = not at all scared/uncomfortable; 100 = the most scared/uncomfortable you could possibly be). This will help to make sure that you have a varied set of scary situations.
3. Place each of the scenarios into one of the following categories according to its score out of 100; try to have at least one situation in each category:

low anxiety/discomfort	*1–19*
medium-low anxiety/discomfort	20–39
medium anxiety/discomfort	40–59
medium-high anxiety/discomfort	60–79
high anxiety/discomfort	80–100

4. Once you have finished creating your hierarchy, put all of the situations in order to create your anxiety/discomfort hierarchy for your particular fear, using Worksheet A9.1.

Facing Your Fears/Discomfort

The next step is to gradually face the fears/discomfort you have identified in this hierarchy. It can sometimes help you to face your fears if you try to use relaxation techniques, whilst you are exposing yourself to the scary/uncomfortable situation. This is because it is not possible for the body to feel anxious and relaxed at the same time. Relaxation also helps to soothe your threat system and provides self-care within the moment. When you expose yourself to your fears, do the following:

1. Practise relaxation techniques (see Appendix 16: *Relaxation Skills: Finding Calm and Balance*) and make sure you can use them effectively. Whilst you are facing your anxieties, make sure you try to relax using these techniques.
2. Expose yourself to each anxiety/uncomfortable situation in turn, starting with what is at the bottom of your hierarchy (the easiest to face). Rate your anxiety at the beginning of the exposure (on a scale from 0 to 100).
3. Continue to expose yourself to each particular situation until you start to notice your anxiety is decreasing to a manageable level, or for as long as you can cope with (rate your anxiety on a scale from 0 to 100).
4. Do not move on to the next step in your hierarchy until your anxiety/discomfort in the situation you have exposed yourself to has reached a manageable level (e.g., 50%) at the beginning of the exposure time. Keep practising until your anxiety reduces to this level.

As you move up the hierarchy towards the more worrying scenarios, each should be easier to face because you have desensitised yourself to the ones before them. Use Worksheet A21.2 to rate your fears before and after you have exposed yourself to the scary/uncomfortable situation.

Worksheet A21.1 Anxiety/Discomfort Hierarchy

Use Worksheet A21.1 to create your hierarchy of scary/uncomfortable situations.

Scary situation	*How scary/uncomfortable the situation is on a scale of 0–100%*

Use Worksheet A21.2 to monitor your anxiety/discomfort levels during exposure to the scary situations. At the beginning of the exposure, rate your anxiety on a scale of 0%–100%, and at the end of the exposure, rate your anxiety on a scale of 0%–100% (0% = not at all anxious; 50% = moderately anxious; 100% = the most scared you could possibly be).

Worksheet A21.2 Anxiety Ratings for Exposure

Scary/uncomfortable situation	*Anxiety/discomfort rating at beginning of exposure (scale: 0%–100%)*	*Anxiety/discomfort at end of exposure (scale: 0%–100%)*

Compassionate Resilient Mind (CRM) Reflection:. "Systematic desensitisation" is not about eliminating anxiety/discomfort or proving you are fearless. It is about teaching your mind and body that you can navigate discomfort with compassion, slowly and step by step. Each time you choose to face fear or discomfort, rather than avoid it, you strengthen your CRM. This is purposeful action in motion driven by adaptation, not avoidance; guided by courage, and rooted in compassion, not criticism.

Caution: After a brain injury some people find it difficult to filter out "environmental noise," making busy environments feel uncomfortable. Some people may, with practice, increase their tolerance for stimulating settings. Others may find that highly busy environments will always remain too draining. In these cases, you may need to adapt wisely, for example, encouraging shopping at quieter times, choosing less busy cafés, or finding alternative ways to engage in valued activities without unnecessary overload.

Appendix 22

Therapeutic Letter for Forgiveness and Healing

Use the template below to help you process the feelings of injustice that you experienced as a result of the traumatic event.

[Date]

Dear [Your name/name of the person who caused you harm],

I write this letter as a way of processing what has happened to me, in the hope that it will help me to move forward with my recovery and my future life.

Describing the Event That Injured You

On [date], something happened that has changed my life. *[describe the event or situation that caused harm]*. As a result, I was injured *[describe your injuries and what happened next, e.g., hospital stay/rehabilitation]*.

This event has had a significant effect on me, *[describe how the event affected your life or changed your beliefs, emotions, physical consequences, changes in cognitive skills]*.

Expressing How You Feel

Thinking about the event and what has happened to me leaves me feeling *[describe any ongoing emotions or feelings]*. I continue to be affected by the consequences of this event, for example *[mention any ongoing challenges, physical or cognitive difficulties, emotional or psychological issues etc.]*. My life is different now because *[report any changes in your life as a consequence of the event]*.

Offering Forgiveness

I have come to understand that holding onto my feelings of injustice or embitterment is having a detrimental effect on me. It holds me back from making a full recovery and getting on with my life. I want to forgive *[you/name of person who harmed you]*, so that I can be free of this negativity. I realise that forgiveness is a gift to myself, which will liberate me from a dark place and allow me to move forward in a positive way in line with my values.

By forgiving *[you/name of person who harmed you]* I do not condone *[actions/behaviour/event]*, but I release the hold that this has on me. This is an act of compassion for myself.

Best Hopes

Making the decision to forgive makes me feel *[describe the feeling of forgiveness and letting go]*.

It is my best hope that by forgiving *[you/name of person who harmed you]*, I can move forward more positively with my recovery and rebuilding my life. I hope that I can experience the happiness that I deserve. *[describe your hopes for your future now that you have forgiven, e.g., improved relationships, better mental and physical health, moving forward with goals]*.

Sincerely,

[Your name]

Notes:

Writing this letter is to help you move forward on your healing and recovery journey. Be honest with yourself as you write it.

You may want to keep this letter for your own reference, or you could ceremonially destroy it (e.g., tear it up or burn it safely).

You can write the letter to yourself, or to the person who harmed you. The template is just a suggestion. Please adapt it to suit your personal needs and situation.

Appendix 23

Pros and Cons of Remaining Embittered

If you have been harmed by an event, situation or person, then it can be normal to have feelings of injustice about this. Often these feelings are transient and pass with time. If they become chronic, then it can lead to embitterment. Feelings of embitterment can feel difficult to let go of, but remaining embittered can have significant negative effects.

Use this worksheet to consider the pros and cons of holding onto your feelings of embitterment.

Step 1: Describe the Situation

Describe the event that caused you to feel embittered (i.e., the accident or situation that led to you being harmed).

What was it about the situation that felt the most unjust?

Describe what is the most upsetting part of this for you.

Step 2: Describe the Benefits to You of Remaining Embittered

Are there benefits to you of being embittered? Consider the points below plus any other benefits that you get from feeling this way.

Protection: Does holding onto feelings of embitterment offer you some protection from future harm? If so, how?

Fairness: Does being embittered fulfil a sense of justice against the person who harmed you?

Witness to harm: Do you feel that your embitterment helps others to see how you have been harmed? Does it enable your suffering to be witnessed?

Other benefits: How else might remaining embittered benefit you?

Step 3: Costs of Embitterment

Are there negative consequences to you from feeling embittered? Consider the costs outlined below and add in any other consequences that you experience.

Physical costs: Do you experience physical symptoms associated with your embitterment? Do you feel stressed, tense, fatigued or in pain?

Psychological costs: How does feeling embittered impact your emotional well-being and mental health? Do you experience difficult thoughts and feelings linked to this, or symptoms of low mood and anxiety?

SUPPORT MATERIAL

Recovery costs: Do your feelings of embitterment get in the way of your recovery? Do you feel worried about recovering?

Relationships: Are your family relationships and friendships affected by your embitterment?

Feeling stuck: Do you feel stuck in the past because of your embitterment? Does it prevent you from moving forward with your life?

Other costs: Are there other costs to you remaining embittered?

Step 4: Your Thoughts

There may be benefits and costs to you of remaining embittered. The following questions might help you to think further about this:

- Where does embitterment fit in with my values?
- What is important to me about embitterment?
- Does embitterment help me to live a meaningful life?
- Do I feel ready or able to let go of my embitterment?
- What feelings arise when I think about letting go of embitterment?
- Do I need some help to process my feelings of embitterment?
- Who can I ask for help with this? (e.g., a friend, therapist, GP)
- How would I like to move forward with this?

Appendix 24

Pros and Cons of Forgiveness

Step 1: List Your Worries about Forgiveness

Considering forgiving someone who has caused you harm may feel very difficult or painful. It might even feel impossible. Use the space below to think about the negative aspects or your worries about forgiveness.

Is this the right time?: Are you ready to consider forgiveness yet? What might be the potential drawbacks of forgiveness for you at this time?

Safety: Do you fear there may be risks involved with forgiving the person(s)? What do you fear could happen?

Justice: Do you worry that your forgiveness may impact on justice? Do you fear that others may view this as you accepting their actions or the consequences of their actions?

Other worries: List any other worries that you might have about forgiveness.

Step 2: List the Benefits of Forgiveness

Forgiveness can feel difficult, but there can be advantages and benefits to you after forgiving the person(s) who caused you harm. Use the space below to reflect on how you could benefit from forgiveness.

Mental health benefits: Could the act of forgiveness allow you to improve your mental well-being, for example, by reducing difficult thoughts, feelings of stress and anxiety, and improving your mood?

Physical health benefits: How might your physical health benefit from forgiveness? Perhaps reduced tension may lead to reduced pain experience, feeling more relaxed and comfortable.

Growth: Could forgiveness free you from the state of embitterment? Could it help you move forward with your recovery and your life?

Other benefits: How else might forgiveness benefit you and improve your life?

Step 3: Your Decision

There will likely be both worries and benefits to forgiveness in your personal situation. No one can decide for you, and it is for you to weigh up the good and bad to decide whether forgiveness is something that feels right for you.

Below are some questions to help you think some more about this:

- Where does forgiveness fit in with my values?
- What is important to me about forgiveness or not forgiving?
- Do I need more help to process my feelings before I am ready to forgive?
- Who can I ask for help with this? (e.g., a friend, therapist, GP)
- If I am ready to forgive, will I choose to communicate this to the person I'm forgiving, or will this be a private mental act just for myself?
- How would I like to move forward with this?

Appendix 25

Recognising the Signs of Fatigue

On Worksheet A25.1, try to note the signs you notice when you get tired. You may want to think about how you think, feel and act differently. It may help if you also get someone else to tell you what he or she notices about you when you get tired.

Worksheet A25.1 "Signs of Fatigue" Monitoring Form

Sign of fatigue	*Sign present when tired (tick if present)*	*Time(s) of day when at worst*	*Time(s) of day when at best*
Body feeling heavier			
Mind feeling "foggy" or "cloudy"			
Slowed thinking			
Feeling confused			
Forgetting things			
Low motivation			
Anxiety			
Frustration			
Low mood			
Slurred speech			
Any other sign(s) noticed:			

Appendix 26

Fatigue Diary: Tracking Patterns to Support Adaptive Pacing

After a brain injury, fatigue can affect you in complex and often unpredictable ways. Monitoring your energy levels throughout the day can help you develop a clearer understanding of:

- When your fatigue is at its worst
- Which activities are most draining
- Whether your day is overloaded or under-stimulated
- Environmental factors (e.g., noise, social demands) that worsen your fatigue

This insight can help you plan your days more compassionately and strategically, aligning your routines with your energy rhythms.

How to Use Your Fatigue Diary

Use Worksheet A26.1 to track your activity and energy levels over the course of the day. Each hour, jot down what you were doing (even if it was "resting" or "doing nothing") and rate your fatigue on a scale from 0 to 10:

0 = not tired at all

10 = extremely tired/would fall asleep if I didn't stop

You can also use your Fatigue Signs Checklist from Appendix 25: *Recognising the Signs of Fatigue*, to guide your ratings, consider how many of those signs you noticed, and how strong they were during each time block.

Top Tip: Try not to become overly focused or self-critical whilst tracking. This is about curiosity, not judgement. One week of gentle monitoring is usually enough to spot useful patterns.

Use mindful noticing (see Appendix 14: *Switching off Automatic Pilot: The Art of Mindfulness*) to acknowledge signs of fatigue with openness, and then gently return your focus to what matters in the moment.

What to Reflect On

After completing a few days of tracking, look for helpful patterns:

- At what times of day does fatigue tend to peak?
- Are your days too full or too empty, leading to energy crashes?
- Are certain environments (e.g., noise, crowds, conversations) making things worse?

- Which activities are the most mentally or physically draining (red activities), and which are restorative (green activities)?
- Are there patterns with more fatiguing activities requiring more physical or cognitive effort? Or are they more emotionally draining?

This kind of self-awareness supports Compassionate Resilient Mind (CRM) informed pacing: choosing actions that are both meaningful and manageable, rather than being pulled around by guilt, pressure or "automatic pilot."

Worksheet A26.1—Fatigue Diary Template

Time block	*What I did*	*Fatigue level (0–10)*
06:00–08:00		
08:00–10:00		
10:00–11:00		
11:00–12:00		
12:00–13:00		
13:00–14:00		
14:00–15:00		
15:00–16:00		
16:00–17:00		
17:00–18:00		
18:00–19:00		
19:00–20:00		
20:00–00:00		
Hours slept (night before)		
Time went to bed		
Total hours of activity today		

Top Tip: Symptom monitoring is like checking the weather. It only needs a glance to help you decide if it is time to carry an umbrella, not a reason to stare at the sky all day.

SUPPORT MATERIAL

Appendix 27

Evaluating Beliefs about Fatigue and Initiating Compassionate-Resilient Change

Why Beliefs about Fatigue Matter

Some people ignore signs of fatigue because they believe pushing through will lead to better outcomes. Whilst this might occasionally be true, rigidly following the rule, "I *always* need to ignore my tiredness to achieve the best outcome" can sometimes lead you further away from your goals. For example, if you do not rest when your body signals you to, you may end up unable to complete your task, feel emotionally drained, or struggle the next day.

Other people respond to fatigue by avoiding activity altogether. This too can become a rigid belief: "If I *always* do as little as possible, I'll preserve energy." Whilst this can be protective short-term, over time it may limit confidence, reduce physical stamina and contribute to low mood or isolation.

The Compassionate Resilient Mind (CRM) helps you reflect on such beliefs, not to label them as right or wrong, but to increase flexibility in your thinking. By examining both sides of your beliefs, you learn when they are useful and when they are not. The goal is to respond to harsh, rigid self-talk with flexible thinking and beliefs that are wise, kind, adaptable and goal-supportive. Use the worksheet below to evaluate the helpfulness of your beliefs about fatigue. Examples of fatigue beliefs have been provided for you.

Worksheet 27.1—Evaluating the Helpfulness of Beliefs

Belief: "I need to ignore my tiredness to achieve the best outcome."

When it has helped (I achieved more by pushing through)	*When it has not helped (Ignoring tiredness caused problems)*

Reflective prompts:

- Has ignoring your tiredness sometimes been useful?
- Has pushing through sometimes affected your mood, patience or relationships later?
- Has it impacted on your concentration, memory or speed of thinking?
- Has it led to poor performance, mistakes or reduced enjoyment?
- Did skipping breaks lead to knock-on effects the next day?
- Has it affected your sleep or recovery time?

Belief: "I'll achieve a better outcome if I try to do as little as possible."

When it has helped	*When it has not helped*

Reflective prompts:

- Has avoiding activity sometimes protected you in helpful ways?
- Has it also caused you to miss out what is meaningful or purposeful to you (e.g., family, friends) or enjoyment (e.g., has it stopped you from doing things you enjoy)?
- Has avoiding tasks made it harder to start again later?
- Has doing very little increased feelings of helplessness or disconnection from life?

Worksheet 27.2—Replacing Rigid Beliefs with Compassionate Resilient Beliefs

"Compassion is the friend who walks beside you with a backpack of snacks and encouragement, reminding you to rest; resilience is the part that laces up your boots and says, 'Let's keep climbing when you're ready.'" Compassionate resilient thoughts therefore help you to adapt to your fatigue. Try and respond to your thoughts about fatigue with a compassionate resilient thought.

Instructions:

1. Write down beliefs about fatigue (e.g., "rest is failure").
2. Explore the emotional and practical impact of that belief.
3. Create a new belief that is wise, kind, realistic and helpful.

Original belief	*What impact does it have?*	*Compassionate resilient belief*
"If I stop now, I'm weak."	"I feel ashamed and push myself too far."	"Stopping when I need to is a sign of self-respect and inner strength."
"I should do more."	"I overdo it and then crash."	"These 'should' rules are pressure talk from the 'Gatekeeper'". "Doing what I can, not what I 'should,' keeps me going steadily."

CRM Inspired Motivational Statements

When it is hard to rest, respond with your CRM. Examples of what it could say, include:

- "It's okay to feel tired. I deserve to have energy left for what matters most."
- "Taking a break is not giving up; it's investing in my energy."
- "Listening to my body is a sign of strength, not weakness."
- "Stopping now helps me keep going later."

Examples of what it could say when it is hard to start, include:

- "I don't need to do it all. I can start with small steps."
- "It's okay to feel tired and still take action."
- "Every step I take, no matter how small, is a step forward."

Worksheet 27.3—Activity Pacing Reflection

Use the following worksheet to identify the advantages and disadvantages of pacing:
Situation/Activity:
E.g., cooking dinner, working at the computer, attending appointments.

Advantages of using pacing	*Disadvantages of using pacing*
Better energy throughout the day	Task might take longer
Less emotional overwhelm	May need to adjust expectations
Greater enjoyment and clarity	Might feel "slower" than before injury

Worksheet 27.5—Reintegrating Meaningful Activities

Even when living with fatigue, you can reconnect with activities that bring joy, meaning and identity. This process may involve adapting, simplifying or asking for help, but it reflects resilient action guided by what you care about. Use the following worksheet to help to reintegrate activities within your life:

Activities I would like to reintegrate	*Strategies for reintegrating or adapting them*
Gardening	Break into 10-minute sessions, sit whilst working
Going to the café with a friend	Choose quieter times, rest before and after
Volunteering	Start with one hour a week, clarify role boundaries

Appendix 28

Breaking Out of the "Boom-Bust" Cycle—Pacing Activities

"Boom-bust" cycles refer to doing too much and then crashing. This is common after brain injury. Pacing is the key to breaking this unhelpful pattern and building a steadier, more manageable rhythm of activity.

Understanding the "Boom-Bust" Cycle

In this cycle:

- You might overexert on a day you feel "better," trying to catch up or get ahead (boom).
- Then, you crash, needing extended recovery, often leading to inactivity and frustration (bust).
- Pacing is about gently finding a "just right" zone, which involves balancing meaningful activity and necessary rest.

General Pacing Strategies

Reflect on Your Habits: Write down the advantages and disadvantages of doing too much or too little (see Appendix 27: *Evaluating Beliefs About Fatigue and Initiating Compassionate-Resilient Change*). What are your usual tendencies? What beliefs or situations contribute to those patterns?

Identify Barriers: What gets in the way of pacing? Is it guilt, pressure, expectations or difficulty saying no? How might you navigate or work around those?

Plan Small Changes: Experiment with subtle shifts in activity, rest or timing. Use pacing as a flexible process, not a rigid rule.

Use a Daily or Weekly Diary: Track energy, activity and rest. Avoid packing the day too tightly, but also try not to under-plan.

Prioritise Meaning: Put your activities in order of importance. Choose 2–3 that either must be done, or would genuinely boost your well-being.

Schedule Around Energy, Not Just Time: Plan higher-demand tasks for when you tend to feel most alert or experience the least pain/fatigue.

Set Regular Goals: Refer to Appendix 3: *Turning Values into Action: Setting SMART Goals*, for SMART goal-setting guidance to stay motivated without overload.

The "Traffic Light" System

To create balance and avoid burnout, it can be useful to colour-code your activities using a simple "traffic light" system.

Red Activities

These are physically, cognitively or emotionally draining. They typically require sustained effort, stimulation or multitasking.
*Examples:

- Shopping
- Cleaning
- Long or emotionally intense conversations
- Problem-solving tasks
- Multitasking under pressure

Amber Activities

These are moderately tiring; they are not as exhausting as red activities, but still require some energy or engagement. They can be a useful bridge or transition between red and green activities.
*Examples:

- Light cooking
- Organising paperwork
- Walking, whilst talking with someone
- Attending a low-demand meeting
- Passive screen time (e.g., watching a familiar TV show)

Green Activities

These are calming, low-effort or pleasurable. They help restore energy, soothe the nervous system and support emotional regulation.
*Examples:

- Having a cup of green tea
- Gentle stretching
- Mindful breathing
- Listening to music
- Engaging in enjoyable hobbies

*The examples may not necessarily be applicable to you; they will be different for everyone.

Top Tips for Integration

Alternate Red and Green: Avoid stacking too many reds in a row. Ideally, follow a red task with a green one, and if needed, insert an amber activity as a gentle bridge.

Use Amber as Transitions: Amber activities can help you wind down from a red, or gradually re-engage after a green.

Use Green as Buffers and Recovery Tools: Schedule green activities proactively to prevent energy crashes.

Review your activity diary (see Appendix 26: *Fatigue diary: Tracking Patterns to Support Adaptive Pacing*) and colour-code tasks to spot patterns and redesign your week with more balance.

If You Tend to Do Too Little:

- Write a list of activities that make you feel better, lighter or more connected.
- Record how much enjoyment and achievement you get from each (see Appendix 4: *Enjoyment and Achievement: Activities to Lift Mood and Motivation*).
- Try to do at least one green or amber activity each day, even if brief.
- Reward yourself, celebrate action, not perfection.
- Build up gradually, using alarms or timers to prompt action.
- Refer to Appendix 11: *Turning Procrastination into Meaningful Action*, if you tend to procrastinate or freeze up.

If You Tend to Do Too Much:

Remind Yourself: "A good day doesn't mean I have to do everything." Progress is about balance, not ticking off every task.

Watch for the "Boom-Bust" Cycle: When you feel good, it is natural to want to catch up or get ahead. But overdoing it can lead to a crash. Aim for steady pacing instead.

Break Tasks into Manageable Steps: Split larger tasks into smaller steps. Use amber and green activities or breaks to pace yourself.

Monitor Symptoms Gently, Not Excessively: Pay attention to fatigue and pain, using a simple 0–10 scale and:

- Treat it as a quiet internal check-in, rather than a constant focus.
- Choose an intensity level (e.g., 6/10) for when to consider a green or amber activity, rather than pushing through.
- Avoid tracking symptoms too often or getting caught up in numbers; just notice occasionally to guide your pacing.

Let Others Support You: Trusted family members or support workers can help notice signs of overdoing it. Let them help identify tasks you can delegate, delay or drop.

Pre-Schedule Rest and Mindful Pauses: Build in regular rest periods, even on good days, not just when you feel exhausted.

Include Mindful Check-Ins: Take three slow breaths, notice body tension and consciously relax (see Appendix 16: *Relaxation Skills: Finding Calm and Balance*, for guidance on relaxation).

Top Tip: Symptom monitoring is like checking the weather just at a glance to help you decide if it is time to carry an umbrella, not a reason to stare at the sky all day.

Compassionate Resilient Mind (CRM) Insight: Using the CRM as your compass, pacing is an act of self-respect and compassion, not laziness or avoidance. It helps you stay in tune with your mind and body, supporting your long-term adaptability, connection and well-being.

Appendix 29

Rebalancing the Volume: Highlighting What Matters, Softening the Noise of Pain and Fatigue

Fatigue after brain injury can take up a lot of mental space, but we can choose how much attention and energy we give it.

This worksheet will help you explore two helpful metaphors:

1. The Internal Social Media Feed
2. The Interference Signal (Radio or Wi-Fi)

Part 1: Spot the "Body Influencer"

Instructions: Think of your body's fatigue signals like a post from a "body influencer" on your mind's social media feed.

You do not need to "like," comment or follow it.

You can just notice, name and scroll past. For example: "Fatigue is posting again!"

Situation	*What was fatigue/ pain "posting"?*	*Your response*	*Could you scroll past? (✓/✗)*
e.g., Getting dressed in the morning	"This is too much. I can't even start."	"I paused and named it:" "Post from Fatigue."	✓

Try This Phrase:

"Here's a post from fatigue/pain again. I see it. I don't need to respond. I'll gently scroll on."

Part 2: Is Fatigue Distorting the Signal?

Now imagine fatigue like radio static or a weak Wi-Fi signal, making it harder to think clearly, feel motivated or follow through on goals. Your Compassionate Resilient Mind (CRM) can help filter the noise and amplify the signal you want to tune into.

Reflection Questions:

1. **What is your signal today?**
   What matters most to you today, underneath the static? For example, "Connecting with my child," "Taking one step towards my rehab goal".
2. **What is the interference?**
   What kinds of thoughts, sensations or stories are muddying the signal? For example "I feel heavy," "This won't work," "Why bother?"
3. **CRM Filter Practice:**
   Choose one CRM response below to help shift the dial:
   - **Compassion:** "It's okay to feel this and still take a small step."
   - **Purposeful Focus:** "I'll do one small thing that aligns with my values."
   - **Flexibility:** "I can adjust my plan without giving up."

CRM Reframe Example

"Fatigue/pain is here, but I can still tune into what matters. I'll adjust the volume and focus on what I can do."

Part 3: Create Your CRM Practice Plan

Trigger situation	*What's the fatigue "post" or "interference"?*	*My CRM response*	*What will I focus on instead?*

Appendix 30

Memory Slip Tracker Form

After a brain injury, it is common to experience more frequent attentional lapses, moments when your focus slips and something gets missed or forgotten. These lapses can feel frustrating, but they are also entirely human. Everyone zones out, forgets things or gets distracted from time to time. After brain injury, however, such lapses may happen more often, making it helpful to track patterns and identify situations where additional support or strategies may be useful.

Instructions

Use the worksheet below to record attentional lapses when they feel meaningful. You do not need to note down every small or everyday mistakes, as this would be overwhelming and unhelpful.

What Counts as a "Meaningful" Attentional Lapse?

A lapse is meaningful if it causes:

- A noticeable consequence (e.g., forgetting food on the stove, missing an appointment)
- A repeated frustration or a pattern that is starting to impact your routine
- A risk to safety or well-being
- Interference with important goals (e.g., social interactions, work, independence)

By identifying meaningful lapses, you give your Compassionate Resilient Mind (CRM) the chance to step in, not with judgement, but with curiosity and adaptability. Use this exercise to build awareness, spot patterns and plan supportive strategies, so that you can respond, rather than react.

Start with the example below:

Table A30.1 Example: Attentional Lapse Monitoring Form

Date	*Attentional lapse*	*What I could do to manage it*
Wednesday, 14 Aug	Forgot to take the roast out of the oven	Set a kitchen timer or use a phone alarm
Friday, 16 Aug	Answered the door and forgot I had something on the hob	Write “pan on” on a sticky note and hold it in hand when leaving the kitchen briefly
Tuesday, 3 Sept	Overflowed the bath by forgetting the taps were running	Don’t leave the bathroom whilst filling the bath; if I must, drape towel over shoulder as a cue
Thursday, 12 Sept	Forgot to take notice of where I parked the car	Take a quick photo of the car and surroundings on my phone

Worksheet A30.1 Attentional Lapse Monitoring Form Template

Date	*Attentional lapse*	*What could I do to manage it*

CRM Insight—Building Awareness without Criticism

From a CRM perspective, attentional lapses are not a reflection of failure or laziness; they are signals from your brain that it needs support, structure and care.

This exercise helps you:

- Recognise what is difficult, without falling into blame
- Stay open and curious, rather than critical or hopeless
- Take purposeful action that supports your functioning
- Train your mind to become more self-aware and flexible, rather than rigid and reactive

Think of these moments not as mistakes, but as opportunities to learn how to work with your brain, not against it. Small adaptations (e.g., cues, routines and reminders) are wise tools for someone responding resiliently to life after injury.

Appendix 31

PQRST Guidelines

Often, when we are watching a TV programme or reading something, our mind begins to wander. This makes it difficult for us to follow the gist of the information that we are trying to take in. In such instances, it can be useful to use the PQRST technique (this stands for preview, question, review, self-recite and test). This is a technique that keeps our minds focused by continually making us review the information with which we are being presented. This technique involves the following steps.

P	**Preview**	To get an overview of what, for example, a TV programme is about, read the summary in the newspaper, or on the internet; or before reading a chapter in a book, go through and read the headings in that chapter.
Q	**Question**	Formulate key questions that you expect to be answered, such as who, when, where and what?
R	**Read/review**	Read or listen to the material.
S	**Self-recite**	Summarise what you have just heard or read.
T	**Test**	Answer the questions you asked yourself and check that you have got them correct by reviewing the material.

Appendix 32

Guidelines for Problem-Solving

Brain injuries can cause problem-solving difficulties. Solving problems before your brain injury may have come very naturally, without having to think about all the steps involved in how to solve a problem. After a brain injury, it is sometimes necessary to break down the steps involved in problem-solving and go through them in a very structured way. Use Worksheet 32.1 as an example to help carry you through these steps. See the following example.

Step 1: Write down the problem.

My problem is: "The neighbour is making noise at night, and has been every night for the last month, and I'm not getting any sleep. I've asked him politely to be quiet and he has ignored me."

Step 2: Write down a number of possible solutions (it sometimes helps to search for the problem on the internet to find potential solutions).

Solution 1: I could go round there and threaten my neighbour with violence.

Solution 2: I could make lots of noise myself to annoy him.

Solution 3: I could report it to the authorities and get advice from them.

Step 3: Consider the pros and cons of each solution and how likely you think each one will be to work on a scale of 0%–100% (0% = it will not work at all; 100% = you are 100% sure it will work).

	Pros	*Cons*	*Likelihood of working (scale: 0%–100%)*
Solution 1: Threaten with violence	He might get scared and stop making noise.	He could call the police.	80
Solution 2: Retaliate by making lots of noise myself	This may make him think about what he's doing to me.	He is likely to retaliate and make even more noise.	20
Solution 3: Report to the local authorities and get advice from them	The local authorities are likely to give me good advice on how to deal with the problem.	It may not work and could take a while to get sorted.	80

Step 4: Choose one possible solution that looks as though it may work, and which will have the most favourable outcome based on advantages and disadvantages.

Chosen solution: "Report to the local authorities."

Step 5: Plan out step by step what you will need to carry out this solution.

	Problem: The neighbour is making noise at night, and has been every night for the last month, and I'm not getting any sleep. I've asked him politely to be quiet and he has ignored me.
Step 1	Log instances of all noise.
Step 2	Look on the internet to see how I can report this to the authorities.
Step 3	Report this to the authorities.

Step 6: Write down how you will know if your solution has worked and a time by which you will evaluate whether it has worked.

"The neighbour will stop making noise. I'll evaluate this in two weeks' time."

Step 7: Carry out your plan.

Step 8: Evaluate whether it has worked.

Worksheet A30.1 Problem-Solving Exercise Template

Step 1: Write down the problem.

My problem is:

Step 2: Write down a number of possible solutions (it sometimes helps to search for the problem on the internet to find potential solutions).

Solution 1:

Solution 2:

Solution 3:

Step 3: Consider the pros and cons of each solution and how likely you think each one will be to work on a scale of 0%–100% (0% = it will not work at all; 100% = you are 100% sure it will work).

	Pros	*Cons*	*Likelihood of working (scale: 0%–100%)*
Solution 1:			
Solution 2:			
Solution 3:			

Step 4: Choose one possible solution that looks as though it may work and which will have the most favourable outcome based on advantages and disadvantages.

Step 5: Plan out step by step what you will need to carry out this solution.

	Problem
Step 1	
Step 2	
Step 3	

Step 6: Write down how you will know if your solution has worked and a time by which you will evaluate whether it has worked.

Step 7: Carry out your plan.

Step 8: Evaluate whether it has worked.

Appendix 33

Guidelines for Planning Essays after Brain Injury

This worksheet will guide you through the process of planning and writing essays, especially if you have difficulties with organisation, memory or focus after a brain injury.

Step 1: Understand the Question

- Read the question out loud.
- Ask yourself: What is the question really asking?
- Break it into smaller parts if needed.

Step 2: Plan Your Answer

- Bullet point your main ideas. These will become subheadings for your essay.
- Write key words or phrases under each subheading.
- Decide the order of the points—what comes first, next, last?
- Estimate how much to write for each point.

Include:

- An introduction (what the essay will cover).
- A conclusion (summary and take-home message).

Step 3: Write Your Essay

- Write one bullet point at a time.
- Tick it off when you finish each paragraph.

After each paragraph, check:

- Have I answered the question?
- Have I repeated myself?
- Do the sentences make sense?
- Is the paragraph the right length?
- Have I added a concluding sentence?

Top Tip: Read each paragraph aloud to hear how it sounds.

Essay Planning Template

Essay Question:

Section	*Key words or notes*	✓ *Tick when done*
Introduction		☐
Subheading 1		☐
Subheading 2		☐
Subheading 3		☐
Subheading 4		☐
Subheading 5		☐
Subheading 6		☐
Conclusion		☐

Appendix 34

Structured Decision-Making Tool: Finding the Best Option for You

Decision-Making

After a brain injury, it is common to experience difficulties with decision-making. You might feel overwhelmed, uncertain or stuck between different viewpoints (e.g., your own or those of others). This worksheet offers a structured way to compare your options and reach a decision that feels right for you.

Step 1: Identify the Options

Write down the different choices you are considering.

Example 1: Relationship Dilemma

Decision: What should I do about my relationship?

- Option 1: Leave my partner.
- Option 2: Stay and attend couples therapy.
- Option 3: Stay, but keep things as they are.
- Option 4: Delay deciding and carry on without making changes for now.

Example 2: Health Decision

Decision: Should I start a new medication?

- Option 1: Take the medication regularly as prescribed.
- Option 2: Don't take the medication at all.
- Option 3: Take it occasionally or only when symptoms feel severe.
- Option 4: Postpone the decision and ask for more advice or information.

Caution: It is essential to discuss the impact of these decisions with a medical professional, who will be able to inform your decision.

Example 3: Returning to Work or Study

Decision: Should I return to work/study?

- Option 1: Return full-time right away.
- Option 2: Try a phased or part-time return with support.
- Option 3: Delay returning until I feel more confident.
- Option 4: Decide not to return and explore other meaningful activities.

Step 2: Use the Decision Table Below

Criteria	*Option 1*	*Option 2*	*Option 3 (if needed)*	*Option 4 (if needed)*
Pros (what is good about this?)				
Cons (what is difficult or risky?)				
Worst-case outcome				
Best-case outcome				
Emotional impact (how might I feel?)				
Rate this option (0 = not good, 10 = best)				
My notes:				

Step 3: Make a Decision

Reflect on the table above. You may wish to talk it through with someone you trust (e.g., support worker, therapist, friend).

Which option do I feel most comfortable with right now?

- Option 1
- Option 2
- Option 3
- Option 4
- Still unsure—I will revisit this later or seek more support.

My next step is:

____

____

CRM Top Tips:

- Instead of looking for the "perfect decision" look for what is most workable or least harmful right now.
- It is okay to change your mind later. Decision-making is a process, not a one-time event.
- Writing it down can help organise thoughts and reduce overwhelm.

Appendix 35

Strengthening Your Mental Brakes with a Compassionate Resilient Mindset (CRM)

Your frontal lobes play a crucial role in self-control. They are the control centre for the "stop and think" part of the brain, which acts as your "mental brakes", and helps you pause, reflect and consider consequences before acting. After a brain injury, these "mental brakes" can be weakened, making it harder to resist strong impulses, delay gratification or weigh up long-term outcomes. When these "mental brakes" are underactive, it can feel like your "primitive brain" (driven by urges, emotions and instant gratification) is in the driver's seat. When unchecked, these strong urges might feel good in the moment, but they can lead to negative consequences later on. The more you act on these urges, the stronger they become, creating habits that pull you further away from balance and well-being.

The frontal lobes are not fully developed in children, and their "mental brakes" do not work efficiently. Consider the consequences of letting them do whatever they want to do. For example, it is likely that they would play all day and neglect their school work, because they would only be able to act on their immediate desires without considering the long term consequences or impact. If an adult has weak "mental brakes" it can lead to addictive, obsessive and hedonistic, risky behaviours. It may also lead to an imbalance between work and play/family life.

The goal of this exercise is to help you:

- Recognise your urges and desires
- Consider their consequences
- Develop strategies to slow down and respond with awareness
- Shift from automatic impulse to intentional action, guided by your Compassionate Resilient Mind (CRM)

Part 1: Noticing Impulses and Their Impact

Use the following table to reflect on situations where your "primitive brain" urges take over, and what the consequences might be when your logical, "stop and think" does not apply the brakes.

Example 1:

Primitive brain: What are your strong urges and desires? What are you passionate about?	**Logical brain "Stop and think about consequences": What are the consequences of not being able to put on the "mental brakes" when you are either engaged in this behaviour or you have the desire to engage in it?**

(*Continued*)

"I get completely obsessed with taking photos and may take the whole day doing this, ignoring everything else."	"My relationship with my partner suffers and I get nothing else done."
Primitive brain: When you are doing a mundane task, what are you likely to get tempted away by?	**Logical brain "Stop and think about consequences": What are the consequences of not being able to put on the "mental brakes" by getting drawn away?**
"When I'm doing my college work, I get distracted by my phone and my guitar."	"If I get distracted, it means that I don't get the work done that I need to do."

Blank template:

Primitive brain: What are your strong urges and desires? What are you passionate about?	**Logical brain "Stop and think about consequences": What are the consequences of not being able to put on the "mental brakes" when you are either engaged in this behaviour or you have the desire to engage in it?**
Primitive brain: When you are doing a mundane task, what are you likely to get tempted away by?	**Logical brain "Stop and think about consequences": What are the consequences of not being able to put on the "mental brakes" by getting drawn away?**

Part 2: Building an Action Plan—Putting on the "Mental Brakes."

Now identify some of your risk desires (these are your very strong desires that are likely to pull you into impulsively responding without stopping and thinking) and develop a clear strategy for applying your "mental brakes." This is how you shift from reactivity to purposeful, adaptive action.

Example 1:

Risk desires	*How to put on the "mental brakes"?*
I get carried away by wanting to take photos all the time.	"Set myself times when I can do this." "Set myself a limit to how long I'm going to spend doing this and set an alarm, which tells me when to stop." "Put my camera in a place out of the way where it's difficult to reach."
Getting distracted by my phone and guitar.	"When I'm doing important tasks, put my phone and guitar in a different room out of the way." "Set myself breaks from work, and as a reward for working, allow myself to use the phone and guitar for set periods of time."
Eating too much food and snacking lots in the day.	"Don't keep unhealthy snacks in the house."

Blank template:

Risk desires	*How to put on the "mental brakes"?*

Part 3: Surfing the Urge—The "Gatekeeper" and the Wave

When urges or impulses arise, (e.g., the pull to shop, snack, snap at someone or avoid a task) you might feel like you are being pushed around by a force stronger than you. That is your "primitive brain" in action, and it is when the survival/protective part of your mind (or the "Gatekeeper") can take over (see Appendix 8: *Unlocking Adaptation: A Practical Guide to the Compassionate Resilient Mind*).

The "Gatekeeper" does not like discomfort. He is rigid, reactive and driven by a need for immediate relief. When an urge shows up, he wants to act fast: "Buy it now!" "Say what you're thinking!" "Avoid it, it's too hard!" He fights for control by trying to eliminate discomfort, without considering long-term consequences.

But you have another part of your mind, the flexible, adaptive part, "Eve Olve" (your CRM). She notices discomfort but does not panic. She steps back, assesses and chooses a wiser path, even when it is hard.

Surfing the urge is a technique to help "Eve Olve" regain the wheel and prevent the "Gatekeeper" from throwing you off course.

What Is Urge Surfing?

Urge surfing is the skill of riding out intense feelings or impulses without reacting to them. You do not fight the urge, but you do not give in to it either. Like a surfer riding a wave, you stay steady as the urge builds. When the wave hits its peak, it can feel overwhelming, but if you hold your balance and ride it out, it will naturally lose power and pass.

The key is to recognise that you cannot control the wave, but you can control how you respond to it.

CRM phrase: "When you ride the wave, you're not at the mercy of your impulses; you are the one creating purposeful action."

Steps to Surf the Urge (with "Eve Olve")

1. Notice the Urge

   Pause and name what is happening:

   "I notice the urge to scroll on social media instead of work" or "I feel the pull to shout back."
2. Acknowledge the "Gatekeeper's" Presence

   You might say:

   "Hello 'Gatekeeper', I see you're fired up and pushing for immediate gratification."

3. Call on "Eve Olve" (your CRM)
   Imagine "Eve Olve" stepping in with calm curiosity. She might say:
   "This is hard, but we don't have to react. Let's just watch what happens."
4. Ride the Wave
   Focus on your breath or ground yourself with your senses.
   Observe the urge, like it is a wave building in the ocean.
   Remind yourself: "This is just a feeling. It'll pass."
5. Redirect Attention
   When the urge, fades, gently return to a meaningful action, something aligned with what is meaningful to you. This could be your work or even a helpful distraction you have planned ahead of time. You could also use mindfulness strategies to help you do this (see Appendix 14: *witching off Automatic Pilot: The Art of Mindfulness*).

CRM Reflection: When you feel an urge, the "Gatekeeper" wants to avoid discomfort at any cost. He may push you to react quickly without taking time to stop and think, or encourage you to carry on automatically without pausing to reflect. This can make it harder to step back, consider your options, and choose a wiser path that is connected to what truly matters to you. Instead, by surfing the urge, you give space for your CRM to respond. You interrupt reactivity and choose adaptation over impulse. By practising this regularly, urges become less overpowering, and your "mental brakes" get stronger.

Appendix 36

Using the Compassionate Resilient Mind (CRM) to Navigate Cognitive Symptoms with ACCEPTS

Cognitive symptoms after brain injury, such as forgetfulness, losing focus, difficulty organising or struggling to plan, can feel overwhelming in the moment. The Compassionate Resilient Mind (CRM) provides a framework for responding wisely and constructively to cognitive problems. With ACCEPTS, symptoms shift from perceived moments of failure into opportunities for growth, learning and resilience.

The ACCEPTS Response to Cognitive Symptoms

A—Awareness and Acceptance

Notice the cognitive slip and your thoughts, feelings and bodily sensations when it appears. Name them without judgment.

Example: "I notice I feel anxious and frustrated because I forgot what I was supposed to do. That reaction makes sense."

C—Cognitive Flexibility

Respond with openness, rather than rigidity. Explore alternative perspectives and approaches.

Example: "Making mistakes is human. It is an opportunity for adaptation and trying a different approach. Next time I will start getting ready earlier and put my bags in front of the door so I do not forget them."

C—Compassion for Self and Others

Soften self-criticism. Offer kindness to yourself and patience to others.

Example: "I'm doing my best. It's okay to ask others to bear with me."

E—Effort with Balance (Compassionate Persistence)

Stay with the task when it feels tough, combining gentleness and grit. Acknowledge limits without giving up, and notice the natural urge to step back or avoid after a mistake. Gently choosing to stay engaged helps learning and makes the task easier next time. Example: "Part of me wants to brush this off or avoid it next time because it feels uncomfortable, but noticing what went wrong helps me learn. I can stay with this gently, try again step by step, and do it differently next time."

P—Purposeful Action

Pause, breathe and choose an intentional response, rather than reacting automatically.

Example: "I've missed a step in a recipe. Getting angry or giving up won't help right now. I'll stop, check the recipe, and work out what can still be salvaged or adapted or learn what I can do differently next time."

Example: "What small, constructive step can I take right now?"

T—Tools and Strategies

Use planners, reminders, checklists or digital aids, not as weaknesses, but as strengths that empower independence.

Example: "I'll set a phone reminder so I don't lose track."

S—Self-Reflection

Turn slips into learning opportunities. Ask: "What contributed to this difficulty?" and "What helped last time?" Reflection builds future resilience.

Example: "I noticed I was most distracted when I was tired, next time I'll rest first."

Quick ACCEPTS Checklist for Cognitive Symptoms

When a cognitive slip arises, move through these steps:

A—Awareness and Acceptance → Pause and notice the symptom/cognitive slip and your feelings.

C—Cognitive Flexibility → Be willing to shift your perspective or approach.

C—Compassion → Be kind to yourself and others involved.

E—Effort with Balance → Stay with it gently; do not abandon the task too soon.

P—Purposeful Action → Take a small, intentional step.

T—Tools and Strategies → Use supports, such as reminders, planners or routines.

S—Self-Reflection → Learn from what happened to build resilience.

Worksheet for Dealing with Cognitive Symptoms

1. Awareness and Acceptance

"What slip or difficulty did I notice (or did others notice)?"

"What am I noticing in my thoughts, body and feelings?"

"Can I name and allow them without judgment?"

____

____

2. Cognitive Flexibility

"Would shifting perspective help me here?"

"Do I need a different approach to this task?"

"Can I try a different strategy?"

____

____

3. Compassion

"What kind words can I offer myself to help myself learn from this task and keep going?"

____

____

4. Effort with Balance (Compassionate Persistence)

"How can I keep going with gentleness and persistence, even though this feels hard?"

____

____

5. Purposeful Action

"Instead of reacting automatically, what small, intentional step can I take now?"

____

____

6. Tools and Strategies

"What tools, reminders or supports can I use here?"

____

____

7. Self-Reflection

"What can I learn from this slip or experience to help me next time?"

____

____

Key Message:

Cognitive symptoms are not signs of weakness or failure. They are invitations to practise awareness, compassion and adaptability. With the CRM, every lapse can become a step towards strength and independence. If you have difficulty thinking of strategies to help you compensate for slips it may be useful to ask your therapist or someone you trust for advice.

Appendix 37

Understanding Your Own Finances

Understanding Your Finances

This worksheet will help you see:

- How much money you have coming in
- What you spend it on
- How much is left over
- What you might need for the future

Step 1: Know Your Income

Write down all the money you receive. Include:

- Type (e.g., wages, benefits, pension)
- How it is paid (e.g., bank transfer, cash)
- Amount

Type of income	*How received*	*Amount*
Total		£________

Step 2: Track Essential Spending

Write down your regular bills and essentials. Include:

- Rent/mortgage
- Utilities
- Food
- Insurance
- Travel costs

Top Tip: Divide yearly costs (like car insurance) into monthly or weekly amounts.

Essential outgoing	*How paid*	*Amount*

Disposable income = total income – total essentials = £________

Step 3: Track Non-Essential Spending

These are things you do not have to buy, but may add to your well-being (e.g., hobbies, meals out, clothes, treats).

Non-essential outgoing	*How paid*	*Amount*

Compare: disposable income £________ vs. non-essential spending £________
Reflection Questions

- Do you have money left over each month?
- If not, where could you cut back?
- Are there costs you cannot explain?
- Do you run out of money at a certain time each month? What happens then?

Step 4: Savings, Assets and Future Needs

List any savings, property or investments. Think about big future costs (e.g., replacing a car, holidays, home adaptations, increased care).

Future expense	*Future amount*

Key Point:

Knowing your income, spending, savings and future needs gives you the power to make informed choices, avoid overspending and plan ahead with confidence.

Appendix 38

Insight and Self-Awareness: Understanding Vulnerability after Brain Injury

This worksheet uses a simple model to help you think about the different factors, linked to brain injury and personality, that can make you more vulnerable to financial mistakes. Building this self-awareness is the first step towards:

- Better strategies
- Stronger habits
- More control over your money and decisions

The Four Categories of Vulnerability

In **Figure A38.1**, the shaded semi-circles show four common areas that can affect decision-making:

1. Thinking skills
2. Emotional factors
3. External factors
4. Physical factors

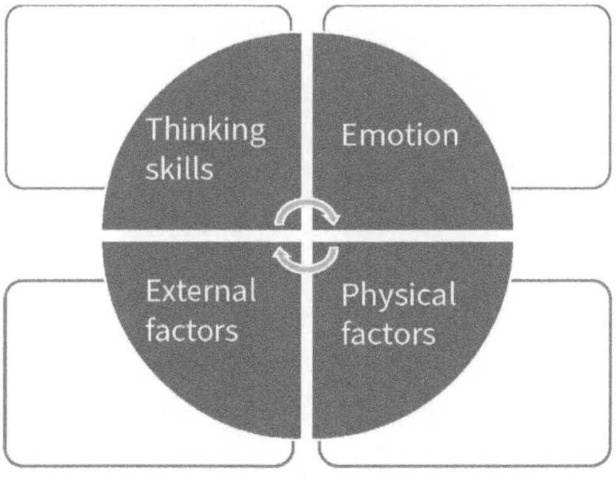

Figure A38.1 Four common areas that can affect decision-making.

How to Use This Model

Write your own examples or possible risk points in the circles in the diagram.

Think about real situations you have experienced, or possible challenges in the future.

Notice how different vulnerabilities can interact and make each other worse.

The aim is to spot patterns and develop strategies to avoid harm or regret.

Top Tip*:* Do this exercise with someone you trust (e.g., a psychologist, support worker or family member).

Review it regularly to track progress and spot new patterns.

Example: Raj's Impulsive Purchase

Raj bought expensive trainers and sports clothes whilst out shopping. Later, he realised he had gone over his monthly budget.

Using the model, he broke it down:

Thinking Skills: "I didn't stop to think before buying." (*Impulsivity*)

Emotional Factors: "I've been feeling low and wanted a quick boost." (*Mood-driven spending*)

External Factors: "The shop was noisy and crowded—I couldn't think straight." (*Sensory overload*)

Physical Factors: "I was tired, which made it harder to make good choices." (*Fatigue*)

Reflect on Your Own Triggers

Here are some ideas to get you started:

Thinking Skills: "I forget what I've already bought."

Emotional Factors: "I give in and spend money to avoid conflict."

External Factors: "I'm easily persuaded by friends or salespeople."

Physical Factors: "I make poorer decisions when I'm tired or unwell."

Appendix 39

Smart Spending and Budget Confidence

(A guide to planning purchases, resisting impulsive urges and building financial control).

This worksheet helps you plan purchases, so you stick to your budget, reduce overspending and feel more in control of your money. You can complete all sections or just the ones most useful for you.

Step 1. Planning a Purchase

Before buying something, take time to check if it fits your goals.

A Clarify what matters (example purchase: holiday)

Quality	**Importance (0–10)**
Close to the sea	8

B Research the price and budget

Price range: £________

My budget: £________

C Shortlist options (up to 4)

1 ____________________________

2 ____________________________

3 ____________________________

4 ____________________________

D Pros and cons

Pros	Cons

My decision: ____________________________

Step 2. Setting a Realistic Budget

Decide how much you can save each month for your goal. Make sure it is:

- **Sensible:** Does not leave you short for essentials
- **Sustainable:** Something you can keep up
- **Balanced:** Still leaves money for daily life

Item	Budget
e.g., Holiday	£______

Step 3. Saving for Your Goal

Total amount needed	________________
Amount to save each month	________________
Time to reach goal	________________
Where I'll keep the money	________________

Top Tip: Use a separate account or savings jar to resist temptation.

Step 4. Staying Motivated

List reasons why sticking to your budget matters:

1. ________________________
2. ________________________
3. ________________________

Top Tip: Keep this list somewhere visible, like on your phone or fridge.

Step 5. Spotting Triggers and Planning Strategies

Trigger/urge	Example	If I overspend	Strategy
Bargains	Can't resist offers	Waste money	Make a list and stick to it

Step 6. Managing Spending Urges—The Inner Salesperson

Imagine your urge to spend is like a pushy salesperson in your head. They say things like:

"This deal won't last!" "You deserve it."

"You'll feel better if you buy it."

But remember, you do not have to buy what they are selling.

Steps to take:

- Notice the urge ("My inner salesperson is at work").
- Pause, you do not need to decide now.
- Talk back: "I don't make money decisions under pressure."
- Acknowledge the feeling, it will pass.
- Shift focus—call a friend, take a walk, check your goals, use a calming activity (see Appendix 9).

Step 7. Practical Strategies for Common Triggers

Trigger	Helpful strategy
Online shopping late at night	No credit card use after 10 pm

Step 8. Quick Tips for Control

- Set clear spending rules.
- Pause before buying.
- Review your spending regularly.
- Talk to someone before big or emotional purchases.
- Focus on what matters most—your long-term goals.

Step 9. Reflection

- When do I usually feel the urge to spend?
- What thoughts go through my mind?
- What emotions or physical feelings do I notice?
- What helps me stay in control?
- What could I put in my "Fed-Up First Aid Kit"?

Key message: Managing spending is about building awareness, planning ahead and protecting what truly matters to you. Every small step towards control builds long-term freedom.

Appendix 40

Safe Action Planning For Finances

This worksheet helps you plan how to deal with personal challenges (vulnerabilities) or build skills. Use it for money-related issues or other situations that could put you at risk.

Example—Sarah's Missing Money

Sarah notices some of her money is going missing. She thinks that carers may have taken her money. The following outlines the steps Sarah took and why.

Vulnerability/Skill: Memory problems and difficulty speaking up

Possible options:

1. Stop using carers (not realistic)
2. Call police immediately (worried I'd be wrong)
3. Talk to care agency manager with support
4. Do nothing

Chosen action: Speak to care agency manager with my sister and keep written records.
Steps:

1. Call my sister to explain situation
2. Arrange a meeting with the care manager
3. Keep all receipts and track my cash
4. Attend the planned meeting with sister, request written summary
5. If money keeps going missing, report to police

Outcome: Money still went missing, so I reported it to the police. My records helped identify the problem. Person responsible was removed, now have reliable carers. I'll switch to debit card/online banking to reduce risk.

Your Turn—Action Planning

Use the following steps to identify financial risk and a strategy to deal with it.
Describe the situation: What's happening that doesn't feel right?
Personal challenges/vulnerabilities: (e.g., memory problems, fear of conflict, trouble tracking spending)

Possible options:

1. ____________________
2. ____________________
3. ____________________
4. ____________________

Chosen option and why:

Steps to take:

1. ____________________
2. ____________________
3. ____________________
4. ____________________

After trying it—What happened?

____

What did you learn?

____

Anything else you will do differently in future?

____

Summary

This worksheet helps you think clearly about a situation where you might feel unsafe or uncertain about your ability to manage money. It guides you to reflect on your personal challenges, explore your options and make a step-by-step plan to protect yourself. You do not need to have all the answers right now—just being willing to think things through and ask for support is a strong and positive step. Remember: noticing a problem, asking for help and making a plan are all signs of strength.

Appendix 41

Key Points for Your Family to Understand about Brain Injury

A brain injury can happen to anyone. For many, the injury occurs in an accident. For others, the brain injury may be the result of a severe illness.

A brain injury tends to affect different people in different ways. Although the person may look the same, they may act differently to how they were before the injury.

The effect of a brain injury can change over time as things settle down. Unfortunately some people do not recover completely and continue to have problems. The person may have something called "rehabilitation", which helps them relearn how to do things or learn how to do things in a different way.

The brain is inside the head and controls everything that the person does. This includes physical skills, thinking and feelings.

What Kind of Problems Can People with a Brain Injury Have?

Physical

- Difficulties walking, running, jumping, throwing and catching
- Changes to sight, hearing, sense of smell, taste or touch
- Tiredness and poor sleep
- Aches and pains
- Dizziness or loss of balance

Thinking and feelings

- Memory problems
- Poor concentration
- Difficulty with planning and organising
- Slurred speech or problems finding the right words
- Problems with following instructions or long sentences
- Processing information slowly
- Mood changes or mood swings
- Feeling sad, anxious or angry

Sometimes, the problems mean that the person cannot do the things they used to do, like work or look after the family. The person with the brain injury may feel sad that they cannot do the things that they used to do. Lots of problems can improve, as ways to do things differently are found.

What Can Help?

Talking to someone about your feelings and worries always helps. Talking to a trusted adult or a close friend may help you to feel better. None of this is your fault. Building your understanding of brain injury may make it easier to cope with some of the difficulties.

Appendix 42

Relationships with Children Worksheet (to Complete with Your Family)

Table A42.1 Example completed family worksheet

Difficulty	*What helps*
I have slow speed of thinking	Write things down for me to read at my own pace Give me just a couple of things to think about at once
I get angry and sometimes shout	Know that the anger is about the brain injury, not about you Allow me a few minutes space to calm down Talk with me about how you feel once we are both calm
I forget about appointments and birthdays	Check that it has been put on the calendar Write it onto the calendar if it is not there Remind me to check the calendar

Table A42.2 Family worksheet template

Difficulty	*What helps*

Appendix 43

Best Memory (for Infant and Primary School Age)

You will need paper and pencil, including colouring pencils or crayons, pictures and glue for this activity.

Ask the child to draw their best memory of something that they have done with you? before your brain injury. Work out together how you could best create this memory through drawings or pictures, and then create it together. Use the picture, whilst creating it to draw out your child's memory using questions:

- Why is it the best memory?
- What did you like most about it?
- What else does it make you think about?

Include in the discussion what happens now and how things might be adjusted to help create new best memories.

Appendix 44

Draw a Family (for Infant and Primary School Age)

You will need a couple of sheets of A4 paper and colouring pencils for this activity.

Ask your child to make a drawing of their family doing something together. When they are finished, ask your child to tell you what is happening in the picture. Ask questions to understand your child's experience. For example, if your child has drawn your family in the garden, some questions might be: "In the picture, you look sad. Do you feel sad?"; "In the picture, you are standing next to daddy. Do you like standing near daddy best?"; "Mummy has a big smile, how do you feel when she smiles?"

You could draw a picture about the same event. This can be useful for discussing how different people see things in different ways.

Appendix 45

Snakes and Ladders (for Primary School Age)

You will need an A3 piece of paper or card, colouring pencils, dice and counters for this activity.

With your child, draw a grid (e.g., six squares across the bottom and five or more squares up; see example grid below). Mark the bottom left hand corner square as "START" and the top right hand corner square as "FINISH." Let your child draw the snakes and ladders on the grid, but help them make sure that the snakes do not end where a ladder starts or vice versa. At the bottom of each ladder, write the behaviour you are trying to encourage (e.g., give mum time to think), and at the top of the snakes, put the unacceptable behaviour you are trying to discourage (e.g., hitting).

To play the game, use the same rules as conventional snakes and ladders. Take turns to roll the dice and move the counter along according to the number shown on the dice. Each time someone lands on a snake or ladder, discuss the reason for moving up or down. Make sure the child understands why the behaviour is there.

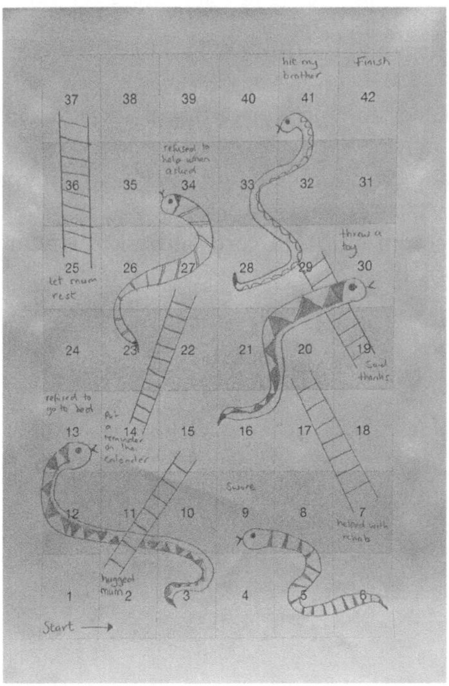

Figure A45.1

Appendix 46

Emotions Cards

It can be difficult for children to understand and express their emotions. When children are relaxed, they are more likely to talk about how they feel, and the emotions cards provide a safe and enjoyable space for children to share their emotions and connect with others.

Preparing Emotions Cards

You will need scissors and crayons/colouring pencils.

Cutting and colouring the cards can be a shared activity.

How to Use Emotions Cards

Lay the cards out on a surface, either facing upwards or facing downwards. Take turns to select a card. You could select a card for each other. You can choose from the following games:

What makes you?—Select an emotion card and ask, "What makes you (emotion from card)?"

Remember when?—Select an emotion card and ask, "When was the last time you felt (emotion from card) and why?"

Making Faces—Select an emotion card and ask, "Can you make a (emotion from card) face?"

Body Language—Select an emotion card and ask, "If you felt (emotion from card) what would your body look like?"

Cut out and colour the emotions cards

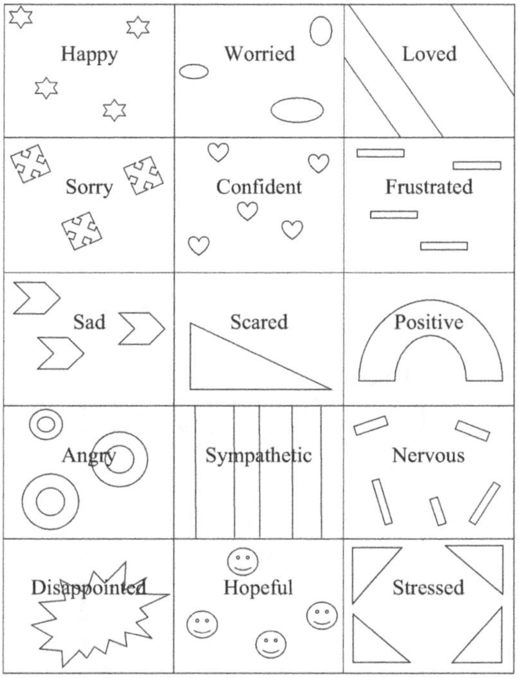

Appendix 47

The Worry Jar

Figure A47.1 Worry Jar

You will need a plastic or glass jar, stickers, card/paper, colouring pencils, scissors and sticky tape. Get your child to decorate it and label it with their name (e.g., "XX's Worry Jar").

A Worry Jar is a safe place for your child to put their worries, so that they do not need to keep thinking about them. It helps to get the worries off their mind by storing them for a particular time. Just knowing that their worries are contained in the jar can free your child from having to replay them over and over in their minds.

Once the jar is finished, help your child write down all his or her worries on paper. You and your child can then cut each worry into its own strip of paper. Fold each worry and put it in the jar. Once all the worries are inside, have your child close the jar.

Schedule a "worry time." A set part of the day when, for 10–15 minutes, your child can worry (not right before bedtime). Write down when "worry time" is on the worry jar (e.g., 4 pm to 4:15 pm). You may want to set a timer or alarm to notify you both that "worry time" has begun and your child can open the worry jar, look inside and worry. Your child can choose to review all the worries or focus on one or two each day. "Worry time" can be spent alone or with you. To end worry time, have a timer or alarm sound to indicate that "worry time" is over for the day. Your child should close the jar to put his or her worries away.

Appendix 48

Creating a "Worry Monster" Worksheet

We all have worries. Worries are a normal part of life, but sometimes, they can get out of hand and get in the way of us doing the things we want.

Externalising is a therapeutic strategy that teaches us to use language to recognise that we are not the problem, and that we are separate from the problem. When we view our worries as separate from ourselves, it becomes easier for us to challenge them, or ignore them. A useful tool to help children externalise their worries is to create their "worry monster." This worksheet aims to encourage your child to identify and discuss their worries with you. It provides guidance for creating a "worry monster" and strategies for using the "worry monster" to address your child's worries.

Create a "Worry Monster"

You will need paper and crayons, pencils, craft materials for this activity.

1. Explain to your child that worries are a normal part of life and that we all have them, and that talking about our worries can help us to feel better.
2. Introduce the "worry monster." Explain that we all have a "worry monster" who visits us, bringing anxious thoughts and feelings.
3. Explain that the "worry monster" might make us feel scared, but we 'do not' have to listen to it.
4. Ask what their "worry monster" might look like, use prompts, such as: Is it big or small? What shape is it? What colour is it? If you touched it, what would it feel like?
5. Support them to draw/create their "worry monster," using crayons, pencils, craft materials.
6. Encourage them to devise a name for the "worry monster," e.g., Mr Mean ……
7. Write the name on the image they produced.
8. Use the name of the "worry monster" from this point onwards to reinforce their worries as separate from themselves.
9. Encourage them to consider the "worry monster's" behaviour, e.g., does "Mr Mean" sneak up on you when you are not expecting it? Does "Mr Mean" say nasty things to you? How does "Mr Mean" sound when he speaks?
10. Encourage them to share how the "worry monster" makes them feel, e.g., does "Mr Mean" make you scared? How do you feel inside your body when "Mr Mean" visits?

SUPPORT MATERIAL

11. Use the "worry monster" to facilitate discussions and gather more information, e.g., When does "Mr Mean" visit? Are there times when "Mr Mean" is not there? Can you remember when Mr Mean first arrived? Who do you think should be in charge of you, you or "Mr Mean"? Is there anything you can do to make "Mr Mean" go away? What things make "Mr Mean" quieter? Louder? What happens when you talk to other people about "Mr Mean"?

Developing a Toolbox of Strategies to Make "Mr Mean" Go Away

Identify a list of trusted adults who your child can talk to about their worries (e.g., My 5 trusted Adults (see Appendix 43: *Relationships with Children Worksheet (to Complete with Your Family)*).

A child-friendly anxiety management technique (e.g., handprint breathing, child mindful breathing (see Appendix 49: *Handprint Breathing*). You could practice this together.

Phrases your child could say to the "worry monster" to make him go away, e.g., "I'm not listening to you," "You're not in charge."

My "worry monster" is called ....

Appendix 49

Handprint Breathing

Mindful breathing can help you to feel calm, even in difficult situations. Using your hand to trace your fingers can help control your pace of breathing. Breathing in, whilst tracing up your finger and breathing out, whilst tracing down, will create a steady breathing pace that regulates your heart rate and can help you to feel calmer.

It is important to learn and practise this technique whilst you feel calm, so that you can easily apply it when needed.

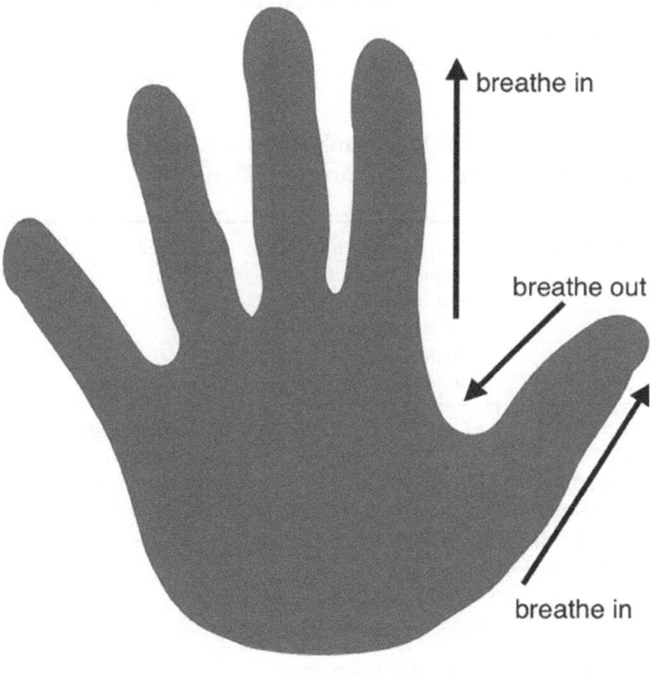

Figure A49.1 Handprint Breathing.

Appendix 50

My Working Week—Potential Challenges and What Helps

You can use this worksheet to help you to plan your return to work. Think about what your working week looks like, and the potential challenges you might face if you were to return to the same working week. You may choose to share this with your employer/manager.

Write down the tasks that you would complete in your day, e.g., admin, meetings, manual work and driving. Then think about what challenges you might face and what strategies you have developed to overcome these, e.g., struggling to remember what is said in meetings—write down notes, ask for minutes to be taken by someone else, ask if you can voice record what has been said.

What are my key difficulties?:

Short-term memory, pain in left leg—can't stand for long duration, harder to think on the spot, lots more worries, more anxious around people.

Day of the week Hours	*Tasks to complete*	*I can do this with no support or additional strategies/I need to use strategies/I need support from someone to do this*	*Potential challenges*	*Strategies/ adaptations*
Monday 9–5 pm	*Catch up with emails Team meeting*	*I need to use strategy*	*Noise in the office Lots of people talking at once*	*Quiet space with no distractions.*
Tuesday 8–8 pm	*Site work—lots of manual work, moving, standing, sitting*	*I need support from others*	*Too long hours*	*Too long hours—graded return needed starting with mornings 8–11 am three days a week.*
Wednesday 8–4 pm	*Drive to client 1–2 hours Meeting Drive back home*	*I need support from others*	*I can no longer be in a car for more than 30 minutes—pain in lower back*	*Only see clients within a 30-minute radius or allow more time so I can stop and stretch for 15 minutes.*

(*Continued*)

Day of the week Hours	*Tasks to complete*	*I can do this with no support or additional strategies/I need to use strategies/I need support from someone to do this*	*Potential challenges*	*Strategies/ adaptations*
Thursday 8–6 pm	Site work—lots of manual work, moving, standing, sitting	I need support from others	Too long hours	Too long hours—graded return needed starting with mornings 8–11 am three days a week.
Friday 9–5.30 pm	Drive to site Site work—lots of manual work, moving, standing, sitting Admin	I need support from others	Fatigue and pain, very tired by Friday	Perhaps reduce hours on a Friday—change tasks to admin only and no driving.
Saturday	Day off	I need support from others	Too fatigued from work—don't do anything else but sleep	Grade return to work further. Discuss with manager.
Sunday	Day off	I need support from others	Worry and anxiety about working week	Speak to my family/friends / employer Talk to a psychologist

SUPPORT MATERIAL

Appendix 51

Employer/Manager Review Meeting Template

You can use this worksheet to help structure a review meeting with your manager/employer. This will help build open, honest and useful conversations about how you are doing at work.

Before you go into the meeting, it is important to give yourself some space to think about how things are going, what would you like to share and what would you like to get out of the meeting.

You can agree the key areas to review with your manager, what might have the biggest impact on your ability to do your work? There is a space for you to rate how you feel this has gone and for your manager to rate this. The manager rating will help you get an outsider's perspective of how things are going. For example, you might be really struggling with fatigue but masking it at work; this might result in your manager thinking everything is okay and giving you more to do. Another example may be that you might worry about your confidence when talking to people, but your manager may feel this is going well.

The idea of the rating scales is to open up a conversation about what is working well and where there is room for improvement to add further support or change the ways you do things.

General check in:

How do I feel work is going?

How does my manager feel work is going?

Key areas to review	*My rating out of 10* *0 = no problem* *10 = significant challenges*	*My manager's rating out of 10* *0 = no problem* *10 = significant challenges*	*Comments* *What's working well?* *What could be improved?*
Fatigue/ tiredness	5	4	Currently working four mornings a week 8 am – 12 pm, managing well—look to increase? Taking regular breaks.
Pain levels	4	4	Pain is manageable, regular breaks help, no prolonged sitting/standing is helpful. May need to change office chair—discuss with occupational health.

(*Continued*)

Key areas to review	*My rating out of 10* *0 = no problem* *10 = significant challenges*	*My manager's rating out of 10* *0 = no problem* *10 = significant challenges*	*Comments* *What's working well?* *What could be improved?*
Short term memory	3	3	Using a diary to write things down, working well. Would help to have agenda for meetings in advance.
Concentration/ focus	4	Unsure	Quieter environments help. Regular breaks helping with focus.
Environment	4	3	Sometimes the office/site is busy and this can impact focus and increase stress.
Confidence with people	7	6	Have returned to work and started to talk to people. Still find it difficult to be in larger groups or speak up in meetings. Work with manager on building confidence in groups.
Add other areas…			

Agreed actions for me:

- Increase hours to five mornings a week and work till 1 pm on two of those days.
- Contact occupational health about my chair.
- Discuss building confidence with psychologist.

Agreed actions for manager:

- Arrange separate meeting to discuss confidence with people.
- Any other important information
- Operation for back pain at the start of June—will be off work for four weeks.

Date of next meeting:

- Next week—Friday 12th April at 1 pm—in person.

Appendix 52

Education Review Meeting Template

This template can help you to structure an education review meeting. This will help build communication about how you are doing. Before you meet, it is important to give yourself time to think about how things are, what you wish to share, and what you want to get out of the meeting.

You can agree together on the key review areas based on what might have the biggest impact on your learning and engagement in education. There is a space for you and the professional to rate how you feel key areas are going. The educational professional's rating will help you get an outside perspective on how things are going. The idea of the rating scales is to open up communication about what is working well, and where there is room for improvement to add further support or change things.

General check in:

- How do I feel education is going?
- How does the educational professional feel it's going?

Key areas to review	*My 0–10 rating (0 no problem; 10 significant problem)*	*Professional's 0–10 rating (0 no problem; 10 significant problem)*	*What's working well? What could be improved?*
Fatigue/tiredness			Currently in three mornings a week 9 am—OK. Taking regular breaks.
Slow processing			Some notes from peers but still missing out. Helpful to have handouts for all lessons from tutors.
Concentration/ focus			Front of class seating helps. Regular changes in task helps with focus.
Confidence with people			Find it difficult to be in large groups or speak up in class. Work on building confidence by speaking up in small group work.
Ensure information shared with all teaching staff			Given detention for missing deadline.

Agreed actions for me:

- Increase hours to four mornings a week.
- Discuss building confidence with psychologist.

Agreed actions for educational professional:

- Arrange separate meeting to discuss confidence with small groups work.
- Speak with member of teaching staff to ensure information shared/retained re: reasonable adjustments in place.

Any other important information:

- July residential rehabilitation—will miss last week of term.

Date of next meeting:

- Next week—Friday 4th May at 12 pm—in person.

Appendix 53

Timetable Worksheet—Potential Difficulties and What Helps

You can use this worksheet to help you to plan your return to education. Think about what your week will look like and the potential issues you might face.

Write down the tasks that you may complete in your day. Then think about what difficulties there might be and what strategies might help (e.g., struggling to remember what is said in class—ask for a handout or notes to be taken by someone else; ask if you can voice record what has been said).

What are my key difficulties:

Slow to process information, short attention span, fatigue, and anxious in groups and busy places.

Time	*Monday*	*Level of support needed*	*Potential Challenges*	*Strategies/adaptations*
8 am	Pack bag for college	I need to use strategy	Limited time, high chance I will forget something	Pack the night before when not in a rush Use a checklist to check that I have everything
10 am	English lesson	I need support from others	Too fast paced to take notes, tend to switch off	Get handout in advance, write bullet points, set watch to vibrate every 5 minutes to refocus
Noon	Lunch	I need support from others	Anxious in busy canteen	Have lunch with friend in quiet room
1 pm	P.E.	I need support from others	Fatigue and pain, very tired by afternoon	Too long hours—not ready for afternoons yet. Discuss with Special Educational Needs or Disabilities Coordinator (SENCO)
2 pm	Travel home	I can do this with no support or additional strategies	Difficulties when fatigued	Ask the bus driver to say when reaching the required stop. Use timer on phone to alert that the journey time is almost up

Index

Note: **Bold** page numbers refer to tables and *italic* page numbers refer to figures.

For Product Safety Concerns and Information please contact our EU representative GPSR@taylorandfrancis.com Taylor & Francis Verlag GmbH, Kaufingerstraße 24, 80331 München, Germany